Using PowerPoint® 3

JAMES G. MEADE
DEBBIE WALKOWSKI

Using PowerPoint 3

Copyright© 1992 by Que® Corporation

Library of Congress Catalog No.: 92-61700

ISBN: 1-56529-102-6

95 94 93   5

Interpretation of the printing code: the rightmost double-digit number is the year of the book's printing; the rightmost single-digit number, the number of the book's printing. For example, a printing code of 92-1 shows that the first printing of the book occurred in 1992.

Screen reproductions in this book were created with Collage Plus from Inner Media, Inc., Hollis, NH.

This book is based on Microsoft PowerPoint Version 3.0.

Publisher: Lloyd J. Short

Associate Publisher: Rick Ranucci

Product Development Manager: Thomas H. Bennett

Book Designer: Scott Cook

Production Team: Jeff Baker, Claudia Bell, Julie Brown, Brad Chinn, Michelle Cleary, Brook Farling, Bob LaRoche, Laurie Lee, Cindy Phipps, Linda Seifert, Sandra Shay, Lisa Wilson, Phil Worthington

CREDITS

Acquisitions Editor
Sarah Browning

Product Director
Shelly O'Hara

Production Director
Cindy Morrow

Editors
Elsa M. Bell
Barb Colter
Brad Sullivan

Technical Editor
Susan K. Lippert

Composed in *Garamond* and *MCPdigital*
by Que Corporation

TRADEMARK
ACKNOWLEDGMENTS

When he is not playing basketball in his backyard, **Jim Meade** spends most of his time writing Que books. His previous Que titles are *Using Freelance Plus, Using MultiMate, Using Peachtree,* and *Using Andrew Tobias' TaxCut.* His company, Meade Ink, has been providing writing services since 1983 to companies such as Lotus Development Corporation, Digital Equipment Corporation, and MCI Communications Corp. His monthly column, "Raw Ink," appears in *Digital Desktop Magazine.* He is a regular software reviewer for *HR Magazine* and has written dozens of columns and articles for computer and technical magazines, such as *Data Communications Magazine* and *Information Week.*

Debbie Walkowski is an experienced technical writer with a degree in scientific and technical communication. She has 12 years experience in the computer industry writing documentation, designing user interfaces, and teaching computer courses. Debbie's company, The Writing Works, specializes in writing computer self-help books and providing writing services to companies such as Microsoft Corporation and Digital Equipment Corporation. She is the author of six books on popular computer software.

CONTENTS AT A GLANCE

TABLE OF CONTENTS

Introduction

Microsoft PowerPoint is aptly named. The "power" in the name refers to all the capabilities loaded into the program. PowerPoint is not one program, but several.

- PowerPoint is a highly efficient drawing program. You can create a variety of shapes or freehand drawings and combine them into any shape you want.

- PowerPoint is a graphing program. You enter the data you want to present (for example, sales for the third and fourth quarters), and then click one of the 84 predefined graph styles to choose the one you want.

- PowerPoint is an executive word processor. You can add text and choose different fonts and type sizes, and you can word wrap. You can indent bulleted lists. You also can use PowerPoint's search and replace feature. PowerPoint can check your spelling as well.

- PowerPoint is an artist's palette that offers you literally thousands of professionally designed color schemes. If these built-in color combinations don't satisfy you, PowerPoint enables you to create your own colors and combinations.

■ PowerPoint is an output program. You can output to your screen, and you can create color slides and overhead transparencies. If you want professionals to create the final output, you can use the GraphicsLink program (included with PowerPoint) to send your file to Genigraphics, a company that will make the slides for you. (The PowerPoint documentation includes the Genigraphics phone number.) PowerPoint, therefore, is also a communications program.

PowerPoint has the power of all these programs loaded into memory and at your service *all at once*. When you use all that power to create your graphics, you do not work with a single chart or drawing, as you might have done with a DOS program. Instead, you can work with an entire multiple-slide presentation at one time. On-screen you can have miniatures of all the slides in your presentation (as many as the memory on your computer can hold).

If you have multiple slides, you can rearrange them, delete them, add to them, change the color scheme, move words and objects from one to the other—all without ever exiting one file or opening another. If you want, you can view all the slides at once by title, or you can view them individually, and then work on them in detail.

PowerPoint, therefore, certainly has immense power, and using this power in your business presentations can help you make your point to your audience. The power available in this program would overwhelm most users without the rest that PowerPoint offers, described by the "point" in its name. You can use all that immense capability by using a mouse to point to options on menus as well as to manipulate the images on-screen.

You may have a task that calls for many different steps, such as creating a scatter chart; importing data from a Lotus 1-2-3 worksheet; using 48-point Helvetica text for the title, a 16-color pastel color scheme, and a rounded rectangle as a frame; importing clip art; setting up the format as a new default; and so on. Your task would be complicated indeed if you had to specify each step by name. When you use PowerPoint, however, you do not have to specify all these steps by name or even know the names of all the steps. You just point and click with the mouse— anyone can do it.

When you point to the feature you want and select it, you are using the graphical user interface (GUI), a user interface that uses the mouse and a graphics display to simplify your use of the computer. When you review what you see on the screen to decide whether you like it, you are using another advanced capability—WYSIWYG ("what you see is what you get"). In PowerPoint, all the colors, typefaces, sizes, and proportions you work with on-screen are those you will see in your final slide.

Thanks to the graphical user interface, PowerPoint is at once powerful and easy to use. What about artistic features for your presentations? You can point to those easily, too. If at first you are not comfortable with the thought of designing the aesthetic aspects of an entire presentation, PowerPoint has found a way to do that for you. Genigraphics artists have created 160 sample templates that have all the features of an outstanding slide show, such as color schemes, fonts for the titles, placement of graphics objects, and the flow of the whole presentation. You can copy the presentation, change the words or objects to suit your purposes, and create a slide show that is just as professional as the one from Genigraphics—without having to know graphic arts.

If the template does not include the image that you need, you probably can find the one you do want. PowerPoint has a clip art library of over 600 color images, drawn by the professional artists at Genigraphics. You can browse through the images, copy one that you want, and paste it into the program.

PowerPoint contains immense power that you can use to make your point in presentations. You are an expert almost as soon as you begin, and using PowerPoint soon becomes second nature. At first, however, you can learn much by reading about the program. PowerPoint offers so much concentrated power that you are almost certain to miss some of its capabilities unless you take a little time to seek them out. Helping you discover PowerPoint's possibilities is the purpose of this book.

What Is in This Book

Like the PowerPoint program itself, *Using PowerPoint 3* attempts to make the power of the program readily accessible. The book begins with basic features and moves toward more advanced features. Start by learning the basics, and then later, when you feel at home with the fundamentals, you can move to advanced features.

Three of the chapters in this book are "Quick Starts," minitutorials that guide you through the steps for accomplishing a particular task. Quick Starts are not cluttered with a lot of detail; they are designed to give you hands-on experience without answering every question you might have. You'll find the answers to your questions in the chapter or chapters that follow each Quick Start.

Other chapters provide detailed explanations and additional tips so that you not only use the features, but understand them and their relation to each other and to the whole program.

Part I, "PowerPoint Basics," introduces you to the basics of PowerPoint.

Chapter 1, "Getting Acquainted with PowerPoint," shows you how to use the mouse and the keyboard, work with the menus, get help, and take advantage of PowerPoint as a Windows program.

Chapter 2, "Quick Start: Creating Your First Presentation," takes you step-by-step through the process of creating a presentation, adding text and graphic objects, and saving the presentation.

Chapter 3, "Creating a Presentation," shows you in detail how to start PowerPoint, create a presentation from scratch, create a presentation by copying a template, view and rearrange the presentation, and save the presentation.

Chapter 4, "Working with Text," demonstrates how to add text to a slide; move, resize, and copy text; and change typefaces, styles, and color. This chapter also explains how to find and change text and how to use the spelling checker.

Chapter 5, "Drawing Objects," introduces you to the drawing tools available in PowerPoint. You draw and delete lines and shapes, move objects, add frames and shadows, and change fill patterns. You learn how to use guides and grids to help you put your drawings exactly where you want them on the slide.

Chapter 6, "Quick Start: Choosing Color Schemes and Creating Graphs," gives you hands-on experience in choosing color schemes, entering data into a graph, and changing the colors within a chart.

Chapter 7, "Working with Color," explains in detail the procedures you learned in Chapter 6. You also see how to color individual objects and text and how to work with patterns.

Chapter 8, "Creating Basic Graphs," shows you how to put your data into a datasheet, choose a graph form from the Chart menu, and include the graph in your slide.

Chapter 9, "Creating Notes Pages, Handouts, and Outlines," tells you how to create each of these elements of a presentation and how to use PowerPoint's outlining feature to create and rearrange a presentation.

Chapter 10, "Creating Output," shows you how to set up your printer. You learn how to output in every possible way—to your screen, to a film recorder, to a transparency, to paper, or to the Genigraphics slide service. You also see how to create and print notes and handouts.

Part II, "PowerPoint Advanced Features," takes you beyond the basics and helps you become familiar with some of the advanced power in PowerPoint.

Chapter 11, "Quick Start: Working with Pictures," demonstrates how to turn objects into a picture and how to retrieve a finished picture from the clip art file and put the picture into your slide.

Chapter 12, "Inserting Objects and Creating Special Effects," takes you a step beyond the capability to work with multiple slides at once. Thanks to Windows, you can work easily with multiple *presentations* at once, or even with multiple applications. This chapter shows you how.

Chapter 13, "Using Advanced Text Features," acquaints you with text capabilities that were not covered in Chapter 4. You see how to use the ruler to set indentations and tabs and how to set line and paragraph spacing. You also learn how to create a custom dictionary for your spelling checker.

Chapter 14, "Using Advanced Graph Features," discusses advanced graphing capabilities available in PowerPoint. You learn how to create custom number formats for the datasheet, how to enhance a graph with special effects, and how to copy a graph to other applications. You also find out how to change the default graph.

Chapter 15, "Using Advanced Color Features," introduces you to advanced color capabilities. You learn how to work with colors that are not in the color scheme, such as those you create yourself. You find out how to recolor a picture you bring in from outside your presentation.

Chapter 16, "Using PowerPoint's Timesaver Presentations," introduces you to the timesaver presentations that come with PowerPoint. You can copy objects or entire slides from these presentations to help you create organization charts, flow charts, calendars, timelines, tables, and graphs.

Appendix A, "Installing PowerPoint," shows you how to install PowerPoint. Appendix B, "PowerPoint Defaults," reviews the PowerPoint default settings—initial settings that are changed (sometimes by accident) as you use the program, but which you may want to restore. Appendix C, "Clip Art," lists the clip art that comes with PowerPoint.

Who Should Use This Book

If a program is "intuitive," as PowerPoint is, why read a book about it? You can use almost anything in PowerPoint—even the most advanced capability, like setting up the color scheme—by browsing through possibilities and making choices. PowerPoint does not require you to know sophisticated commands, as do many non-Windows programs. Nor does PowerPoint require you to know graphic arts.

Read this book to become acquainted with the many possibilities that are available in PowerPoint. You easily can copy a presentation template and use it as your own. To use a presentation template, however, you must know that it is available to use. Any book about PowerPoint, therefore, is more a catalog of possibilities than an instruction manual.

If you start using PowerPoint and never read anything about it, you can perform well. Much of the power in the program, however, almost certainly will be lost to you. Gradually, you may make discoveries. You can continue to make them for months and months, because the program has so much to offer.

When you read this book, you do not need to wait until you happen upon such capabilities by accident. You can find out about Power-Point's easy-to-use possibilities, learn the simple steps for using them, and discover shortcuts and special tips.

This book is not aimed toward the software expert or the graphic artist, although either one can profit by reading it. A software expert can learn about PowerPoint and receive advice on doing graphics well. A graphics expert can learn about the software and get advice on using it well. *Using PowerPoint 3*, however, is written primarily for business presenters who want to create their own presentations. *Using PowerPoint 3* shows you how to use the program step-by-step in a business context. Simple guidelines and explanations keep you steadily on course and help you get the most out of PowerPoint in the least amount of time.

How To Use This Book

PowerPoint is not difficult to use. You do not have to think hard about each feature to be able to use it. You do need to know, however, what the feature is and understand what it does for you. (A Slide Master, for example, is a great concept, but you must know what it is and how to use it.) Read this book to find out what PowerPoint has to offer.

You probably will not read this book as you would a novel, from beginning to end. Keep it available as a reference whenever you use the program. You may use some features often, others only rarely. *Using PowerPoint 3* can serve as a reference for features you only partially remember. Even if you use a feature often, you may want to check this book for shortcuts and special tips. A feature-rich program, no matter how easy to use, deserves a feature-rich book to help you get the most from it.

No matter how intuitive the program, you still must go through a series of steps to perform even the most basic operations. Before you create a slide, for example, you should install and set up your printer, because your printer setup influences how the slide looks on the screen and determines what fonts are available. If you do not follow a procedure step-by-step, you may find out that you have omitted a step and must go back. When you read a Que book such as *Using PowerPoint 3*, you learn all the right steps to follow and the sequence in which to follow them.

Conventions Used in This Book

Several conventions are used in this book to help you learn to use Microsoft PowerPoint quickly. These conventions are as follows:

- The names of dialog boxes and their options, as well as menu names and their options, are in initial capital letters.

- Tips for using Microsoft PowerPoint are included in gray boxes. These tips can help you become more efficient in using the program.

- Cautions are included in outlined boxes. Pay close attention to these warnings, because they may save you from losing data or creating other problems for yourself.

- Anything you should type is in *italic type* or on a line by itself.

- Messages that appear on-screen are in a special typeface.

PowerPoint Basics

PART

I

OUTLINE

Getting Acquainted with PowerPoint

The beauty of any Windows application is that you probably know a great deal about using the application before you even begin. Windows' greatest value is its *graphical user interface (GUI)*. Known as "gooey" throughout the computer industry, the GUI provides a common method for interacting with all Windows applications.

Chances are that PowerPoint is not your first Windows application. Many people use a Windows word processor or a Windows spreadsheet before they begin to use a Windows graphics program. You probably already know how to move the cursor with the mouse or keyboard, how to make menu selections, how to save your document, and much more. You probably know how to use the Windows File Manager for copying files and directories. And you probably know the basics about using the Program Manager to work with multiple programs.

If you know how to use Windows for word processing, creating spreadsheets, or managing files, you also know how to use it for your graphics application. You move the cursor in the same way for any Windows application. You choose from menus in the same way. You shrink and expand windows on the page in the same way. After you know any Windows application, then in a sense you truly do know *any* Windows application. Navigating in PowerPoint is like navigating in other Windows applications.

If you don't know how to use Windows or a Windows application, learning to do so is easy. This chapter reviews Windows features—using the mouse, changing and moving windows, using the Maximize and Minimize buttons—and explains how to start PowerPoint. As you become comfortable with these capabilities, you will become increasingly comfortable with PowerPoint and all other Windows applications.

In the following sections, you become acquainted with the PowerPoint screen and with certain tools—such as the slide changer and the view buttons—that you find in PowerPoint but not elsewhere in Windows. As you work in PowerPoint, you often make changes to slides on the screen, and in this chapter you see how to change the text on a slide. You become familiar with PowerPoint's basic capabilities and with the features PowerPoint brings to all your presentations. You learn how to use PowerPoint menus, view buttons, and Toolbars. (You must have Windows and PowerPoint installed on your computer before you can do any of the exercises in this chapter. Appendix A tells you how to install PowerPoint.)

Using Standard Windows Features

Certain basic screen features are standard to Windows—clicking with the mouse, dragging, choosing from menus by using the mouse or keyboard, controlling the size of windows, and so on. You should be familiar with these basic operations already. If not, you might want to refer to your Windows manual for complete explanations of Windows features before you proceed with this chapter. The following sections give brief descriptions of the Windows functions you will use most often when working with PowerPoint.

Using the Mouse

To perform many PowerPoint actions, you can use either a mouse or the keyboard. Because you can do some things in PowerPoint *only* by using a mouse, a mouse is required for PowerPoint. For this reason, this book emphasizes mouse instructions. The keyboard, however, is sometimes more convenient to use and provides valuable shortcuts. When appropriate, these shortcuts are described in the text, but standard keystrokes (such as choosing commands from a menu) are *not* provided. The level of this book assumes that you know how to use the keyboard to choose menu commands and how to maneuver a dialog box. The remainder of this section briefly reviews the use of the mouse.

To move the mouse pointer on-screen, slide the mouse on your desktop. As you move the mouse, the pointer moves accordingly. To point with the mouse, move the mouse until the tip of the on-screen pointer is at the position you want. To select an item, click the left mouse button once. Selected items appear highlighted on-screen. "Selecting" is often referred to as "highlighting." To choose an item, double-click it. (To double-click, click the left mouse button twice in rapid succession.)

When you choose rather than select an item, you initiate an action. For example, a single click on the PowerPoint icon only selects (or highlights) the icon. To choose the PowerPoint icon (and thereby start the program), you must double-click the PowerPoint icon. In certain situations, you may need to drag the mouse. You drag the mouse by holding down the left mouse button while moving the mouse to another location. For example, you might drag an item to move it to another location or you might drag the mouse to select multiple objects at once.

Using the mouse, you can move to any area that is visible on-screen by moving the pointer to that position and clicking. At times, however, your entire slide may not be completely visible on-screen, particularly if you have been moving and resizing windows. To "scroll" through a slide, use the scroll bars on the right and bottom sides of the window. Each scroll bar contains two scroll arrows and a scroll box that enables you to see nonvisible contents of the window.

The mouse pointer can take several shapes as you use it. The arrow is the most common shape. Use the arrow for pointing—choosing from menus, selecting objects, and so on. When the mouse pointer resembles an uppercase I (called the *I-beam*), use it to highlight text or to tell PowerPoint that you want to type new text. As you type, the insertion point is indicated by a vertical bar. In text mode, this bar is commonly called the *cursor*. For drawing shapes such as rectangles, lines, ovals, and freeforms, the pointer appears as a *crosshair*. As you will see in Chapter 11, the mouse pointer assumes a special shape when you use the Cropping tool to crop (cover over) the outer parts of a graphic. When the program is completing a task and you have to wait, the pointer appears as an hourglass. When you are resizing windows, the pointer appears as a two-headed arrow. The two-headed arrow appears diagonally when you are resizing horizontally and vertically at the same time. A four-headed arrow enables you to move items with the keyboard rather than drag them with the mouse.

Manipulating Windows

One of Windows' most useful features is the capability to display multiple windows on-screen at one time. By opening multiple windows, you can have PowerPoint running in one window and a word processor running in a second window. You also can have several PowerPoint windows open at the same time.

Two especially valuable Windows features, maximize and minimize, are explained in this section. At the top right of each window you find the Maximize and Minimize buttons, identified by black pointers against white backgrounds (see fig. 1.1). As their names imply, these buttons enlarge or shrink open windows. There are two sets of maximize and minimize buttons: one for the application window, and one for the presentation window. The buttons at the far right end of the PowerPoint title bar control the application itself. The buttons at the far right of the presentation window title bar control the presentation window. Maximizing a window causes it to fill all the available space on-screen. Minimizing a window reduces its size or reduces it to an icon so that you can begin a new task. When a window is reduced to an icon, the task is still running.

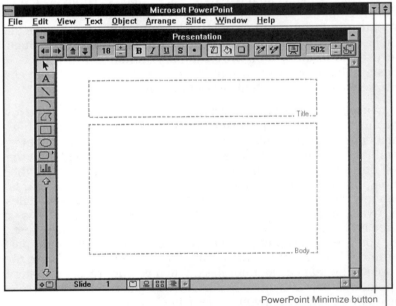

Fig. 1.1

The Maximize and Minimize buttons.

PowerPoint Minimize button

PowerPoint Maximize/Restore button

You can open and close windows, change the scale of windows (from full size to 50 percent, for instance), and arrange windows with

PowerPoint menu commands, as explained in later sections of this chapter.

Starting PowerPoint

Because PowerPoint is a Windows application, you can only use it within Windows. (PowerPoint 3.0 requires Windows Version 3.1.) After you install PowerPoint, the Microsoft PowerPoint group window is created automatically in the Windows Program Manager. The window contains three icons: Microsoft PowerPoint, PowerPoint Viewer, and GraphicsLink. The Microsoft PowerPoint icon starts the program.

 If you have not yet installed PowerPoint, see Appendix A for installation directions.

To start PowerPoint, follow these steps:

1. At the DOS prompt, type *win* and press Enter to start Windows.

   The Windows Program Manager appears. Your screen should resemble (but not be identical to) figure 1.2, which shows the Microsoft PowerPoint group window in the Program Manager. (If the PowerPoint window is not open, you see an icon labeled Microsoft PowerPoint.)

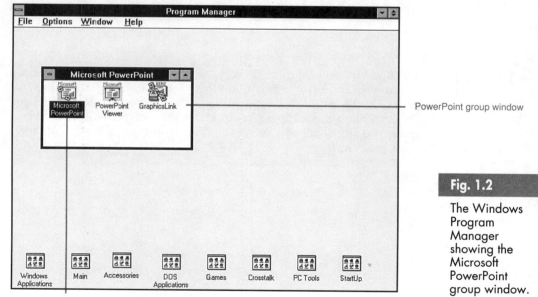

PowerPoint group window

Click here to start PowerPoint

Fig. 1.2

The Windows Program Manager showing the Microsoft PowerPoint group window.

2. If the Microsoft PowerPoint window is not open, double-click the Microsoft PowerPoint group icon to open the window.

3. In the Microsoft PowerPoint window, double-click the Microsoft PowerPoint icon.

The PowerPoint program starts. Figure 1.3 shows the PowerPoint opening screen.

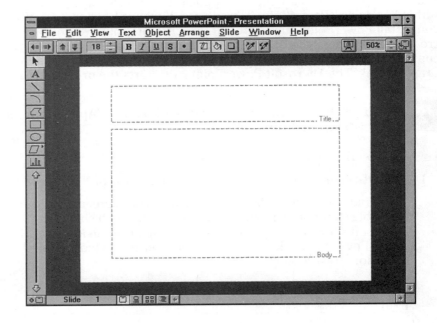

Fig. 1.3

The PowerPoint opening screen.

T I P

To start PowerPoint from the keyboard, type *win* at the DOS prompt to enter Windows. When you see the Program Manager window, press Ctrl-F6 until the Microsoft PowerPoint group is selected. Press Enter to open the window. In the Microsoft PowerPoint window, press the arrow keys to select the Microsoft PowerPoint icon, and then press Enter.

Getting Familiar with the PowerPoint Screen

In this section, you look at the PowerPoint screen and begin to understand some of its features that are distinct from Windows features.

Across the top in the title bar, the PowerPoint screen displays the words Microsoft PowerPoint. Just below the title bar, you see the PowerPoint menu bar, with the choices File, Edit, View, Text, Object, Arrange, Slide, Window, and Help. Below the menu, you see the word Presentation in the presentation window's title bar. (If the presentation window is maximized, the word Presentation appears next to the words Microsoft PowerPoint in the application title bar.) Figure 1.4 shows these parts of the PowerPoint screen. When you name and save a presentation to disk, the name you assign replaces the word Presentation.

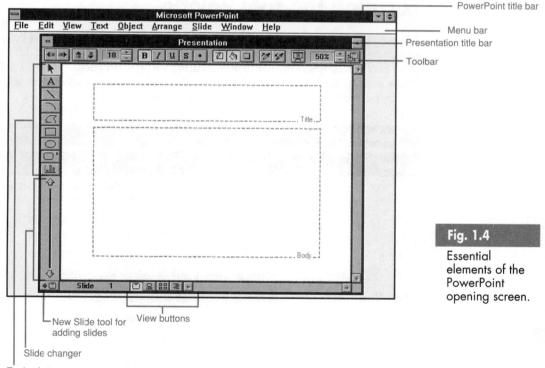

Fig. 1.4

Essential elements of the PowerPoint opening screen.

When you first start PowerPoint, the screen is blank except for a box labeled Title and a box labeled Body. The slide you see is the first slide in an unnamed presentation. On the bottom left of the screen, you see the words Slide 1. The current slide number always appears in this location.

On the lower left side of the screen is a vertical slider with arrows at either end; this slider is called the *slide changer*. You use it to change slides within a presentation by clicking the arrows or by dragging the side bar, much as you do with vertical and horizontal scroll bars. Click the top arrow to move back one slide; click the bottom arrow to move forward one slide. To display a specific slide, move the slide bar along the slide changer until the slide you want is displayed.

At the bottom of the slide changer is the New Slide tool (a + sign to the left of a slide icon). You use this tool to add a new slide to your presentation.

Locating the Tool Palette

Above the slide changer on the left side of the screen is the tool palette (again see fig 1.4). The tool palette contains the Selection, Text, Line, Arc, Freeform, Rectangle, Ellipse, Shape, and Graph tools. These tools allow you to select objects, draw, graph, and add text to your slides. Table 1.1 explains the function of each of these tools.

Table 1.1 Tools on the Tool Palette

Tool	Function
Select	Selects objects so that they can be moved, copied, deleted, or resized. This is the default tool.
Text	Enables you to enter text—such as a caption for a graphic—anywhere on a slide.
Line	Creates horizontal, vertical, or diagonal lines.
Arc	Creates arcs, such as half-moons.
Freeform	Creates free-hand drawings, such as script.
Rectangle	Creates rectangles, squares, or boxes.
Ellipse	Creates ellipses, circles, or ovals.
Shape	Creates various shaped objects, such as starbursts, arrows, stars, and triangles.
Graph	Creates charts such as bar charts, line charts, graph charts, and area charts.

To select a tool other than the default Selection tool, move the mouse pointer over the tool and click once. The tool you select is highlighted. When you select the Text tool, the mouse pointer changes to an I-beam, enabling you to enter text on the slide. When you select any of the drawing tools or the Graph tool, the mouse pointer changes to a crosshair.

Using the Toolbars

As with most Windows programs, you choose menu commands to initiate an action of some kind or to apply an attribute to text or an object. The same is true in PowerPoint, but the Toolbar gives you quick access to some of the most commonly used menu commands, enabling you to bypass common menu commands. For example, suppose that you want to set text in boldface type. Without the Toolbar, you would select the text you want to change, choose the Style command from the Text menu, then choose the Bold menu item. Using the Toolbar, you simply select the text to change, and then click the Bold tool (the tool with the capital B).

Because a mouse is required for PowerPoint, this book places a greater emphasis on using the Toolbar rather than using menu commands. Clicking a tool is generally faster than choosing a menu command, and for most users, learning to use PowerPoint efficiently is a primary goal.

Using the Toolbar, you first select the object or text to edit, and then click a tool. The tool you select is highlighted. Some tools toggle on and off, such as those that you use to apply attributes to an object or to change text format. Click the tool once to turn the tool on, click it again to turn it off. Other tools simply initiate an action or change a setting of some kind.

In PowerPoint, there are three Toolbars:

■ The Toolbar in Slide view and Notes view

■ The Toolbar in Outline view

■ The Toolbar in Slide Sorter view

The Toolbar changes depending on the view you are using. (You learn about views in the next section.) Figure 1.5 illustrates the Toolbars used in each of the four views: Slide and Notes view, Outline view, and Slide Sorter view.

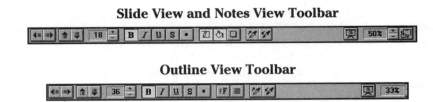

Slide View and Notes View Toolbar

Outline View Toolbar

Fig. 1.5

The PowerPoint
Toolbars.

Slide Sorter Toolbar

Tables 1.2 through 1.4 list the various tools available on these three
Toolbars.

Table 1.2 Tools on the Slide View and Notes View Toolbar	
Tool	**Function**
Promote	Moves selected paragraphs to the left in an outline. Used with bullet charts.
Demote	Moves selected paragraphs to the right in an outline. Used with bullet charts.
Move Up	Moves selected text up one paragraph at a time.
Move Down	Moves selected text down one paragraph at a time.
Font Size	Changes the font size of text. Text size can be increased or decreased by clicking the + to increase or the – to decrease.
Bold	Makes selected text bold.
Italic	Makes selected text italic.
Underline	Makes selected text underlined.
Text Shadow	Applies a shadow to the selected text.
Add Bullet	Adds or removes a bullet from the beginning of the selected paragraph.
Line	Draws a line around a selected object.
Fill	Makes the selected object opaque (solid filled) and filled with the default fill color.
Object Shadow	Applies a shadow to the selected object.
Pick Up Styles	Copies all the attributes of the selected object.

Tool	Function
Apply Styles	Applies the "picked up" attributes to the selected object. If no style has been picked up, the default attributes are applied.
Slide Show	Runs a slide show starting from the currently selected slide.
View Scale	Zooms in (+) or out (–) on a section of the slide.
Home View	Toggles between the last view scale size and the fit-in-window view size.

Table 1.3 Tools on the Outline View Toolbar

Tool	Function
Promote	Moves selected paragraphs to the left in an outline. Used with bullet charts.
Demote	Moves selected paragraphs to the right in an outline. Used with bullet charts.
Move Up	Moves selected text up one paragraph at a time.
Move Down	Moves selected text down one paragraph at a time.
Font Size	Changes the font size of text. Text size can be increased or decreased by clicking the + to increase or the – to decrease.
Bold	Makes selected text bold.
Italic	Makes selected text italic.
Underline	Makes selected text underlined.
Text Shadow	Applies a shadow to the selected text.
Add Bullet	Adds or removes a bullet from the beginning of the selected paragraph.
Draft Text	Displays the outline as unformatted plain text. Used in Outline view.
Titles Only	Displays only the slide titles in Outline view.
Pick Up Styles	Copies all the attributes of the selected object.
Apply Styles	Applies the "picked up" attributes to the selected object. If no style has been picked up, the default attributes are applied.

continues

Table 1.3 Continued

Tool	Function
Slide Show	Runs a slide show starting from the currently selected slide.
View Scale	Zooms in (+) or out (–) on a section of the slide.
Home View	Toggles between the last view scale size and the fit-in-window view size.

Table 1.4 Tools on the Slide Sorter View Toolbar

Tool	Function
Transition Dialog	Sets timings and transitions for each slide in a presentation.
Transition Effect	Specifies the selected transition effect.
Build Dialog	Creates a slide that appears to build on itself. For example, slide one appears with the first bullet, slide two appears with the first and second bullets, and slide three appears with the first, second, and third bullets.
Pick Up Color Scheme	Copies the color scheme of the current slide.
Apply Color Scheme	Applies the "picked up" color scheme to the selected slide.
Slide Show	Runs a slide show starting from the currently selected slide.
View Scale	Zooms in (+) or zooms out (–) on a section of the slide.
Home View	Toggles between the last view scale size and the fit-in-window view size.

Using the View Buttons

When you work with presentations in PowerPoint, you might find viewing a presentation in several ways helpful. As you're entering data, you probably only want to see one slide at a time. After the presentation is complete, however, you might want to view multiple slides to get an overview of the presentation. With PowerPoint, you can display a presentation from four different perspectives, called *views*:

- Slide view
- Notes view
- Outline view (Version 3.0 only)
- Slide Sorter view

The buttons for controlling these views are shown in figure 1.6. You'll learn more about working with each of these views in Chapter 3.

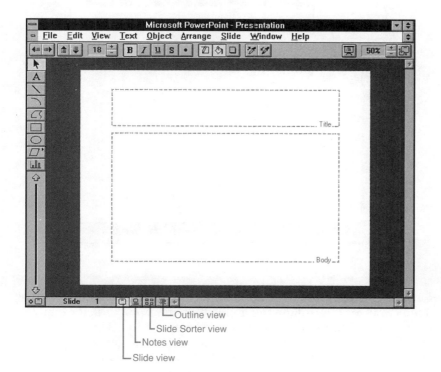

Fig 1.6

The four view buttons.

Using PowerPoint Menus

If you have used other Windows applications, you're familiar with the Windows operating environment. Some of the menus in PowerPoint 3.0—such as the File menu—are similar to those in other Windows applications. You use the same techniques to open menus and select commands in PowerPoint that you use in other programs.

Reviewing PowerPoint's Menus

The basic menu in any Windows application is the Control menu, which is located in the upper left corner of the screen. You identify the Control menu by the horizontal line on the Control menu button. You can use the Control menu options shown in figure 1.7 to close, resize, and move the window.

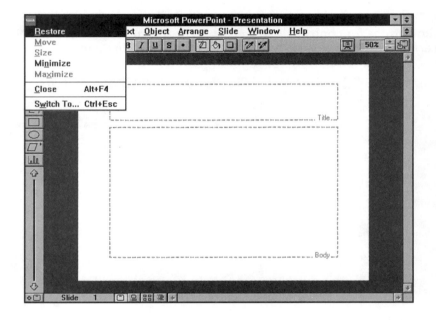

Fig. 1.7

The Control menu.

T I P Remember that in most Windows applications, there are *two* Control menus: one for controlling the application itself, and one for controlling the presentation window within the application. The Control menu button to the left of the application title bar controls the application; the Control menu button to the left of the menu bar controls the presentation window.

Control menus are "special" menus in that they are used to control the windows; they do not affect the workings of the application.

The application menus appear in the menu bar. Table 1.5 lists the available PowerPoint menus.

Table 1.5 PowerPoint Menu Bar—Summary of Functions

Menu	Function
File	Provides access to the disk and lets you open a new or existing presentation, close a presentation, save a presentation, and apply a template. From this menu you also set up the slide dimensions, set up and run the printer, run a slide show, and exit PowerPoint.
Edit	Provides options for manipulating text and objects in slides.
View	Enables you to show slides at different scales and from different views. Use this menu also to display Slide, Notes, Handout and Outline Masters.
Text	Enables you to change the font, size, color, and style of text in a slide. From this menu you can also place and find text in a slide and check spelling.
Object	Lets you control line styles, patterns, and background effects for drawn objects. You can also crop, scale, rotate, or flip objects from this menu.
Arrange	Provides options for rearranging objects, such as aligning, grouping, and ordering. In addition, use this menu to display grids, guides, and edges.
Slide	Enables you to add or delete slides, change color schemes, set timing and transitions for slide shows, and reapply Masters.
Window	Enables you to move between windows and arrange windows.
Help	Provides access to on-line help for PowerPoint.

Choosing a Menu Command

To select any PowerPoint menu by using the mouse, point to the menu and click the left mouse button once. To cancel any menu, use one of the following methods: click the menu again, click the mouse anywhere in the screen outside the menu, or press the Esc key.

To select a menu by using the keyboard, hold down the Alt key and type the underlined letter in the menu, such as the F key for the File menu. You can select the presentation Control menu by pressing Alt--(hyphen). Select the application (PowerPoint) Control menu by pressing Alt-space bar. To cancel a menu from the keyboard, press the Esc key.

Menu commands that appear dimmed are temporarily unavailable— generally because they don't relate to the current task. When an ellipsis (...) appears after the name of a command, choosing that command brings a dialog box on-screen. A check mark next to a command name indicates that the command is active. When a triangle appears to the right of a menu command, choosing that command leads to a drop-down box with additional available commands. If a command has a key combination listed after it, you can use that key combination as a short-cut for choosing the command. For example, to cut a selected object, press Ctrl-X. The shortcut Ctrl-A can be used to select all the objects on a particular slide.

After a menu is open, you can use one of several methods to choose a command:

- Point to the command with the mouse and click.
- Use the arrow keys to highlight your selection, and then press Enter.
- Press the underlined letter in the menu command.
- Press the keyboard shortcut (when listed).

You will become familiar with all the menu options as you read this book.

Getting Help

PowerPoint comes with an on-line Help feature that you access through the Help menu (Alt-H) or by pressing the F1 key. The Help facility provides concise information about a wide variety of PowerPoint topics. Help does not provide comprehensive details for performing complex tasks; it does, however, aid you in remembering procedures and short-cuts, and it can get you safely through the steps for tasks that you perform infrequently.

Using the Help Menu Options

The Help menu has five options: Contents, Search for Help On, Keyboard Guide, How to Use Help, and About PowerPoint. When you choose any of the Help options, a separate Help window opens on-screen.

Help in PowerPoint works just the way Help does in other Windows applications. If you have never used Windows Help before, you might want to click the How to Use Help option to familiarize yourself with the basics of using this feature. The Help Contents window is shown in figure 1.8. The following sections describe each of the Help options.

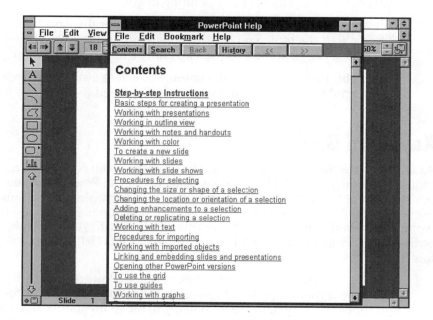

Fig 1.8

The Help
Contents
window.

Search for Help On

When you're looking for a specific topic, it's often more efficient to select the Search for Help On option than to look through the Contents. The Search option displays a separate search window in which you can type any word or topic. To use this option, follow these steps:

1. From the Help menu, choose Search for Help On. The Search dialog box appears and the cursor is blinking in a text box in the upper half of the dialog box.

2. In the text box, type a word or phrase for which to search and press Enter, or double-click an item in the list. The box in the lower half of the dialog box is filled with subtopics.

3. Choose a subtopic from the lower box, and then click the Go To button. PowerPoint displays the topic you choose.

Contents

The Contents option on the Help menu lists a variety of topics grouped under broad categories.

1. From the Help menu, choose Contents. PowerPoint displays the Help contents in a separate Help window. Topics are displayed on-screen in green. When you move the mouse pointer over a topic, the pointer changes to a pointing finger.

2. Click any topic in the list. The Help window either displays information about the topic you chose, or displays another list of subtopics (in green) from which you can choose more specific help.

3. When subtopics are displayed, continue to select a subtopic from the list until the information you want is displayed.

Keyboard Guide

As you work through this book, you will learn all the menu commands and mouse procedures for selecting options, maneuvering in PowerPoint, and initiating actions. Many menu commands, maneuvering tasks, and actions are represented by keyboard shortcuts—key combinations you can use to work with PowerPoint more quickly and efficiently. The Keyboard Guide option on the Help menu lists each shortcut. To use this Help option, follow these steps:

1. From the Help menu, choose Keyboard Guide. PowerPoint displays five keyboard guide categories in the Help window. Categories appear on-screen in green. When you move the mouse pointer over a category, the pointer changes to a pointing finger.

2. Click a category. PowerPoint lists all keyboard shortcuts for the selected category. If necessary, use the scroll bar to view the complete list.

About PowerPoint

The About PowerPoint option on the Help menu lists copyright and version information about PowerPoint. This screen also displays the serial number for your copy of PowerPoint.

Exiting Help

Each option on the Help menu opens a Help window. While the window is displayed, you can maximize, minimize, move, or resize it. When you want to exit Help, you close the Help window by double-clicking the Control menu button or choosing Exit from the File menu.

Chapter Summary

In this chapter, you reviewed some of the standard features of Windows and you learned how to start PowerPoint. You became familiar with the menus, tools, and buttons on the PowerPoint screen, and you learned how to enter and change text on a slide. This chapter showed you how to make selections from PowerPoint menus and helped you become familiar with the menus you are most likely to use each time you work with PowerPoint: the File, View, and Window menus. Finally, you saw how to turn to the Help files for on-line guidance with your PowerPoint tasks. In Chapter 2, you will put your knowledge to use by creating an actual presentation.

Quick Start: Creating Your First Presentation

I n this Quick Start, you get hands-on experience with some of the basic concepts you read about in Chapter 1. As you work through the steps in this chapter, you will develop a familiarity with PowerPoint that will make you more comfortable with the program.

This Quick Start walks you through some basic steps for creating a simple presentation: entering and formatting text, applying a template, creating objects, altering the Slide Master, and viewing slides. You will learn how to use the Text tool and two drawing tools. You finish this Quick Start session by saving your work and exiting PowerPoint. Keep in mind that you might have questions as you work through these steps. Quick Starts guide you through the steps without necessarily explaining all the details. Chapter 3 answers specific questions you might have about creating a presentation.

Starting PowerPoint

PowerPoint must be installed on your system before you can use this Quick Start. See Appendix A if you need help with installation. Because

PowerPoint is a Windows application, you must first open Windows to start PowerPoint. Follow these steps:

1. At the DOS prompt, type *win* to start Windows.

   Windows opens and displays the Program Manager group window. Your own screen will be similar, but not identical to, figure 2.1.

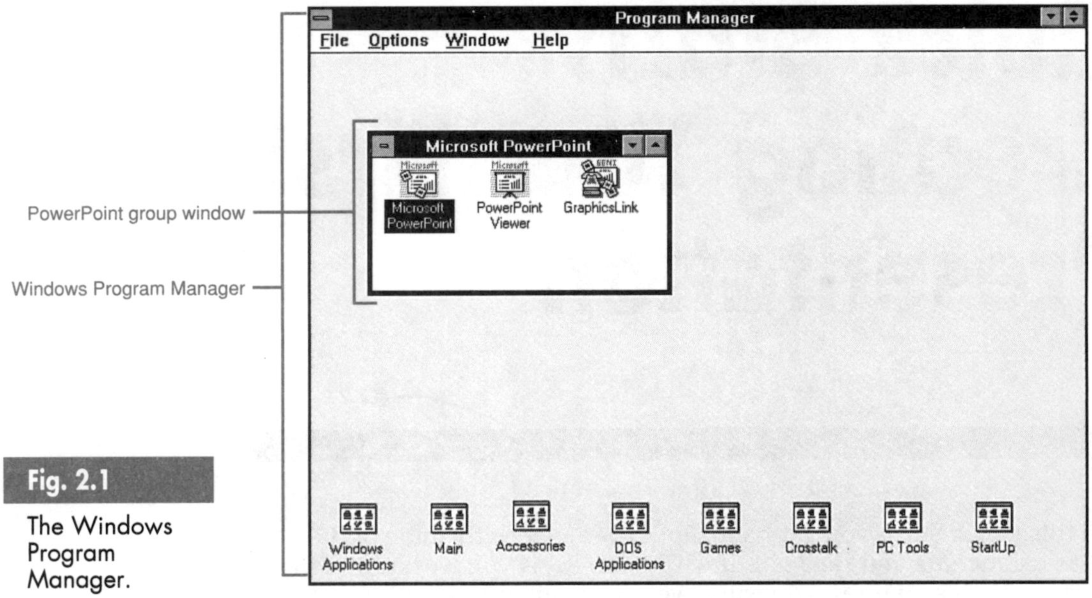

PowerPoint group window ⎯⎯

Windows Program Manager ⎯⎯

Fig. 2.1

The Windows Program Manager.

2. If the Microsoft PowerPoint window is not open, double-click the Microsoft PowerPoint group icon to open the window.

3. Double-click the Microsoft PowerPoint program icon within the Microsoft PowerPoint window. The PowerPoint opening screen appears (see fig. 2.2).

Working with Slides

Each time you open PowerPoint, a new presentation is created for you. A *presentation* is a file that contains an entire set of related slides. The new presentation that PowerPoint creates initially contains one slide. Normally, you add additional slides to the initial slide that PowerPoint creates. Whenever you open PowerPoint, the first screen you see shows the first slide of a new presentation. The slide number appears in the lower left corner of the Presentation window in the *slide counter*.

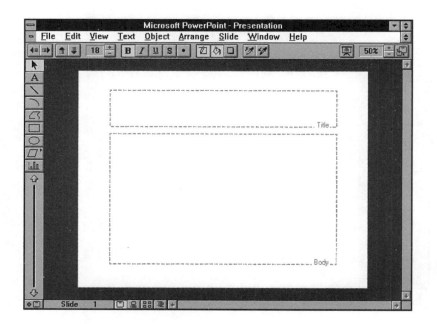

Fig. 2.2

The PowerPoint
opening screen.

Adding a New Slide

The new presentation, which contains only one slide, takes on
PowerPoint's default settings: a simple color scheme and no text. You
build a presentation by adding slides whenever and wherever you want
them. PowerPoint inserts a new slide immediately following the current
slide. So, for example, if your presentation contains eight slides and
you want to insert a new slide between slides 3 and 4, select slide 3
before adding a new slide. When a presentation contains only one slide,
PowerPoint automatically adds the new slide following the first. To add
a slide, click on the New Slide tool (located at the bottom of the slide
changer), or choose New Slide from the Slide menu.

PowerPoint adds to the presentation a new slide *immediately following*
the slide that was previously displayed. Note the new slide number at
the bottom of the window.

The keyboard shortcut for adding a slide is Ctrl-N.	T I P

When you want to insert a slide in a presentation that contains multiple
slides, select the slide that precedes the slide you want to insert, and
then click the New Slide tool. The new slide, shown in figure 2.3, is identical to the first slide. The slide counter now displays Slide 2.

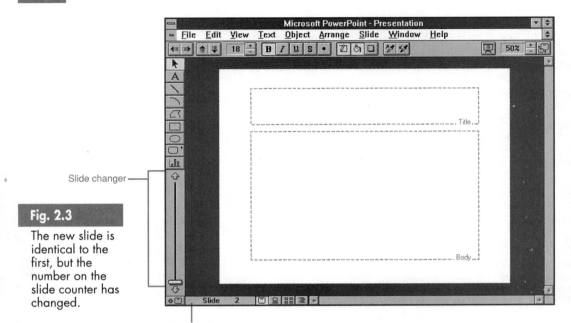

Slide changer

Fig. 2.3

The new slide is identical to the first, but the number on the slide counter has changed.

Slide number

Moving from One Slide to Another

In PowerPoint, you do not work with a single slide (as was often the case with pre-Windows graphics programs) but with a complete presentation made up of more than one slide. You can move from one slide to another in a number of ways. The following lists the most common methods:

Use the slide changer. To return to the first slide, click the top arrow of the slide changer (refer back to fig. 2.3). Slide 1 returns to the screen. When your presentation contains more than one slide, drag the slide changer bar until the slide you want is displayed. The slide counter shows the number of the slide currently displayed.

Use the Page Up and Page Down keys. You can also use the Page Up key to move back one slide and the Page Down key to move to the next slide. The disadvantage to this method is that you can only move one slide at a time.

Working with Text

Each new slide you add contains a title box and a body box, referred to as *objects*. You enter the title for a slide in the title object and the content for the slide in the body object. The title and body objects are the only two objects that PowerPoint creates automatically for you. You can add and edit text in the title and body objects. If you add other objects to a slide, such as circles or rectangles, you can also add text to those objects. In this section you learn how to work with text in the title and body objects; later in this Quick Start you will add text to other objects.

Adding Text

When you want to add text anywhere on a slide in PowerPoint, you use the Text tool. The Text tool contains the letter A; it is the second tool on the tool palette (see fig. 2.4). Follow these steps to add a title to the title object on Slide 1:

1. Use the slide changer to move to Slide 1, if it is not already displayed.

2. Click the Text tool; then click anywhere. The text cursor is blinking in the title object. Double-click in the title object.

3. Type *Exotic Winds Travel Agency* as the title for the first slide.

4. Click anywhere outside of the title object to deselect the object. Your screen now resembles figure 2.4.

> You can use the Text tool by simply double-clicking anywhere in the object in which you want to add text. The blinking text cursor appears.
>
> **T I P**

The procedure for entering text in the text object and the body object is the same. Follow these steps to enter information into the body object:

1. With Slide 1 displayed, double-click anywhere in the body object. The box shrinks to one line, and PowerPoint automatically inserts a bullet preceding the text. The bullet is part of PowerPoint's default settings for the body object.

Text tool

Title in title box

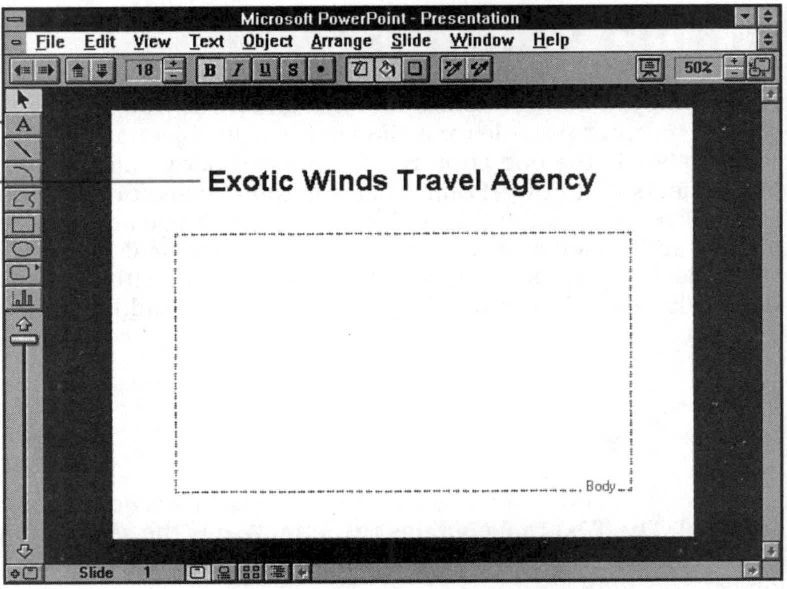

Exotic Winds Travel Agency

Fig 2.4

The title you typed is displayed in the title object.

2. Type *Established in 1934*; then press Enter. A bullet for the second line is inserted automatically.

3. On the second line, type *200 domestic offices, 50 international*; then press Enter.

4. On the third line, type *Specializes in recreational travel*. Don't press Enter.

5. Click anywhere outside the body object to deselect the object. Your screen now resembles figure 2.5.

Formatting Text

Format refers to any attributes that affect the appearance of text: the font style and size; alignment; and attributes, such as bold, italic, or color. You can change the format of any text on a slide. To change the font of the title on the first slide and then underline the text, follow these steps:

1. Click the Text tool on the tool palette.

2. Point to the *E* in *Exotic*, and then click and drag the mouse across the entire title, releasing the mouse button when the title is highlighted.

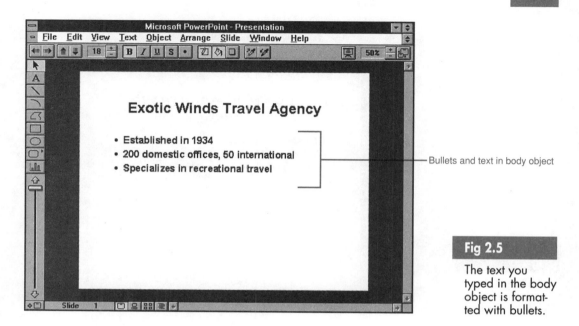

Fig 2.5

The text you typed in the body object is formatted with bullets.

3. Choose Font from the Text menu. A drop-down menu containing a list of fonts is displayed.

4. Click the Lucida Calligraphy font, or any other font if that one is not available. The drop-down menu closes and PowerPoint reformats the selected text using the font you choose. The title text is still selected.

5. Choose Style from the Text menu. A submenu containing style options is displayed.

6. Choose Underline from the submenu. PowerPoint reformats the title text. Your screen now resembles figure 2.6.

Notice that four of the options listed on the Style submenu have corresponding tools on the Toolbar (see fig. 2.7). To use these tools, select the text, and then click the tool.

T I P

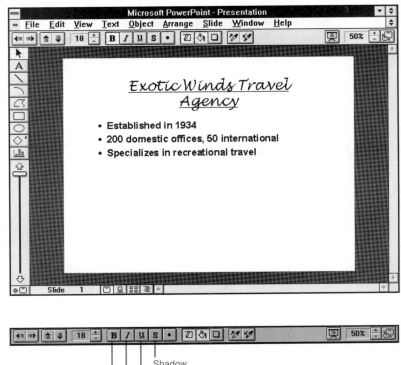

The title text is underlined in a new font style.

Four text style tools on the Toolbar.

Changing the Slide Master

To maintain consistency, most slides in a slide presentation have some common elements. For example, you might want your company or organization logo to appear on each slide. You could include the date or other pertinent information as well. So that you do not have to create these elements on each slide, you can define these elements on a *Slide Master*. All elements of the Slide Master appear on each slide in the presentation. (Every presentation has a Slide Master whether or not you alter the master.) In the following sections, you learn how to add a simple border to the Slide Master and add a simple company logo. Chapter 3 explains specific details about the Slide Master.

To alter the Slide Master for a presentation, you must first display the Slide Master. Click the Slide Master button. You also can choose Slide Master from the View menu. A Slide Master is shown in figure 2.8.

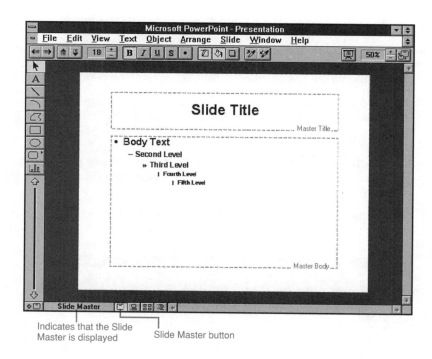

Indicates that the Slide
Master is displayed

Slide Master button

Fig 2.8

The Slide Master
for the active
presentation.

Notice that the Slide Master is almost identical to slide 1. The style of
the title, including the font and size, is the same for other slides as for
the Master. (Recall that you changed the font on slide 1, so it looks
different.)

On the Slide Master, make any changes that you want to apply to each
slide. When you return to Slide view, the slides reflect the changes you
made to the Slide Master.

Drawing a Rectangle

The tool palette, introduced in Chapter 1, contains six drawing tools. In
this section, you use the Rectangle tool to draw a border around the
Slide Master. Follow these steps:

1. Click the Slide Master button or choose Slide Master from the
   View menu. PowerPoint displays the Slide Master for the current
   presentation.

2. Click the Fill tool on the Toolbar to turn off the fill. This step is
   necessary so that the rectangle you draw is transparent.

3. Click the Rectangle tool on the tool palette.

4. Place the mouse pointer (now in the shape of a crosshair) in the upper left corner of the slide, about one-half inch inside the corner of the white background.

5. Click and drag to the bottom right corner of the slide. As you drag the mouse, you see an outline of the rectangle you're creating.

6. Release the mouse button.

   The rectangle is selected after you draw it. If you are not satisfied with the rectangle, press the Delete key, and then repeat steps 4, 5, and 6.

7. Click any blank area of the screen to deselect the rectangle. Your screen now resembles figure 2.9.

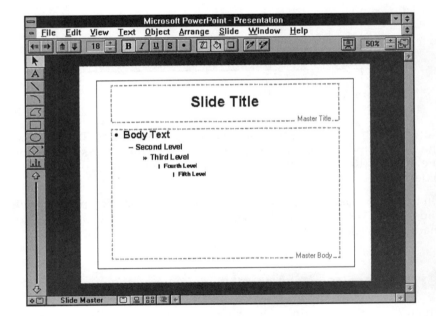

Fig. 2.9

The Slide Master includes a rectangular border drawn using the Rectangle tool.

Adding Text to an Object

In this section, you use another drawing tool to draw an object and add text to it. In the following steps, you draw a diamond shape for a company logo and type the company name inside the diamond. Using this method, the text is attached to the object; when you move or copy the object, the text moves with it.

The Shape tool, which offers 24 different shape options, is the eighth tool on the tool palette. The tool has a right-pointing arrow in the upper right corner, indicating that a submenu is displayed when you select this tool. To add an object with text, follow these steps:

1. Move the mouse pointer to the Shape tool; then press and hold the mouse button until the menu of drawing shapes is displayed.

2. Click the diamond shape (the fourth shape on the top row). The menu disappears and the tool on the tool palette now displays a diamond shape.

3. In the upper left corner of the slide near the border you drew earlier, click and drag a diamond shape large enough to hold the words *Exotic Winds* (on two lines). Release the mouse button when the shape resembles the one shown in figure 2.10. The shape is selected.

4. Type *Exotic* and press Enter.

5. Type *Winds*. Don't press Enter. Click any blank area of the screen to deselect the diamond.

6. To position the diamond as shown in figure 2.10, click the Selection tool, and then click the diamond shape. The mouse pointer arrow returns. Point to the border surrounding the diamond, and click and drag the diamond to reposition it. When the diamond is positioned correctly, release the mouse button.

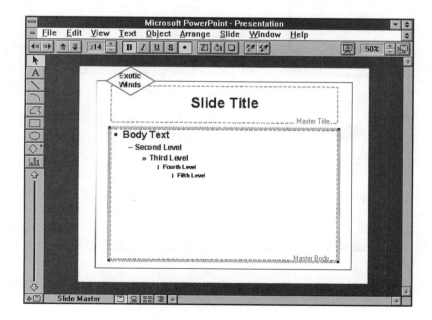

Fig 2.10

The simple logo box on the Slide Master is an object with attached text.

The logo completes the changes to the Slide Master. To return to Slide view, click the Slide View button or choose Slides from the View menu. Each slide now contains the logo you created.

Viewing Slides

At any point while you are creating a presentation, you can view all slides in the presentation by using the Slide Sorter. To select the Slide Sorter view, click the Slide Sorter button (the button that contains four small boxes). Figure 2.11 illustrates the active presentation displayed in Slide Sorter view. (This presentation contains additional slides. On your screen, you will see the first slide that contains text and one additional slide that is blank.) Notice that the Slide Sorter button is highlighted (indicating that it is selected). Using the keyboard, you can switch to Slide Sorter view by choosing the Slide Sorter command from the View menu.

Notice that all the elements you added to the Slide Master are included on every slide in the presentation. The actual text on each slide is probably indistinguishable when displayed at 33 or 50 percent.

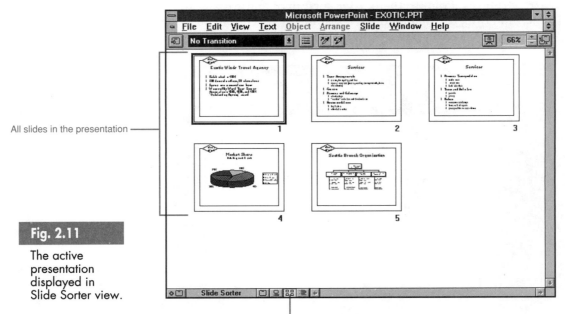

All slides in the presentation ——

Fig. 2.11

The active presentation displayed in Slide Sorter view.

Slide sorter view button

To return to Slide view, click the Slide View button at the bottom of the screen. Using the keyboard, choose the Slides command from the View menu. To return to a specific slide in Slide view, double-click the slide. PowerPoint displays the selected slide in Slide view.

Saving a Presentation

Until you actually save your presentation using the Save or Save As command, the changes you make to the active presentation are not stored on disk. The following steps briefly describe how to save the active presentation for the first time. For a detailed discussion of file names, directories, and drives, refer to Chapter 3. To save a presentation, follow these steps:

1. Choose Save from the File menu. Because you are saving for the first time, PowerPoint displays the Save As dialog box (see fig. 2.12). The cursor is positioned in the File Name text box.

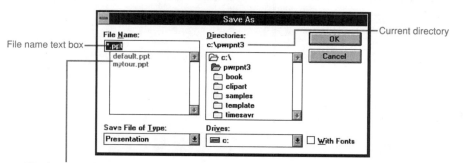

Fig 2.12

The Save As dialog box.

2. Type *myfile* as the file name. PowerPoint adds the .PPT file extension to the file name.

3. Click OK or press Enter. PowerPoint saves your presentation and continues to display it in the active window. Notice that the file name you used is now reflected in the title bar.

Exiting PowerPoint

When you're ready to close PowerPoint, choose the Exit command from the File menu. PowerPoint closes and your screen returns to the Windows Program Manager.

If you try to exit the program before saving any open presentations, PowerPoint displays a message asking whether you want to save the active presentation (and other presentations, if other files are open). Respond to the message for each file displayed. PowerPoint then exits the program as usual.

Chapter Summary

This chapter gave you hands-on experience using some of the basic procedures in PowerPoint. You started PowerPoint from the Windows Program Manager and created new slides in the active presentation. You learned how to enter and edit text in text objects, and you drew new objects on the Slide Master using PowerPoint's drawing tools. Finally, you saved the presentation for future use and exited the program.

You now have the basics skills for using PowerPoint. In Chapter 3, you will learn more detail about the basic functions you used in this Quick Start.

Creating a Presentation

The Quick Start in Chapter 2 gave you some hands-on experience creating an actual presentation, and you probably developed a list of questions along the way. In this chapter, you find the answers to those questions by learning more details about creating a presentation. You begin by learning a step-by-step procedure for creating a presentation. This chapter covers each step in the process: creating a new file, setting defaults, applying templates, editing the Slide Master, and so on. By the time you finish reading this chapter, you will feel comfortable not only creating a presentation, but creating a polished, professional presentation that contains impressive design elements.

Understanding the Presentation Process

Whether you're using a spreadsheet application to create a financial spreadsheet or a desktop publishing application to create a newsletter, it's always best to follow a logical process from beginning to end. The same is true when creating a presentation in PowerPoint. The general steps to follow when creating a PowerPoint presentation are outlined next. Note that some of the steps—for instance, steps 2 and 3—are more advanced. These steps are not covered in detail in this chapter, but they are noted here because they are part of the overall process. Note, also, that some steps (including some of the advanced steps) are optional. Because PowerPoint is flexible, you are in control of the presentation you create, and you can make it as simple or sophisticated as you choose.

To create a PowerPoint presentation, follow these general steps:

1. Begin a new presentation or make an untitled copy of an existing presentation.

2. Set up your printer. (For more information about setting up your printer, see Chapter 9.)

3. Choose the slide setup settings (such as the dimensions and numbering of your slides). This topic is also discussed in Chapter 9.

4. Use PowerPoint's defaults settings or *(optional)* customize the settings. You can change default settings for the current presentation or for all future presentations.

5. *(Optional)* Select a template. You can use PowerPoint's default template, select a specially-designed template, or copy the template from an existing file.

6. Review and/or edit the masters for your presentation: the Slide Master, the Notes Master, the Outline Master, and the Handout Master.

7. Create the slides for your presentation.

8. *(Optional)* Display the presentation from different views and use the Slide Sorter to rearrange slides, if necessary.

9. *(Optional)* Add, delete, copy, or rearrange slides.

10. *(Optional)* Create a Notes page for each slide.

11. Save the presentation and exit PowerPoint.

Beginning a New Presentation

When you start PowerPoint, the presentation that appears on-screen is a new presentation. To work with this presentation (called *Presentation* until you rename it), you simply begin adding slides and filling them in with text, objects, and graphics. This presentation uses PowerPoint's default settings, which are set in the template default.ppt.

In some cases, however, you will want to copy an existing presentation rather than start with a new one. For instance, suppose that you created a presentation three months ago that summarized sales activity for the previous quarter. You could simply copy that presentation and update it with new sales activity for the current quarter. To open an untitled copy of an existing presentation, follow these steps:

1. Choose Open from the File menu. The Open dialog box appears (see fig. 3.1).

The Open dialog box.

The dialog box lists the directory that you specified the last time you used any of the File menu options; in figure 3.1, the directory is c:\pwrpnt3. The Files box on the left displays all .ppt files in this directory. (Other presentations in this directory might have extensions other than .ppt, but PowerPoint does not recognize them. If you want to see a presentation file that has an extension other than .ppt, type the full name in the File Name box and click OK. If the file exists, it is displayed on-screen.)

2. If necessary, select a different directory for the file you want to open.

3. Select a file from the list of files that appears.

4. Click the Open Untitled Copy check box in the lower right corner of the dialog box.

> **CAUTION:** Step 4 is extremely important. If you fail to check the Open Untitled Copy check box, PowerPoint opens the original file. If you alter the file and save the changes, the original presentation is permanently changed.

5. Click OK or press Enter. The file you chose appears on-screen. The file is called Presentation2 until you save and rename it.

T   I   P To open a file quickly, display the Open dialog box and double-click the name of the file that you want to open. The dialog box closes and the file appears on-screen.

When you work with a copy of a presentation, the new presentation contains all the content and the same number of slides as the original. Rather than create a presentation, therefore, you edit an existing one. The remainder of this chapter specifically addresses how to *create* a presentation, although you can easily apply the concepts to editing a presentation.

T   I   P When you want to make changes to an existing presentation, follow the preceding steps, except skip step 4.

Setting PowerPoint Defaults

If you have used other computer programs, you are probably familiar with defaults. *Defaults* are initial program settings that are used in all PowerPoint presentations unless you change them. For example, PowerPoint has an initial color scheme; initial font settings; and an initial format for text, ruler settings, and default settings for each master (the Slide Master, the Notes Master, the Outline Master, and the Handout Master). These default settings are stored in a file called *default.ppt*.

If you're new to PowerPoint, use the defaults until you get to know the program. Until you understand the default color scheme in PowerPoint, for example, you may not want to set up a color scheme of your own. For future reference, however, this section explains the *process* for saving new default settings. You haven't yet learned how to change specific settings, such as color, formatting, or ruler settings; you learn these skills in later chapters. This section tells you how to save settings as defaults after they have been changed.

PowerPoint enables you to change the default settings for the current presentation or for all future presentations (by altering the *default.ppt* file). To save new default settings for the current presentation, follow these steps:

1. Select the Arrow tool on the tool palette. This step ensures that no objects or text in the active presentation are selected.

2. Use the commands on the Text, Object, and Slide menus to select the settings you want to change.

   Because you change the settings without selecting text or an object first, PowerPoint automatically saves the new settings as defaults for the active presentation.

To save new default settings for all new presentations, you alter the default.ppt file. Follow these steps:

1. Open a new presentation and use the commands on the Text, Object, and Slide menus to select the settings you want to change.

   Or

   Open an existing presentation that contains the settings you want to use as defaults.

2. When all settings are correct, choose Save As from the File menu. The Save As dialog box appears.

3. Verify that the current directory is the PowerPoint directory (c:\pwrpnt, unless you renamed it).

4. In the File Name box, type *default.ppt*; then choose OK or press Enter.

Using these steps, you overwrite the default.ppt file with the new settings you chose; the format you saved becomes PowerPoint's default. Whenever you create a new presentation and choose the Use Default Format option from the New dialog box, the new presentations will assume these edited defaults.

The PowerPoint defaults are the product of much collective expertise at Microsoft Corporation. The defaults conform to standards of good usage and design. Until you believe that you have mastered such standards yourself, don't change the default format. A safer method is to copy the default format as a new file and alter the copy. (For information about the default file, refer to Appendix B; this appendix summarizes the default settings in default.ppt.)

T I P

Using Templates

Many people who use presentation graphics programs (such as Power-Point) would like to enter the substance of their presentation and have the program do the design work for them. They want their presentations to look great, but they don't have the graphic arts expertise to create powerful, impressive, professional-quality slides.

PowerPoint provides templates to meet the needs of these users. PowerPoint *templates* are complete collections of masters, designed by professional artists at Genigraphics Corporation. A presentation you create with PowerPoint rivals the quality of any presentation you could commission from a third-party design agency. You don't need to be a graphic arts expert to use PowerPoint, and you can easily make changes to a template.

You can apply a template to an existing presentation, or you can create a new presentation using the template of an existing presentation. Both of these methods are described later in this section. First, however, you take a look at the elements of a template.

 **NOTE** Often new users are not sure how defaults relate to templates. The answer is simple: the default.ppt file that contains PowerPoint's default settings is, itself, a template. When you use PowerPoint's default settings, you are actually using a template, but PowerPoint applies it to your presentation automatically. When you choose one of PowerPoint's custom-designed templates, you must apply it to your presentation, as you learn shortly.

Reviewing the Elements of a Template

Every PowerPoint template consists of a set of masters. A *master* contains common items (such as text or objects) that you want to appear on every slide or page. Each master contained in a template is described in table 3.1.

Table 3.1 Masters in a Template	
Master Type	**Description**
Slide Master	The Slide Master sets up the design of every slide in the presentation. Text and objects that you place here appear on every slide. For more information, refer to the section "Editing a Slide Master" later in this chapter.

Master Type	Description
Outline Master	The Outline Master determines how each outline page will look. (Refer to Chapter 9 for more information about the Outline Master.)
Notes Master	A notes page for a given slide contains a reduced image of the slide at the top of the page and your notes about the slide at the bottom of the page. The Notes Master contains the elements that appear on every notes page. (Refer to Chapter 9 for more information about the Notes Master.)
Handout Master	PowerPoint enables you to create handout pages to distribute to an audience. The Handout Master determines the format and layout of handout pages and the elements that appear on every page, such as a company logo. (Refer to Chapter 9 for more information about the Handout Master.)

Every template also includes settings for a color scheme, background items, and text format.

Choosing a Template

PowerPoint contains a wide variety of templates. Each template was designed with a particular type of output in mind, so the templates are grouped into four categories:

- 33mm slides
- Black-and-white overheads
- Color overheads
- Video screen

Each category contains 40 templates.

PowerPoint's template files are stored in a subdirectory of the PowerPoint directory, usually c:\pwrpnt\template, unless you renamed your PowerPoint directory. The subdirectories for the categories are 35mslide, b&wovrhd, clrovrhd, and vidscren. A video screen template, for example, is found in the directory c:\pwrpnt\template\vidscren.

To browse through PowerPoint's templates, follow these steps:

1. Open a new presentation.
2. Choose Apply Template from the File menu. The Apply Template dialog box appears.

3. In the Directories box, double-click the Template directory (a subdirectory under your PowerPoint directory).

4. Double-click the vidscren subdirectory. (You can choose a different template directory, but the vidscren files are best for on-screen display.)

5. Select any of the files in the Files list. A miniature version of the template appears on the right side of the dialog box.

6. Repeat Step 5 to preview as many templates as you like.

7. To return to your presentation without applying a template, click Cancel.

Figure 3.2 illustrates a sample template displayed in the Apply Template dialog box. The template is more difficult to see on the page of this book than it is on your screen.

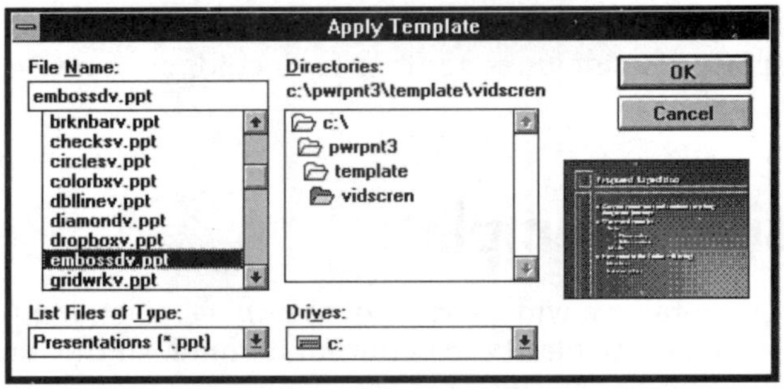

Fig. 3.2

The Apply Template dialog box.

Each subdirectory contains the same—or nearly the same—file names for templates. For example, one of the template files in the vidscren subdirectory is named bludiagv.ppt. This template displays blue diagonal lines in the background of the slide. The same template file can be found in each of the template subdirectories. In the b&wovrhd subdirectory, this file is named bludiagb.ppt; in the 35mslide sub-directory, it is named bludiag3.ppt; in the clrovrhd subdirectory, the same file is named bludiagc.ppt. The last character in the file name reflects the subdirectory in which the file is located. Although the names are nearly the same, the templates are slightly different for each category. Each template has been optimized for the type of output it provides.

Applying a Template

To apply a template to the active presentation, follow these steps:

1. With the presentation in the active window, choose Apply Template from the File menu. PowerPoint displays the Apply Template dialog box (again see figure 3.2).

2. In the Directories box, double-click the template directory.

3. Double-click a subdirectory, such as vidscren. A list of file names appears in the Files box.

4. Click any of the files in the list. A miniature version of the template appears on the right side of the dialog box.

5. Click OK. When PowerPoint returns to the Presentation window, you see a brief message on-screen as the slides in your presentation are updated with the template's attributes.

Sometimes the miniature preview of a template on the Apply Template dialog box is difficult to see. To view a template on an actual slide, follow the preceding steps. If you don't like the template you selected, you can change the template by repeating the steps with a different template file. (After you apply a template, you cannot use the Undo command on the Edit menu to remove the template.)

T I P

Working with a Slide Master

In the previous section you learned that each template contains a Slide Master. A Slide Master contains the elements that you want to appear on every slide. These elements might include a border, a background, the company logo, the date of the presentation, and so on. These elements are automatically transferred to each slide in a presentation so that you don't have to re-create them.

Editing a Slide Master

Technically, you cannot *create* a Slide Master because each template (including the default.ppt template) already contains one. You can, however, *edit* any template's Slide Master. Editing a Slide Master is no more difficult than editing any slide. Follow these steps:

1. Open the presentation for which you want to edit the Slide Master.

2. If you are already using Slide view, click the Slide View button at the bottom of the window. The Slide Master appears in the active window and the slide counter reads Slide Master (see fig. 3.3).

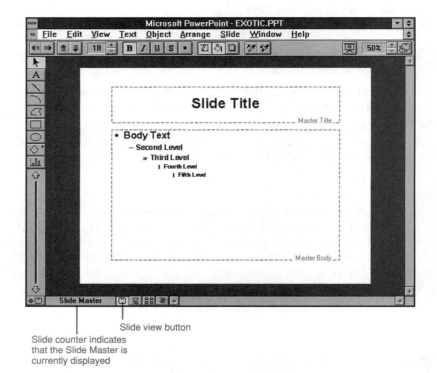

3. To change text formatting in either the Title Master or Body Master, click anywhere in the text object.

4. Choose any of the commands on the Text menu (such as Font, Size, Style, and so on) to reformat the text in the selected object. (Chapter 4 discusses text formatting in detail.)

5. To insert objects on the Slide Master, select any of the drawing tools and draw the objects that you want to appear on each slide. (Refer to Chapter 5 for a detailed explanation of drawing and moving objects.) Choose commands on the Object menu to define characteristics such as Fill, Line, Line Style, Shadow, and so on.

6. To define a color scheme, choose Color Scheme from the Slide menu. (Color schemes are covered in Chapter 7.)

7. When your Slide Master looks the way you want it, return to Slide view by clicking once on the Slide View button at the bottom of the window. The number of the current slide appears in the slide counter.

You can also add an image file, such as your logo, to the Slide Master by using the tools for importing and cropping an image. These tools are explained in Chapter 11.

Adding Special Text to the Slide Master

PowerPoint provides special codes that you can place on the Slide Master to enter slide numbers, the time, and the date automatically. You can either type these codes or use the Insert command to enter them into your file. The number code is ##, the time code is :: and the date code is //. To enter any of these codes, follow these steps:

1. Open the Slide Master.

2. Click on the Text tool. The mouse pointer changes to an I-beam.

3. Click the mouse pointer in the location on the slide where you want the date, time, or page number to appear.

4. Choose Insert from the Edit menu. PowerPoint displays a submenu.

5. From the submenu, choose Date, Time, or Page Number. PowerPoint inserts the code into the slide as a text object.

6. Click in any blank area of the screen to deselect the text object.

The code you inserted appears when you view the slides. When you print the slides, the actual page number, date, or time is printed.

Turning Off Elements of a Slide Master

Even though you define a Slide Master for a presentation, you can change slides individually. To do so, simply display the slide and make the changes you want. PowerPoint also lets you remove selected attributes and elements of the Slide Master from individual slides. You can "turn off" the Slide Master's Color Scheme, Background Items, Title Style, or Body Style on individual slides. Follow these steps:

1. Display the slide you want to change.

2. Choose Follow Master from the Slide menu. A submenu appears displaying a check mark beside each of the four options (Color

Scheme, Background Items, Title Style, Body Style). The check marks indicate that each of these attributes from the Slide Master is currently applied to the selected slide (see fig. 3.4).

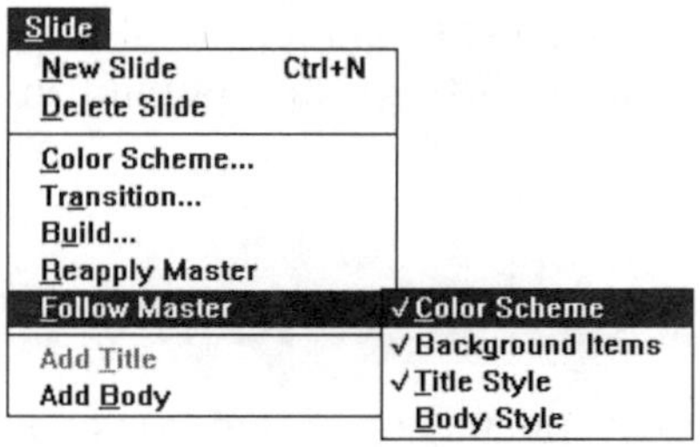

Fig. 3.4

Attributes from the Slide Master for each checked option are applied to the current slide.

```
 Slide
 New Slide          Ctrl+N
 Delete Slide
 ───────────────────────
 Color Scheme...
 Transition...
 Build...
 Reapply Master
 Follow Master          ┌──────────────────────┐
 ───────────────────────│ √ Color Scheme       │
 Add Title              │ √ Background Items    │
 Add Body               │ √ Title Style         │
                        │   Body Style          │
                        └──────────────────────┘
```

3. On the submenu, click the options you *don't* want applied to the current slide. If you don't want the selected slide to use the color scheme defined by the Slide Master, for example, click the Color Scheme option so that the check mark disappears. The current slide changes to reflect your choices.

4. Repeat steps 2 and 3 to turn off other attributes on the current slide.

Reapplying Slide Master Attributes

To reapply Slide Master attributes to slides you have modified, select the correct slide, and then choose the Reapply Master command from the Slide menu. PowerPoint reapplies all attributes that are currently checked on the Follow Master submenu.

After you have edited a Slide Master, you can then use the same Text, Object, and Slide menu commands to edit your changes. When you change the Slide Master for an existing presentation, all the slides in the presentation are reformatted to reflect the new Slide Master. This rule does have one exception: if you have reset the color scheme on one or more slides, those slides will not be changed by the new Slide Master settings. In other words, if you want the slides you altered individually to look like the other slides, you must reset the color scheme on those slides individually.

Creating the Slide Content

At this point, you're ready to add content to the slides. As you have already learned, you can add text, objects, graphs, charts, images, or other types of data to slides. Refer to Chapters 4 and 12 to learn how to work with text elements in a slide. Chapters 5 and 13 explain how to create graphs and charts and insert them in slides. Finally, refer to Chapter 10 for a discussion of importing images and data from other applications.

Viewing a Presentation

You can use the View buttons (Slide View, Notes View, Outline View, and Slide Sorter View) to change your view of a presentation. In this section, you learn how to select the various views and you see how each view helps you manage a presentation.

The View buttons all toggle: one click displays a given view, another click displays the corresponding master. Because the Slide Sorter has no master, there is one exception to this rule: a second click on the Slide Sorter button displays the Handout Master. The View button functions are summarized in table 3.2.

Table 3.2 The View Button Functions

Button	Toggle Positions
View	Individual slides/Slide Master
Notes	Individual notes pages/Notes Master
Outline	Presentation in outline form/Outline Master
Slide Sorter	Multiple slides on one screen/Handout Master

Using Slide View

Slide view needs little explanation; you have been working almost exclusively in Slide view throughout Chapters 1, 2, and 3. Use this view to see individual slides. Use the slide changer to move from one slide to another. When Slide view is already active, click once on the Slide view button to display the Slide Master. To select Slide view or the Slide

Master by using the keyboard, choose the appropriate command from the View menu.

Using Notes View

PowerPoint automatically creates a Notes Master for each presentation. The Notes Master defines the format for the notes pages of a presentation. The standard format displays a reduced view of the slide in the upper half of the page. The bottom half of the page contains a body object (see fig. 3.5). Use this object to enter speaker's notes that pertain to the selected slide. When Notes view is already active, click the Notes View button to display the Notes Master. To select Notes view or the Notes Master by using the keyboard, choose the appropriate command from the View menu.

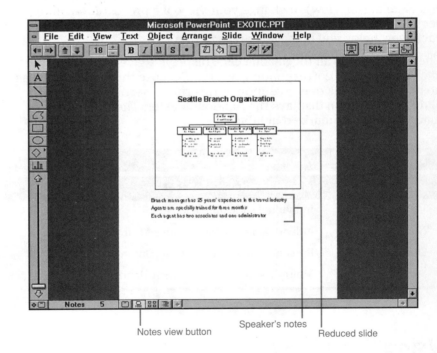

Notes view button   Speaker's notes   Reduced slide

Using Outline View

A new feature with Version 3.0 of PowerPoint enables you to work with slides in Outline mode. If you have worked with Outline mode in Word for Windows, you already know how to use this feature. In Outline view, only the title and text from a slide are displayed in the form of an outline. Any objects, figures, graphs, or charts contained in a slide are *not* displayed.

In Outline view, the contents of multiple slides are shown on the screen at once. Each slide is indicated by a slide icon to the left of the title. When the slide contains graphical objects, the slide icon also includes a graphical representation (see fig. 3.6).

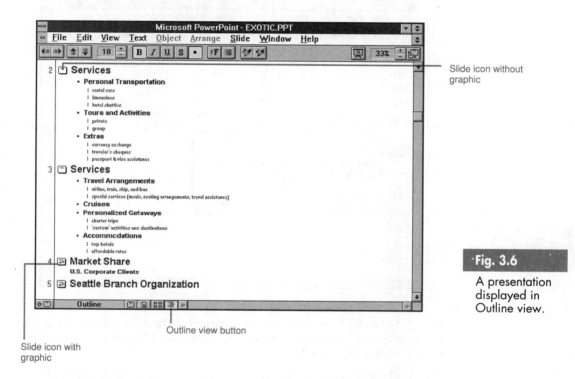

Slide icon without graphic

Outline view button

Slide icon with graphic

Fig. 3.6

A presentation displayed in Outline view.

Some people find Outline view very efficient to use, especially when first entering the content of a slide. When Outline view is active, a single click on the Outline View button displays the Outline Master. Commands for the outline and Outline Master are available on the View menu as well.

Using Slide Sorter View

Slide Sorter view is most useful for getting an overall perspective of a presentation and for rearranging slides in a presentation. In this view, a miniature version of each slide is displayed (see fig. 3.7). The slide number appears near the bottom right corner of each slide. This view also allows you to set timing and transitions between slides for an automatic slide show. For instance, you might want each slide to remain onscreen for 30 seconds, and then "dissolve" into the next slide. When timing has been set between slides for an automatic slide show, the time appears at the bottom left corner of each slide.

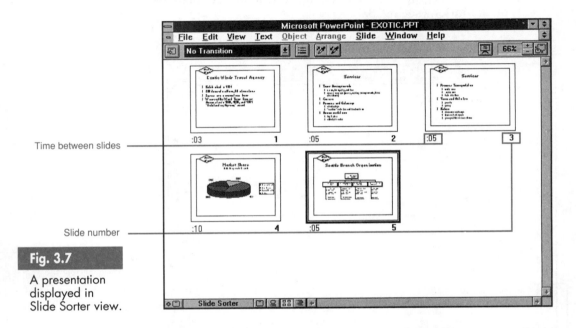

Time between slides

Slide number

Fig. 3.7

A presentation displayed in Slide Sorter view.

After Slide Sorter view is active, you can click the Slide Sorter button to display the Handout Master. (Using the keyboard, you can select either of these views from the View menu.)

You define elements of the Handout Master the same way you do for the Slide, Outline, and Notes Masters. The dotted lines that appear on the Handout Master illustrate where slides will be printed on a handout, depending on the number of slides you choose per page. When you choose two slides, they are arranged vertically on each page. When you choose three slides, they are arranged vertically down the left side of each page. When you choose six slides per page, they appear in two vertical columns of three slides each.

The exact number you see depends on the scale you are using and the size of the window. The slide number appears at the bottom right of each minislide. When timing between slides has been set for an automatic slide show, the time also appears near the bottom of each slide.

Changing the Scale of the Display

You can view the contents of a PowerPoint window at 25%, 33%, 50%, 66%, Actual Size, 200%, or 400%. Using one of these options is called *scaling* the window. At actual size (100%), a slide appears in the window at the size it will be when printed. To see an entire slide in Slide view, select 25%, 33%, 50%, or 66%. When you select Actual Size (100%), 200%, or 400%, you may not be able to see an entire slide in the window at once. Use the scroll bars to see sections of the window that aren't visible on-screen.

You scale a window using the Scale tool on the Toolbar, or by choosing a scale option on the View menu. The current scale is always displayed next to the Scale tool on the Toolbar. (The tool itself contains the + and – signs; the scale display appears to the left of the tool.) The current scale is also indicated in the View menu by a dot to the left of the active scale option.

Figure 3.8 shows how a normal slide looks when displayed at 100%. Compare this slide to the scale display for most of the previous figures in this chapter, which are displayed at 50%.

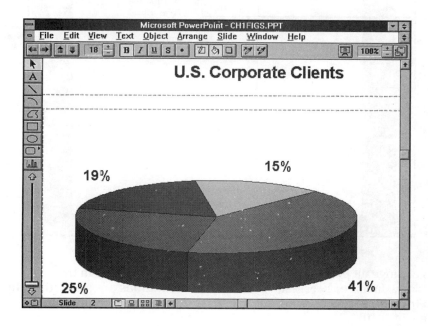

Fig. 3.8

A slide containing a pie chart displayed at 100%.

To change the scale of the active presentation, click the + or – sign on the Scale tool, or choose a percentage from the View menu. The contents of the window are immediately resized according to the scale you choose.

You can scale any PowerPoint window regardless of the view you are using. For example, when using Slide Sorter view, the contents of a single slide generally are not readable. You can "zoom in" to read the contents of a slide by selecting a larger scale such as 200%.

Viewing More Than One Presentation

A powerful feature of Windows is its capability to have more than one application file open at once. In PowerPoint, this capability means that you can work on more than one presentation at a time. You can have more than one file open at once, even if you don't see both files on-screen simultaneously. Whenever you have multiple presentations open at one time, you use the Window menu to manage those presentations on-screen. Figure 3.9 shows the Window menu.

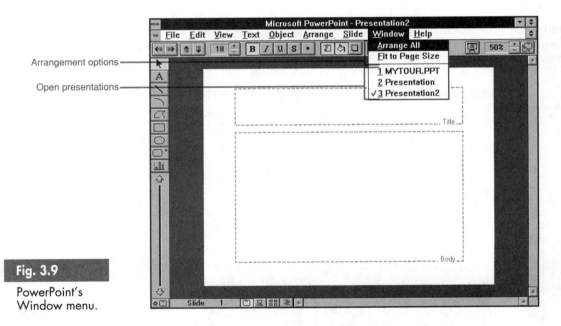

Fig. 3.9

PowerPoint's Window menu.

To arrange all presentations on-screen, click Arrange All in the Window menu or press Alt-A. All open presentations are stacked neatly on top of one another with the title bars displaying each file name (see fig. 3.10).

Using the mouse, you can move quickly between presentations when they are stacked in this way. Click any Presentation window once to activate the presentation. Whenever any portion of a Presentation window is visible, you can click it to make that presentation the active window. Using the keyboard, you can move quickly between windows by pressing Ctrl-F6 until the window you want is highlighted.

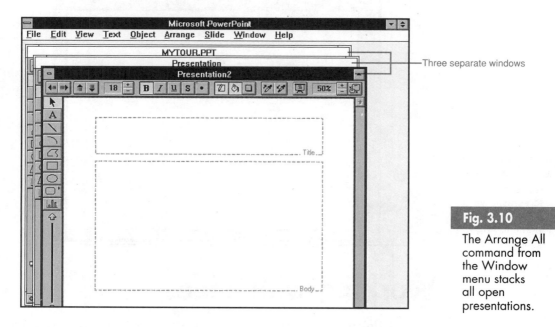

Three separate windows

The Arrange All command from the Window menu stacks all open presentations.

NOTE When you have many open files, some might become ob-scured, especially when you frequently resize windows. To verify which files are open at any given time, always check the list at the bottom of the Window menu.

The other command on the Window menu, Fit to Page Size, makes the active presentation expand to fill the available room on-screen—a useful capability when you want to give all your attention to one pre-sentation and need the maximum space in which to work. Open the Window menu and choose Fit to Page Size. The result should resemble figure 3.11.

Below the separator line in the menu is a list of all open presentations. In the example, three presentations are open: MYTOUR.PPT, PRESEN-TATION, and PRESENTATION2 (see again fig. 3.9). The check mark to the left of PRESENTATION2 indicates that it is the active presentation. (The name also appears in the title bar.)

To move between Presentation windows, open the Window menu and click a file name. To use the keyboard, press the underlined number that precedes the file name.

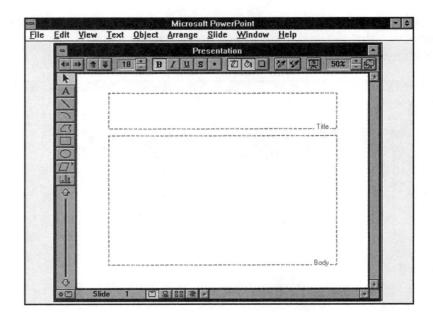

Fig. 3.11

A presentation screen showing the result of using the Fit to Page Size command.

Working with Slides

You can delete, copy, or add slides no matter what view you are using. This section describes the method for Slide view or Slide Sorter view. (In general, you can apply the same principles when using Notes or Outline view.) See Chapter 12 for specific instructions on deleting, copying, and adding a slide in Outline view.

Adding a Slide

You can add a new slide to a presentation no matter which view you are using. To add a slide when using Slide view or Slide Sorter view, follow these steps:

1. Select the slide that precedes the slide where you want to insert.

2. Click the New Slide tool at the bottom of the Slide Sorter. PowerPoint adds a new slide immediately following the current slide.

To use the keyboard to add a slide, choose the New Slide command from the Edit menu or press Ctrl-N.

T I P

Deleting a Slide

To delete a slide, follow these steps:

1. Using either Slide view or Slide Sorter view, select the slide you want to delete.

2. Choose Delete Slide from the Slide menu, or press the Delete key. PowerPoint deletes the slide from the presentation.

If you inadvertently delete the slide and want to restore it, choose the Undo command from the Edit menu or press Ctrl-Z.

This method permanently deletes the slide from the presentation—the only way to bring it back is to use the Undo command immediately. If you're not sure that you want to delete a slide permanently, choose the Copy command from the Edit menu to place a copy of the slide on the Clipboard.

Copying a Slide

In some cases, you might want to make a copy of a slide and insert it elsewhere in a presentation. The following steps describe how to copy and paste a slide:

1. Using Slide Sorter view, select the slide you want to copy.

2. Choose Copy from the Edit menu, or press Ctrl-C. PowerPoint places a copy of the slide on the Clipboard.

3. Position the mouse pointer between the two slides where you want to insert a copy.

4. Choose Paste from the Edit menu or press Ctrl-V. A copy of the slide is inserted at the new position.

Rearranging Slides

No matter how carefully you plan a presentation, sooner or later you will want to rearrange your slides. Fortunately, you can complete this task easily in Slide Sorter view. In this view, you're able to see multiple slides at once, and moving a slide from one location to another couldn't be easier.

Moving a Single Slide

To move a single slide, follow these steps:

1. Click the Slide Sorter button to display your presentation in Slide Sorter view.

2. Select the slide you want to move. In figure 3.12, slide 3 is selected.

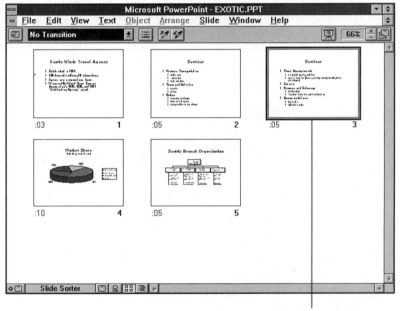

Fig. 3.12

Slide 3 is selected to be moved between two other slides.

3. Click the slide and drag it to the space between the two slides where you want to insert it. Notice that the mouse pointer changes to a small slide with a downward pointing arrow.

4. Release the mouse button. The selected slide is repositioned in its new location.

The text on individual slides is virtually illegible when displayed at 66% in Slide Sorter view. If readability is important, you can increase the scale to 100% and still see multiple slides on one screen. If seeing many slides on-screen is more important, however, change the scale to 50%.

T I P

Moving Sequential Slides

Using methods similar to those in the preceding steps, you can rearrange multiple slides, whether or not they are in sequence. To move a sequence of slides to a new location, follow these steps. In this example, you move slides 1 and 2 so that they follow slide 4:

1. Position the mouse pointer outside the upper left corner of the slide you want to move—for this example, slide 2.

2. Click and drag the mouse around the other slide—in this example, drag just outside the lower right corner of slide 3. As you drag the mouse, PowerPoint draws a selection box around both slides (see fig. 3.13). Release the mouse button.

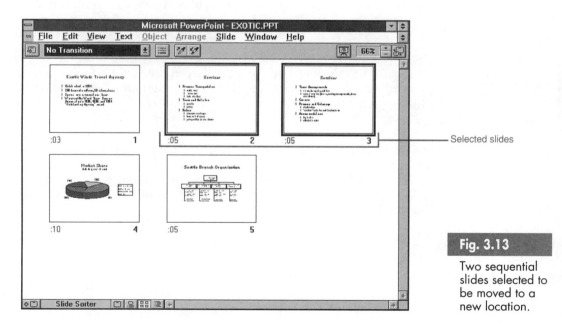

Selected slides

Fig. 3.13

Two sequential slides selected to be moved to a new location.

3. Click on either one of the slides and drag them to the new location—for this example, drag them to the space between slides 4
and 5. Notice that as you drag the selected slides, the mouse
pointer changes to two small slides with a downward-pointing
arrow. The form of the mouse is dependent on the number of
slides you select. If you had selected three slides, for example,
the mouse pointer would change to three small slides.

4. Release the mouse button. Both slides are moved to the new
location.

Moving Nonsequential Slides

The method for moving multiple, nonsequential slides is slightly different. To move the slides shown in figure 3.14, follow these steps:

1. Select the first slide that you want to move. In this example, select
slide 1.

2. Hold down the Shift key and select a second slide. In this example,
select slide 5.

3. Release the Shift key.

4. Point to either of the selected slides and drag them both to the
new position. For this example, drag the slides between slides 2
and 3.

5. Release the mouse button. The slides are moved to their new
position.

T I P   For any of these steps, if you want to return the slides to their original positions, choose Undo from the Edit menu immediately before
initiating any other action.

The preceding steps have shown you how to rearrange slides in Slide
Sorter view. You can also rearrange slides in Outline view. To use this
method, however, you need to be somewhat familiar with PowerPoint's
outlining functions. (For more information about these functions, see
Chapter 12.)

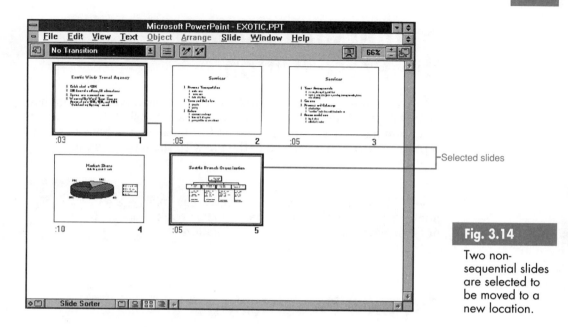

Fig. 3.14

Two non-
sequential slides
are selected to
be moved to a
new location.

Creating Notes Pages

Having impressive slides helps to make a presentation more successful,
but if you must struggle with awkward, poorly written, or unorganized
notes, the presentation can be a disaster. You learned earlier in this
chapter that PowerPoint includes a Notes Master. The Notes Master
contains a reduced slide and a body object in which you can insert
speaker's notes. To create a notes page, follow these steps:

1. Select the slide for which you want to create notes.

2. Click the Notes View button at the bottom of the window.
   PowerPoint displays the notes page for the current slide.

3. If the current scale is smaller than 66%, click the Scale tool to
   raise the scale to 66% or higher.

4. Double-click anywhere in the body object.

5. Type the notes that apply to the current slide.

6. Click anywhere outside the body object; this step deselects the
   object.

7. To return to Slide view, click the Slide View tool at the bottom of
   the window.

Saving and Closing the Presentation

After you enter information into PowerPoint, the information is displayed in the slides on-screen; it is not a file on disk until you save it. After you have saved a file for the first time, using the Save command replaces the original version of the file with the new version.

> **T I P**   Save a file frequently as you work; saving regularly (every 5 to 15 minutes) ensures that your changes are preserved and that you will not lose work in the case of a power failure.

Saving a Presentation

To save a presentation, follow these steps:

1. Choose Save from the File menu.

   The first time you save a file (using the Save or the Save As command), PowerPoint displays the Save As dialog box (see fig. 3.15).

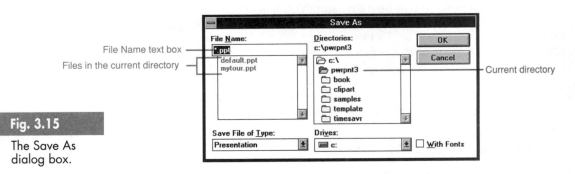

Fig. 3.15

The Save As dialog box.

The current directory name is shown under the heading Directories. In figure 3.15, the current directory is c:\pwrpnt3 because the directory was renamed during installation. In most cases, however, the current directory name is c:\powerpnt.

2. If necessary, change the directory. You can select a different directory by navigating the Directories box using standard Windows

procedures: click the C:\ icon to move to the C:\ directory or double-click a subdirectory name to select it as the current directory.

> From the keyboard, press Alt-D to select the Directories list box.   **T I P**

3. To save your presentation on a different drive, select the drive from the Drives drop-down list.

4. Type the file name.

   When naming a file, the normal DOS file name rules apply: you can use up to eight characters before the dot separator and up to three after the dot separator. PowerPoint assigns all its presentation files the extension ppt, unless you specify otherwise. You should use this extension so that PowerPoint recognizes your file as a PowerPoint presentation. (If you omit the .ppt extension, PowerPoint adds it for you automatically.)

   In the file name text box, type the file name in upper- or lowercase letters; DOS makes no distinction between them in file names.

5. If you want to change the file type, select a type from the Save File of Type drop-down list. If you will be running a slide show presentation on a different computer, you might want to select the With Fonts box to save the fonts with the presentation. This option ensures that the presentation will display correctly in the event the other computer does not contain the correct fonts.

 NOTE Only use a file type other than .ppt in one of two situations: when you want to save the current slide as a metafile (.wmf) for use in Microsoft Word, or when you want to save only the text in a presentation as an outline (.rtf) file.

6. Click on OK.

After you have named and saved the new presentation, the new name replaces the word Presentation at the top of the screen.

The Save As function works like the Save function except that Save As always asks for a file name. Save asks for a name only when you save the new presentation for the first time. The next time you save the file, Save will save the file on disk with the name displayed at the top of the screen.

Use Save As when you want to create a new presentation similar to one already on file. Open the existing presentation and, as soon as it appears on-screen, use the Save As option to rename the presentation and save it to disk. (The original presentation remains unchanged under its original name.) Change the new presentation as necessary.

Closing a Presentation

To close the currently displayed presentation, choose Close from the File menu or double-click the Control menu box for the Presentation window. If you have made any changes to the presentation, PowerPoint asks whether you want to save them. Choose Yes, No, or Cancel.

Note that the Close command does *not* close PowerPoint. To close, or exit, PowerPoint, choose the Exit command from the File menu or double-click the Control menu box for the PowerPoint window. Chapter 1 covers exiting the program.

Chapter Summary

In this chapter you learned the process for building a complete presentation. To begin the process, you learned how to open a new presentation or copy an existing one. You learned how to change default settings, review and apply templates, and alter a Slide Master. You learned about the various ways in which to view a presentation. Finally, you discovered how to delete, copy, and add slides, and how to create notes pages.

At this point, you have reached your first milestone in working with PowerPoint. You should now be feeling relatively comfortable with the program. In the remainder of Part I, you learn about the specific tools for developing slides. The next chapter tells you how to work with text.

Working with Text

I n this chapter, you learn how to add text to a presentation by using PowerPoint's Text tool, and how to manipulate text after you have entered it. You learn how to change the font style and size and how to add special enhancements, such as boldface, underline, shadows, and color. Because knowing *how* to change text isn't very useful if you don't know *when* to change it, this chapter provides some basic guidelines for using different text styles. You also learn how to change the alignment of text to suit the content of the slide. Finally, you learn to use two tools becoming widely available in graphics packages: the find and replace feature and the spelling checker.

Creating Text

Earlier versions of PowerPoint offered two tools for entering text: the Labeler tool and the Word Processor tool. Confusing the two and forgetting the uses for each tool was easy. In Version 3.0, the Text tool replaces the Labeler tool. The combination of the two tools eliminates confusion about the functions of each. The Text tool enables you to "label" objects (just as the Labeler tool did) and enter text into text objects. The Text tool is the second tool on the tool palette; the Text tool is marked with an uppercase letter *A*.

The next two sections describe how to use the Text tool to label objects and to compose larger blocks of text.

Labeling Objects

Suppose that you are designing a slide show to introduce a new product. One of your slides contains a picture of the product imported from another application (see fig. 4.1). You want to label the product on the slide.

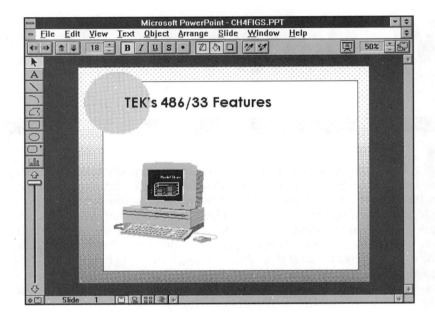

Fig. 4.1

A slide containing an imported picture.

Follow these steps to label the picture:

1. Click the Text tool. The mouse pointer changes to an I-beam.

2. Place the mouse pointer where you want the label to begin.

3. Click the left mouse button once and begin typing the label.

4. After you finish typing the label, click anywhere away from the text to rechoose the default Selection tool.

Figure 4.2 shows how the label looks when added to the slide shown in figure 4.1.

If the label isn't positioned exactly where you want it, don't worry for now. Later in this chapter, you will learn how to move the text.

 Because text entered as a label has no right margin, PowerPoint cannot automatically wrap text. To enter text on more than one line, press Enter and continue typing.

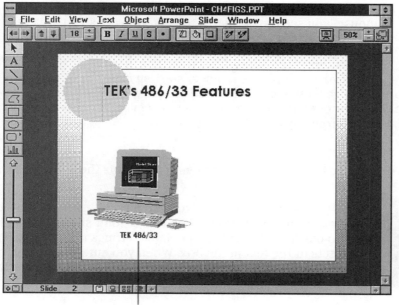

A typed label

Fig. 4.2

A text label
added to the
picture on the
slide.

Creating Text Objects

When you want to enter a larger block of text—that is, something larger
than a label—you use the Text tool to draw a text object. A *text object*
is a rectangular shape that covers the approximate area in which you
want your words to fit. Creating a text object enables you to position
text more precisely on a slide.

Creating a text object also enables you to control the width of the text.
For example, you might want to add a column of text next to a large
picture. When you draw a text object, the width is the important dimen-
sion to specify; the length is less important, as you'll see when you
create a text object yourself. If necessary, you can change the size of
the text object later.

Suppose that you want to add a product description to the slide shown
in figure 4.2. Because the description is longer than a few words, you
create a text object first and then enter the text. Follow these steps to
insert a text object:

1. Choose the Text tool. The mouse pointer changes to an I-beam.

2. Position the mouse pointer on the slide where you want to locate
    the upper left corner of the text object.

3. Drag the mouse pointer down and to the right. As you drag the mouse, you see the outline of the text object as you are creating it.

T   I   P   Step 3 tells you to draw a text object starting from the upper left corner. For most users, this method seems to be the most comfortable way for drawing objects. You can, however, begin drawing a text object from any one of its four corners.

4. Release the mouse button when the object is the width you want.

 NOTE   If you draw a text object to accommodate several lines of text, don't be alarmed when PowerPoint shrinks the object to one line. PowerPoint's default settings make all text objects fit the text in the box. When you enter more than one line of text, the text object is resized to accommodate the additional lines.

You can find more on this subject later in this chapter. You can now begin entering text in the text object. Follow these steps:

1. Type the text that you want to appear in the text object.

2. Click in any blank area of the slide to deselect the text object.

The sample slide in figure 4.3 shows how a text object looks on-screen.

If you use the PowerPoint defaults, the text in the object is left-justified with a ragged right margin. In Chapter 13 you learn how to set the indentation in text objects.

In this section, you have learned how to create text in two ways: by creating a label for an object, and by creating a text object and inserting text into it. Although you didn't create a text object before you created the label, the label became a text object after you created it. You can resize or move any text object regardless of the method you used to create it.

Manipulating Text Objects

After you have created a text object, you can change and manipulate it in many ways. Text objects are like any other type of object; you can resize them, move them, and apply special attributes, such as a frame, color, a shadow, a pattern, and so on. In the following sections, you will learn how to do these tasks.

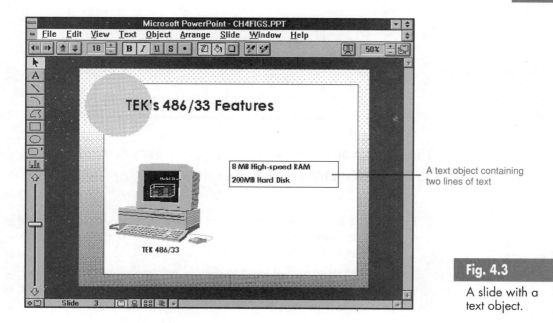

A text object containing
two lines of text

Fig. 4.3

A slide with a
text object.

Resizing a Text Object

As you have just learned, PowerPoint's default setting adjusts the size
of a text object to fit the text inside. The object shrinks or expands to
fit precisely around the words you type. This resizing occurred when
you drew the text object in the preceding section. Resizing is controlled
by the Fit Text command on the Text menu. The Fit Text dialog box
contains an option called Adjust Object Size to Fit Text. This box is
checked by default.

You might not want to use the Adjust Object Size to Fit Text option. For
example, suppose that you know that you will add more text to a text
object later. You want the object to appear on the slide in the correct
size so that you can design the remainder of the slide.

To cancel the Adjust Object Size to Fit Text option, follow these steps:

1. Choose the text object you want to resize.

2. Choose Fit Text from the Text menu. The Fit Text dialog box, as
   shown in figure 4.4, appears.

3. Click the Adjust Object Size to Fit Text check box to turn off the
   option.

4. Click OK.

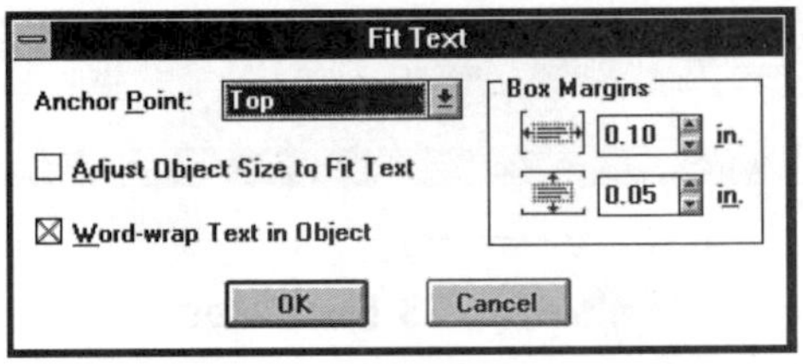

Fig. 4.4

The Fit Text
dialog box.

The option is no longer selected, and you can resize the text object.

To resize a text object, follow these steps:

1. Click the Selection tool.

2. Click the text object you want to resize. The object is surrounded by a gray border with black *handles* in each corner. The handles enable you to resize the object.

3. Click and drag any of the handles to change an object's height (drag a handle up or down), width (drag a handle right or left), or both (drag a handle diagonally).

4. Release the mouse button when the object is the size you want.

In figure 4.5 the text object has been resized to make room for additional text. (The object in the figure is selected so that the borders are visible.) The Adjust Object to Fit Text option was turned off before resizing.

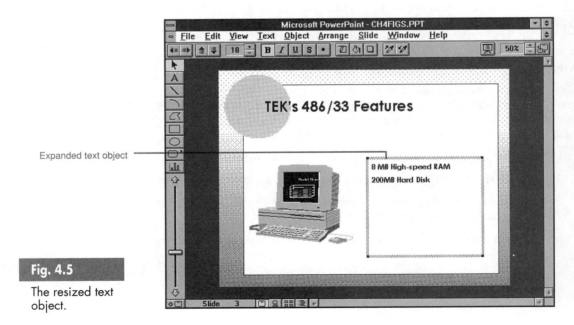

Expanded text object

Fig. 4.5

The resized text
object.

The steps for resizing an object are brief. Chapter 5 explains more about resizing objects—including some tricks for resizing only horizontally or only vertically, or for maintaining the same height-to-width ratio.

T I P

Moving a Text Object

Often you want to move a text object after creating it. You can move a text object anywhere on the slide by following these steps:

1. Click the Selection tool.

2. Click the text object you want to move. The selected object is surrounded by a gray border with black handles in each corner.

3. Click and drag any part of the gray border (*not* on the black handles), repositioning the object on the slide.

4. Release the mouse button when the object is positioned where you want it.

These steps are brief. Moving objects is discussed in greater detail in Chapter 5.

T I P

Enhancing Text Objects

The Object menu contains commands that enable you to enhance the appearance of objects. You can, for example, fill an object with a colored, shaded, or patterned background. You can *line* (or frame) an object using various line styles, and you can add a shadow to a text object. You can use Object menu commands to enhance the appearance of any object, not just text objects. In this section, you are introduced to the steps for applying some of these attributes to text objects. These techniques are discussed in greater detail in Chapter 5.

To apply any of the Object menu's attributes, choose the text object first; then choose the appropriate command from the Object menu. Most commands lead to submenus that display a complete list of choices. The Line, Fill, and Object Shadow options have corresponding tools on the Toolbar (see fig. 4.6). To apply these attributes quickly, use the tool on the Toolbar rather than the menu command.

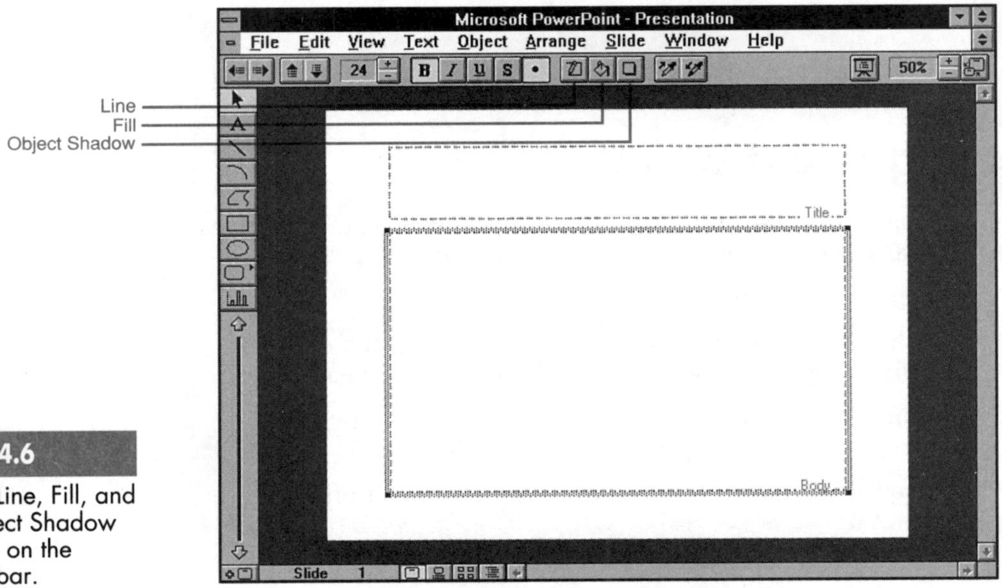

Fig. 4.6

The Line, Fill, and Object Shadow tools on the Toolbar.

To add a frame (line) to the text object in the example, follow these steps:

1. Click the Selection tool.

2. Click the text object to select it.

3. Click the Line tool, or choose Line from the Object menu and then choose a color for the line or frame. The object is now surrounded by a narrow line or frame. (Note that when you use the Line tool on the Toolbar, you cannot select a color.)

4. Click anywhere on the slide to deselect the text object. (The frame is more visible when the object is not selected.)

You can choose a different line style for the same object. Follow these steps:

1. Click the Selection tool.

2. Click the text object to select it.

3. Choose Line Style from the Object menu. A submenu displays all available line styles (see fig. 4.7). The currently selected line style is indicated by a dot to the left of the style.

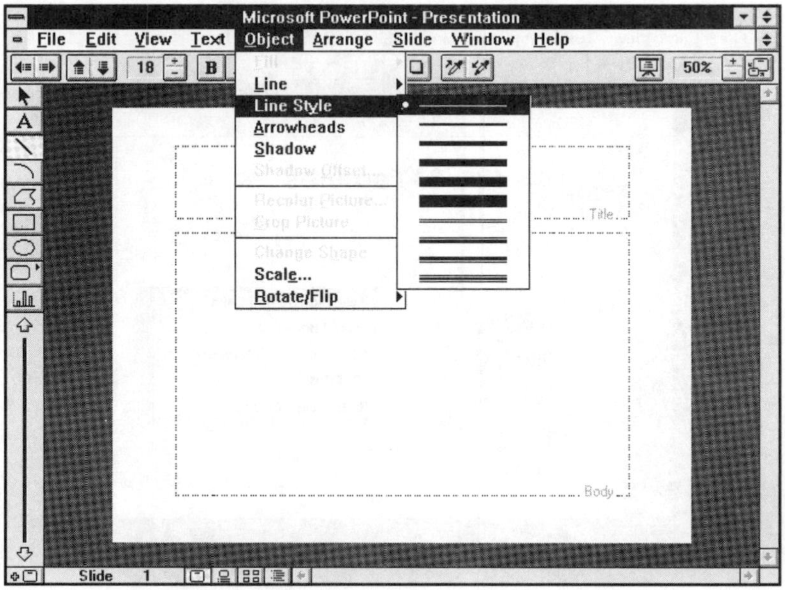

Fig. 4.7

The Line Style
submenu.

4. Click the style you choose. The text object is immediately reformatted with the new line style.

5. Click anywhere on the slide to deselect the text object and make the new line style more visible.

In figure 4.8, the text object in the sample slide is shown with a triple border.

Selecting Text

When the action you want to initiate involves text, you must select the text first and then start the action. For example, if you want to edit, delete, add to, or apply an attribute to text within a text object, you must select the text first. The text you enter into an object does not become part of that object; the text and object remain distinct elements, although both move when you move the object. You must know how to select the text without selecting the object.

You can select text in a text object in several ways. The method you choose depends on the action you want to take next. These actions are summarized in table 4.1.

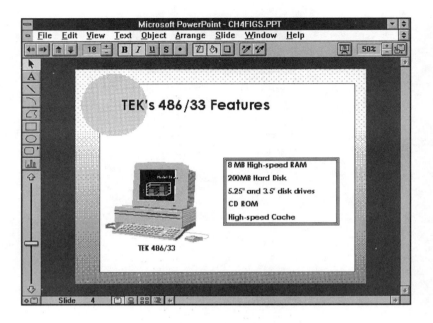

Fig. 4.8

The text object is
outlined by a
triple border.

Table 4.1 Selecting Text in a Text Object

Select	If you want to...
All text in a text object	Apply an attribute (such as color or a different font) to all text in the object
Specific text in a text object	Apply an attribute to the selected text only
One word in a text object	Replace the word or apply an attribute only to that word

To select all text in an object, simply select the object. Any text attribute, including changes in font type or size, the color of the text, the alignment, the style (such as boldface and underline), and so on, that you choose while the object is selected is applied to all text in the object.

To select specific text in an object, follow these steps:

1. Select the text object.

2. Click the mouse pointer a second time on the text object so that the mouse pointer changes to an I-beam.

3. Click and drag the mouse over the text you want to select. The text is highlighted.

To select one word in a text object, follow these steps:

1. Double-click the text object. The vertical line cursor appears in the box.

2. Double-click the word you want to select.

Changing Text Style and Color

The Text menu contains all the commands you need to change the style and color of text in a text object. In this context, *style* refers to font style and size and to features such as boldface, italic, underline, shadow, emboss, superscript, and subscript. You can apply one or more of these styles to the same text. And text in any of these styles can be changed to the color you choose.

You apply all style options to text the same way: select the text you want to change; then choose a style option from the Text menu. (For some options, you need to choose from a submenu.) In the following sections you learn how to apply all the styles.

The PowerPoint Toolbar was designed to simplify the tasks involved in creating slides. The Bold, Italic, Underline, and Text Shadow commands have corresponding tools on the Toolbar, as shown in figure 4.9.

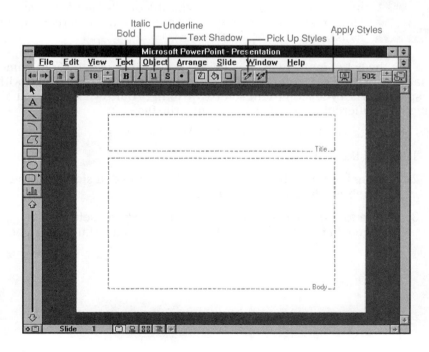

Fig. 4.9

The text attribute tools on the Toolbar.

Two other tools on the Toolbar—Pick Up Styles and Apply Styles—are especially useful for copying styles from one area of text to another. A special section on using these tools follows the sections on applying styles and color.

Changing a Font

A *font* refers to a particular design or style of character that PowerPoint displays on-screen and prints on paper. Fonts are available in different point sizes. When you run the setup program during installation, PowerPoint installs its TrueType fonts. These fonts are especially designed to be used on any printer and in any type style. On your system, additional fonts might be available if you have installed them. When you work with PowerPoint, however, use a TrueType font in your presentations to ensure reliable screen and printed results. (Other fonts might produce unpredictable results when printed because what you see on-screen is not necessarily what you get when the presentation is printed.)

 Point size refers to the height of characters for a given font style. One point is equal to 1/72 inch. A 72-point font produces letters one inch high. Most documents such as business letters are produced with a 10- or 12-point font. On a slide, text is usually at least 18-point so that it is readable at a distance.

To see the list of fonts available on your system, choose the Font command from the Text menu (see fig. 4.10). TrueType fonts are noted with a special TrueType icon to the left of the font. (Your own Font menu might by different from the one shown in the figure.)

To change the font for selected text, follow these steps:

1. Select the text you want to change.

2. Choose Font from the Text menu. A font submenu similar to the menu shown in figure 4.10 appears.

3. Click a font to choose it. The font for the text you selected is changed. In figure 4.11, the title text is changed to Lucida Bright.

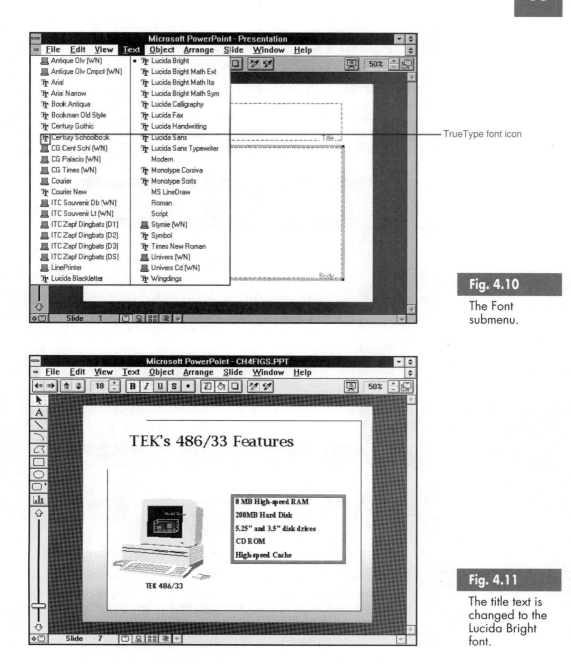

TrueType font icon

Fig. 4.10

The Font submenu.

Fig. 4.11

The title text is changed to the Lucida Bright font.

Changing Font Size

To change the font size of selected text, use the Font Size tool on the Toolbar (see fig. 4.12). With this tool, you can choose a font size without using the menu command. You use the menu command only if you want to set a custom font size. With the Font Size tool, for example, you can choose 18 points or 20 points, but you need to use the menu command if you want to use 19 points.

Font Size tool ——

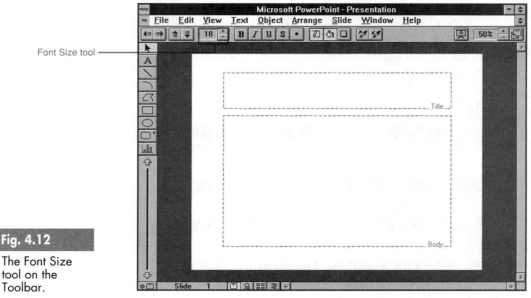

Fig. 4.12

The Font Size tool on the Toolbar.

You change the font size in the same way that you change the font style: select the text first; then select the font size. To change the font size using the Font Size tool, follow these steps:

1. Select the text for which you want to change the font size.

2. To choose a larger font size, click the plus (+) sign on the Font Size tool. To choose a smaller font size, click the minus (-) sign. The next available size appears in the font size window next to the tool (refer back to fig. 4.12).

3. Repeat step 2 until the font size you want appears in the font size window. The selected text is resized on-screen each time you choose a new size.

4. Click anywhere outside the text object to deselect the text.

   In figure 4.13, the title text was changed from 36 points to 48 points.

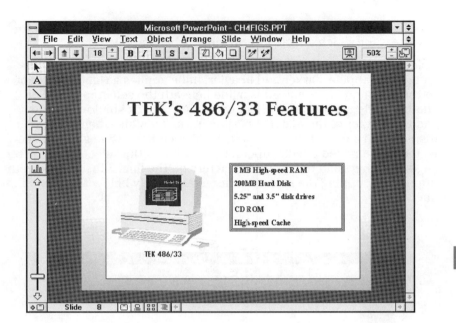

Fig. 4.13

The title text is enlarged to 48 points.

To create a custom font size, follow these steps:

1. Select the text for which you want to change the font size.

2. Choose Size from the Text menu. A submenu of font sizes is displayed.

3. From the bottom of the submenu, choose Other. The Other Size dialog box appears (see fig. 4.14).

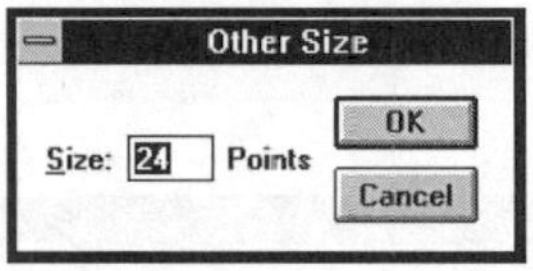

Fig. 4.14

The Other Size dialog box.

4. In the Size box, type the point size you want to use; then click OK. The dialog box closes, and the selected text changes to the size you specified.

Applying Text Styles

PowerPoint's eight available text styles are bold, italic, underline, shadow, emboss, superscript, subscript, and plain. Because the first four styles have corresponding tools on the Toolbar, these styles are quick and easy to apply (see fig. 4.15). The plain style enables you to reset text for which a style has previously been applied.

Bold, italic, and underline are widely used styles. Bold makes the selected text appear darker and heavier, italic applies a rightward slant to the text, and underline adds a line beneath the selected text. The shadow style creates a 3-D effect by adding a black shadow behind each character of the text. (This style is most visible when the text is displayed in a color other than black.) The emboss style gives the selected text a raised effect. Superscript positions the selected character slightly higher than the other characters on the line. Subscript does the opposite, dropping the selected character slightly below the normal line.

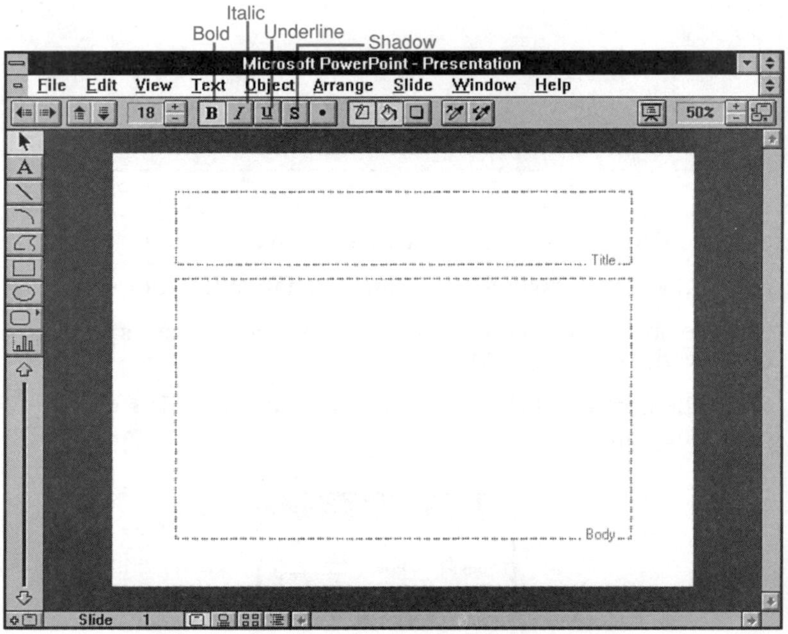

Fig. 4.15

The Bold, Italic, Underline, and Shadow tools.

To apply a style to text, select the text; then select the style. To apply a style using the style tools on the Toolbar, follow these steps:

1. Select the text to which you want to apply a style.

2. Click the Bold, Italic, Underline, or Shadow tool on the Toolbar.

3. To apply an additional style while the text is still selected, repeat step 2.

4. Click anywhere outside of the text object to deselect the text.

Follow these steps to choose a text style from the Text menu:

1. Select the text to which you want to apply a style.

2. Choose Style from the Text menu. A submenu appears.

3. From the submenu, click the style option you want to use. PowerPoint reformats the text; the text is still selected.

4. Repeat steps 2 and 3 to apply additional styles to the text.

5. Click anywhere outside the text object to deselect the text.

Figure 4.16 illustrates a title that has been italicized.

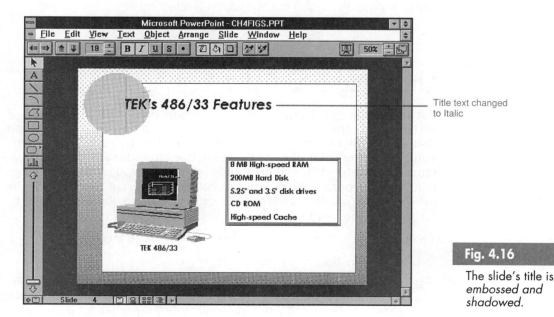

Title text changed to Italic

Fig. 4.16

The slide's title is *embossed and shadowed.*

When you displayed the Style menu, you might have noticed that some styles have keyboard shortcuts. Table 4.2 lists these shortcuts. To use the shortcuts, select the text; then press the keyboard shortcut.

Table 4.2 Text Style Keyboard Shortcuts

Text Style	Keyboard Shortcut
Plain	Ctrl-T
Bold	Ctrl-B

continues

Table 4.2 Continued	
Text Style	**Keyboard Shortcut**
Italic	Ctrl-I
Underline	Ctrl-U

T I P   Do not apply styles to text randomly. Follow the guidelines on the use of styles, discussed in the section "Following Style Guidelines."

Changing Text Color

Besides changing text styles, you can change the color of text on-screen. This capability is especially useful for enhancing presentations that will be displayed as slide shows. Remember, however, that when you change the color of text on-screen, the printed results might be more difficult to read. You need to experiment if you intend to print handouts of your slides; or you can choose a different template for the presentation (one listed in the *b&wovrhd* template subdirectory) just for printing the handouts.

To change the color of text on-screen, follow these steps:

1. Select the text you want to change.

2. Choose Color from the Text menu. The submenu shown in figure 4.17 appears. This submenu lists all available colors in the current color scheme. (Refer to Chapters 6 and 7 for more information about color and color schemes.)

3. Click a color in the list, or choose Other to define a new color. (Refer to Chapters 7 and 15 for detailed instructions on defining new colors.) PowerPoint changes the selected text to the color you choose.

4. Click anywhere outside of the text object to deselect the text.

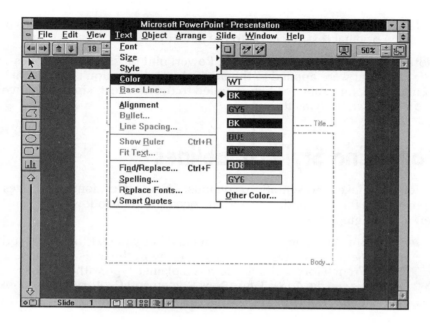

Applying Styles

As you have learned, the Toolbar in PowerPoint was designed to simplify the task of creating presentations. The Pick Up Styles and Apply Styles tools certainly live up to that expectation. These tools enable you to "pick up" all the attributes of selected text and apply them instantly to other text. For example, suppose that you have carefully chosen a font style, size, and custom text color for the title of a slide. In addition, you have embossed and italicized the text. Now you want another selection of text to have exactly the same style and attributes. Without the Pick Up Styles and Apply Styles tools, you would have to select the text and then apply each attribute individually to the new text. With these tools, however, you simply "pick up" the styles (collectively) and apply them to the new text. A process that might have taken six or eight steps is reduced to two steps.

To use the Pick Up Styles and Apply Styles tools, follow these steps:

1. Select the text from which you want to copy text styles and color.

2. Click the Pick Up Styles tool.

3. Select the text to which you want to apply the styles you picked up.

4. Click the Apply Styles tool. PowerPoint applies all the styles from the original text selection to the new text.

Note that when you use these tools, PowerPoint picks up and applies *all* styles that were applied to the original text. If you don't want a particular style, for example, italic, applied to the new text, simply remove the style after applying it.

Following Style Guidelines

When you make a presentation, you must select styles, fonts, and sizes appropriate for your audience and the occasion. The following are a few general guidelines:

■ Serif fonts are much easier to read in a body of text than sans serif fonts. *Serif* fonts have small cross strokes at the ends of letters. *Sans* (French for "without") *serif* is a plainer type without cross strokes (see fig. 4.18). Times New Roman and Century Schoolbook are examples of serif fonts; Arial is a sans serif font.

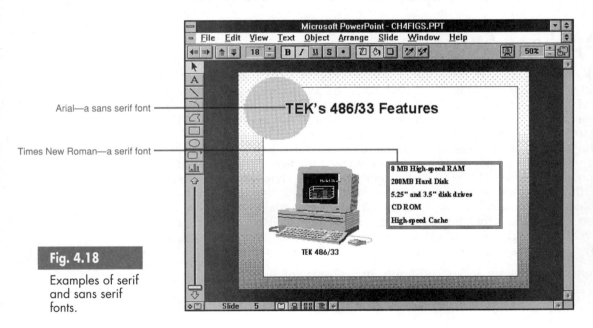

Arial—a sans serif font

Times New Roman—a serif font

Fig. 4.18

Examples of serif and sans serif fonts.

■ Serif fonts work well for smaller text sizes, such as text in the body of a slide. Sans serif fonts are best for headings and subheads.

- All-uppercase headings and subheads are hard to read and should be avoided. Use large size type in uppercase and lowercase letters with boldface to emphasize headings.

- In most presentations, three fonts and three sizes suffice for headings. Select one size for each subhead, and put all body text in a single font and point size.

- Use underlining sparingly. Too much underlining is hard on the eyes. Limit underlining to body text rather than titles and headings. Underlining titles and headings, especially in larger point sizes, makes them more difficult to read.

- Be cautious about italicizing body text for emphasis. Boldface, and even underlining, are often easier to read because italic text is often fainter than plain text. In general, reserve italic in text for foreign or specialized words.

- When you use color in text, use light colors against dark backgrounds and dark colors against light backgrounds to maintain a high contrast.

Aligning Text

Alignment refers to the way text is positioned within a text object. Unlike style and color options, which you can apply to selected areas (that is, a word or a phrase) of text, alignment options apply to entire paragraphs.

PowerPoint's Text menu gives you four options for aligning text: Left, Right, Center, and Justify. Using the Left option aligns text along the left edge of the text object. Right alignment aligns text along the right edge of the text object. Choosing the Center option centers text from the center point of each line, placing an equal number of characters to the left and right. The Justify option aligns text along both the left and right edges so that the text on a line covers the full width of a text object.

The most common alignment style is Left, but often the other alignment options are useful. You can use Right alignment for visual effect. For instance, when a caption for a picture or graph appears to the left of the figure, the caption looks better right-aligned. Center alignment is most commonly used for slide titles or for centering headings over a column or a paragraph. Justified text is more formal; it is often used in newspapers where columns of text are printed close together. In slides, justified text has fewer applications.

> **NOTE** The Justify alignment style can be applied only to text for which a text object was created first. Text created as a label (that is, text you typed without first creating a text object) cannot be justified because the label has no right margin.

If you don't remember the difference between labels and true text objects, refer to the section "Labeling Objects" earlier in this chapter.

You use the same basic steps to apply alignment options regardless of the option you choose. The amount of text you select, however, is determined by the amount of text you want to realign. For example, if you want to realign a single paragraph, you don't need to select any text; just place the cursor anywhere within the paragraph. PowerPoint assumes that you want to realign that paragraph. If you want to realign more than one paragraph at once, select all the text in all paragraphs.

To apply alignment options, follow these steps:

1. Choose the text object that contains the text to realign.

2. Select the paragraphs you want to realign. If you want to realign only one paragraph, just place the text cursor anywhere within that paragraph.

3. Choose Alignment from the Text menu. The Alignment submenu appears.

4. Choose an alignment option from the submenu. The submenu disappears, and the paragraph is realigned.

Figure 4.19 illustrates several alignment styles. Try using the preceding steps to experiment with alignment styles in a sample presentation of your own.

You might have noticed that the alignment submenu displays keyboard shortcuts for alignment styles. These shortcut keys are summarized in table 4.3. After you learn these shortcuts, they are faster to use than the menu commands.

Table 4.3 Alignment Style Keyboard Shortcuts

Alignment Style	Keyboard Shortcut
Left	Ctrl-[
Right	Ctrl-]
Center	Ctrl-\

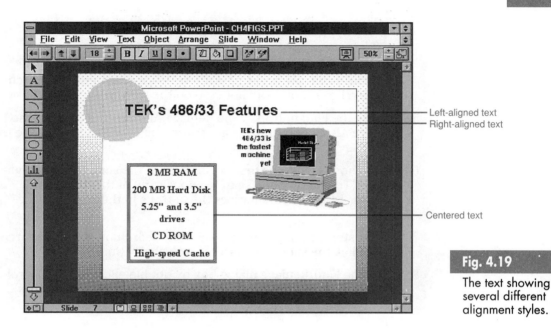

Left-aligned text
Right-aligned text
Centered text

Fig. 4.19

The text showing several different alignment styles.

Finding and Replacing Text

The Find/Replace option on the Text menu enables you to make individual and global changes to the text. Suppose that you discover a misspelled proper name in your presentation. Rather than search through your entire presentation and change each occurrence of the name, you can make a global change. You can use Find/Replace to make the changes throughout the presentation, including on your notes, outline, and handouts pages.

To search the entire presentation, start at slide 1; then follow these steps:

1. Choose Find/Replace from the Text menu. The Find/Replace dialog box appears (see fig. 4.20).

2. In the Find Text box, type the text you want to find.

3. In the Replace With box, type the replacement text.

   Note that both the text you search for and the replacement text need not be single words. You can search for up to 256 characters.

4. Choose Match Whole Word Only if you want an exact match and not the same series of letters in another word. For example, if you

search for *car*, this option finds *car* but not *carpet, cartoon,* or *career.*

Choose Match Case if you want to find only text that matches uppercase and lowercase characters. If, for example, you search for *Gray*, PowerPoint will not stop on the word *gray.*

5. Choose the Find button or the Replace All button. If you choose Replace All, all occurrences are automatically replaced and the search ends.

6. If you choose Find, the first occurrence of the search text is highlighted. To continue the search, choose any of the four search buttons. Table 4.4 summarizes the buttons in the Find/Replace box.

7. Repeat step 6 until you want to end the search or until the search ends. Click the slide to end the search at any time.

8. Close the Find/Replace dialog box by double-clicking the control-menu button or by choosing Close from the Control menu.

The Find/
Replace dialog
box.

Table 4.4 The Find/Replace Command Buttons

Button	Function
Find	Finds specified text. PowerPoint searches for and highlights the text but does not replace it.
Replace then Find	Replaces the current occurrence of the text you entered; then finds but does not replace the next occurrence.
Replace	Replaces a single occurrence of the text without automatically continuing the search. You must click another search button to restart the search.
Replace All	Replaces all occurrences of the text you entered. Replace All searches the Slide Master, Outline Master, and Notes Master as well as the body of the presentation on each slide.

T I P

If the Find/Replace dialog box gets in your way as you search, move it to another part of the screen by dragging the title bar. When the search is over, you don't have to close the dialog box. If you plan to use the dialog box repeatedly, drag it to the edge of your Presentation window. Leave a small portion of the box visible so that you can click it when you want it. If the box becomes obscured, bring it to the foreground by pressing Ctrl-F or by selecting the box from the Window menu.

NOTE After you have used Find/Replace, you cannot use the Undo command on the Edit menu to change the text back to its original form. You must use Find/Replace again.

Using the Spelling Checker

To find and correct spelling or typographical errors in your presentation, use the Spelling option on the Text menu. The spelling checker searches all pages in your file and highlights words not found in its dictionary.

NOTE The spelling checker checks the spelling of all words in labels, text, and objects, but not in objects that have been pasted into your presentation from other applications.

Table 4.5 describes the six command buttons in the Spelling dialog box: Check Spelling, Change, Ignore, Suggest, Add, and Dictionary.

Table 4.5 Spelling Options

Option	Function
Check Spelling	Starts or restarts the spelling checker.
Change	Changes the misspelled word on the slide to the correct word shown in the text box. Click the Check Spelling button to resume the search.
Ignore	Leaves the misspelled word unchanged and restarts the spelling checker automatically. Use this option for words that are spelled correctly but used too infrequently to add to the dictionary. (Proper names are a good example.)

continues

Table 4.5 Continued	
Option	**Function**
Suggest	Displays a list of suggested alternative spellings in the list box. Scroll through the list and choose the correct word.
Add	Adds the misspelled (or unrecognized) word to the custom dictionary file. All future occurrences of the word are presumed to be spelled correctly. Use this option to add correctly spelled but unfamiliar words to the dictionary so that the spelling checker will not question them in the future.
Dictionary	Enables you to edit your custom dictionary or open a different dictionary. To learn how to create a custom dictionary and work with other dictionaries, refer to Chapter 13.

To use the spelling checker, follow these steps:

1. Choose Spelling from the Text menu. The Spelling dialog box appears (see fig. 4.21).

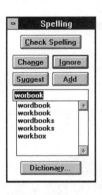

Fig. 4.21

The Spelling
dialog box.

2. Choose Check Spelling to start the spelling checker. The first misspelled word is displayed in the text box near the middle of the dialog box, as in figure 4.21.

When you click the Suggest button, suggested replacement spellings are displayed in the list box just underneath the word box. In Figure 4.21, the misspelled word is *worbook*. Notice that *workbook*, the correct spelling, is included in the list of suggested replacements.

3. Take one of the following actions:

   To retain the original spelling of the word, click Ignore; then repeat step 2 to continue checking the current presentation.

   To add the word to the dictionary, click Add; then repeat step 2 to continue checking the current presentation.

   To display a list of suggested alternative spellings, click Suggest; then continue with step 4.

4. Scroll down the suggestion list and click the correct word. The word you choose replaces the misspelled word in the word box.

If the correct word isn't on the suggestion list, consult a regular dictionary. If you know the correct spelling, replace the word in the word box with the correct spelling.

T I P

---

5. Click the Change button. PowerPoint changes the current spelling of the word.

6. Repeat steps 2 through 5 until the entire document is spell-checked or until you want to stop spell-checking the current presentation.

7. To stop spell-checking a document at any point, close the Spelling dialog box by double-clicking the Control menu box or by choosing Close from the Control menu.

If the Spelling dialog box is in your way, you can move it to another part of the screen. You can also keep the box open if you plan to use it frequently. If the PowerPoint window blocks the Spelling dialog box, choose the Spelling dialog box from the Window menu to bring the dialog box to the foreground.

T I P

Chapter Summary

This chapter introduced you to the Text tool, the basic tool for creating text in a presentation. You have learned how to label objects and how to create text objects and then insert text by using the Text tool. You know how to apply the different styles, fonts, and sizes, and how to align text in text boxes. Finally, you learned the steps for finding and replacing words in a presentation, and you learned how to run the spelling checker to find and correct misspelled words.

In most cases, text objects make up the majority of the slides' content. To enhance your text, however, you might want to add graphic objects, such as pictures, geometric shapes, or other objects to your slides. In the next chapter, you learn how to use PowerPoint's drawing features.

Drawing Objects

I f you know how to work with Windows, you already know much about working with objects in PowerPoint. You are familiar with techniques for selecting, resizing, and moving objects, and you probably know a good bit about changing or deleting them. This chapter teaches you the basics of manipulating objects.

In this chapter, you learn to draw the many varieties of shapes: basic shapes such as squares, ovals, rectangles, and circles, as well as special shapes such as stars, arrows, starbursts, and hexagons. Next you learn to manipulate the shapes. You can move and resize your drawings—often in specific and refined ways, such as outward from a central point or, for a line, from one end or from both ends simultaneously.

Drawing objects with PowerPoint can be confusing if you are not familiar with the basics. If you draw an unfilled object without a frame, you cannot see the object on-screen. If you have one object stacked beneath another, you cannot see the bottom object and might not be able to work with it. If the Snap to Grid option is turned on, your objects automatically snap to invisible lines as you move them—a useful feature if you know how to use it, but a confusing feature if you don't. This chapter discusses these capabilities.

You also learn how to fill shapes that enclose space, such as ovals, with color and how to change the fill pattern. You learn to add shadows to shapes in order to produce a three-dimensional effect, and to apply different line styles to a frame or line. PowerPoint provides refined tools, such as guides and grids, to help you align objects precisely, and this chapter teaches you about these specialized tools.

In Chapter 4, you learned a little about manipulating text objects drawn with the Text tool. Most of the techniques covered in this chapter, such as moving, filling, and framing, also apply to text objects; the techniques work in exactly the same way.

Using Drawing Tools

With PowerPoint, you can draw straight lines, arcs, and freeform objects, and you can draw a variety of shapes including ovals, circles, rectangles, and squares with rounded corners. The tool palette contains the tools for drawing lines and shapes (see fig. 5.1).

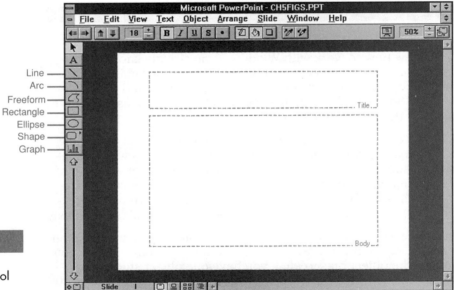

Fig. 5.1

The drawing tools in the tool palette.

The first three drawing tools on the tool palette enable you to draw lines, arcs, and freeform drawings. The fourth drawing tool lets you draw rectangles, and the fifth tool is for drawing ellipses. The final drawing tool is called the Shape tool because you can use it to draw a variety of shapes. Notice that the tool has a small right-pointing arrow in the upper right corner. When you click this tool, a submenu appears that displays 24 different shapes you can draw (see fig.5.2).

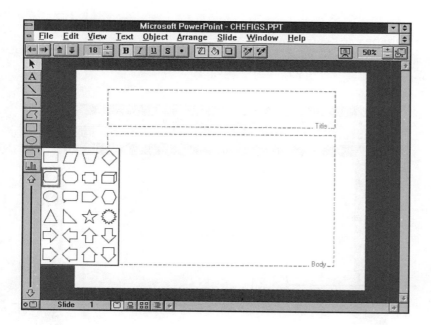

Fig. 5.2

The Shape submenu.

Drawing Shapes, Lines, and Arcs

You need only follow a few simple steps to draw shapes, lines, or arcs. In general, you create any shape by selecting the drawing tool from the tool palette, positioning the pointer where you want the shape to appear on the slide, and dragging with the mouse until the shape is the size you want.

The following steps describe how to draw a shape using the Rectangle tool. Use the same steps to draw ovals with the Ellipse tool, lines with the Line tool, or arcs with the Arc tool. In the next section, you learn how to draw uniform shapes such as circles and squares.

1. Click the Rectangle tool. The tool is highlighted and the mouse pointer changes to a crosshair.

2. Position the mouse pointer approximately where you want the rectangle to appear on the slide.

3. Press the left mouse button and drag the mouse in any direction. As you drag, the screen displays a solid outline of the rectangle you're drawing.

4. When the rectangle is the shape and size you want it, release the mouse button to make the shape permanent. The shape is selected automatically.

5. Click anywhere on-screen, except on the shape, to deselect the shape.

Figure 5.3 illustrates how the screen looks while you're drawing a rectangle.

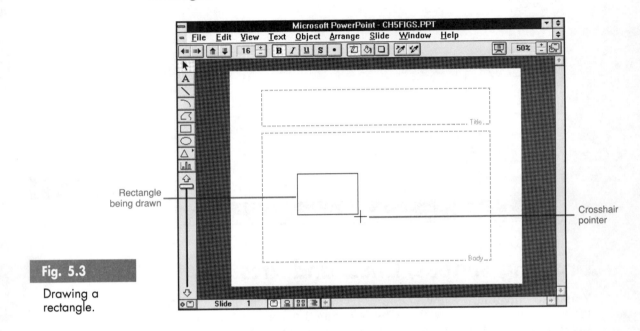

Rectangle being drawn

Crosshair pointer

Fig. 5.3

Drawing a rectangle.

To draw a shape using the Shape tool, the steps are almost identical to those for drawing a rectangle, except that you must select a shape from the Shape submenu. Follow these steps:

1. Click and hold the mouse button on the Shape tool until the submenu appears; then release the mouse button.

2. On the submenu, click the shape you want to draw. The shape you choose replaces the shape in the Shape tool. The mouse pointer changes to a crosshair.

3. Position the mouse pointer approximately where you want the shape to appear on the slide.

4. Press the left mouse button and drag the mouse in any direction. As you drag, the screen displays a solid outline of the shape you're drawing.

5. When the shape is the size you want, release the mouse button to make the shape permanent. The shape is selected automatically.

6. Click anywhere on-screen, except on the shape, to deselect the shape. Figure 5.4 illustrates a starburst drawn with the starburst shape tool.

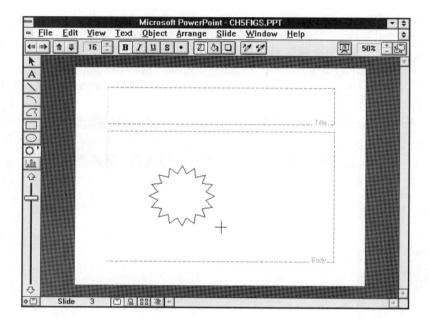

Drawing a starburst.

When a shape is selected, you can manipulate it in many ways, including changing its size, color, and location on the slide. Later sections in this chapter discuss these activities.

> To deselect an object without inadvertently selecting another, click the Selection tool on the tool palette.
>
> **T I P**

Drawing Uniform Shapes

To draw a uniform shape, you use the same basic steps for drawing a shape, except that you also employ a "constraint" key. The constraint key—Shift—keeps the horizontal and vertical distance from the mouse pointer uniform as you draw a shape. To draw a perfect circle, for example, you hold the Shift key while using the Ellipse tool. To draw a perfect square, you hold the Shift key while using the Rectangle tool.

To draw a circle, square, or other uniform shape, follow these steps:

1. Click the Ellipse, Rectangle, or Shape tool. The tool is highlighted and the mouse pointer changes to a crosshair.

2. Position the mouse pointer where you want to begin drawing the shape.

3. Hold down the Shift key, press the left mouse button, and then drag the mouse as you draw the shape. This step maintains a height-to-width ratio. Figure 5.5 shows a 3-D box being drawn.

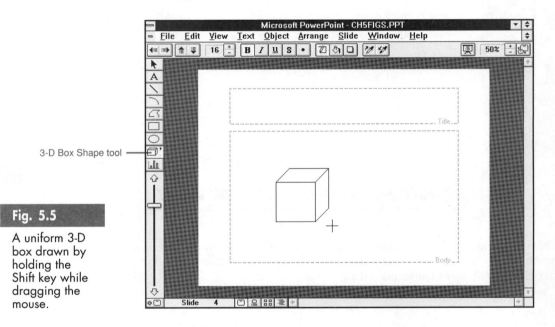

3-D Box Shape tool

Fig. 5.5

A uniform 3-D box drawn by holding the Shift key while dragging the mouse.

4. When the shape is the size you want, release the mouse button and the Shift key. The shape is selected automatically.

5. Click anywhere on-screen, except on the shape, to deselect the shape.

You use a similar technique to draw lines with specific properties, as you learn in the next section.

Drawing Vertical, Horizontal, and 45-Degree Angle Lines

The Shift constraint key helps you draw perfectly vertical, horizontal, and 45-degree angle lines. To draw a vertical line, hold down the Shift key and drag vertically. To draw a horizontal line, hold down the Shift key and drag horizontally. To draw a line at a 45-degree angle, hold down the Shift key and drag diagonally in the direction you want the line drawn. To experiment with this technique, hold down the Shift key and drag the mouse in a circular direction (clockwise or counterclockwise) from the starting point. You can draw the line in one of eight directions from a starting point: 45, 90, 135, 180, 225, 270, 315, and 360 degrees.

In certain situations, you might want to keep an object in the same position relative to other objects on the slide. In these cases, you can draw the object from the center outward, as explained in the next section.

Drawing Shapes, Lines, and Arcs from a Center Point

You have seen how to draw lines and other shapes by starting at one of the corners (or ends, in the case of lines) of the shape. Sometimes, however, you might want the *center* of a shape, line, or arc located in a particular position. Another constraint key—Ctrl—enables you to draw a shape, line, or arc outward from the center point.

To draw any shape outward from the center point, follow these steps:

1. Click any drawing tool. The tool is highlighted and the mouse pointer changes to a crosshair.

2. Position the mouse pointer at the point where you want the center of the object to be.

3. Hold down the Ctrl key, press the left mouse button, and then drag the mouse as you draw the shape. As you drag, you see a solid outline of the shape you're drawing. Notice that the center point does not move.

4. Release the mouse button and the Ctrl key when the shape is the size you want. The shape is selected automatically.

5. Click anywhere on-screen, except on the shape, to deselect the shape.

You have seen examples of how to draw uniform shapes using the Shift key and how to draw from the center point out using the Ctrl key. You can use *both* constraint keys to draw uniform shapes and lines from the center point outward. To draw a circle or square from the center point, or lines at certain angles from the center point, follow these steps:

1. Click a drawing tool.

2. Position the mouse pointer at the point where you want the center of the shape, line, or arc to be.

3. Hold down the Shift and Ctrl keys together, press the left mouse button, and then drag the mouse to begin drawing. As you drag, you see a solid outline of the shape you're drawing. Notice that the center point does not move.

4. Release the mouse button when the shape is the size you want.

Table 5.1 summarizes how you use Shift and Ctrl when drawing shapes and lines.

Table 5.1 Using the Shift and Ctrl Keys in Drawing

Use	With Line Tool	With Other Drawing Tools
Shift	To draw vertical, horizontal, and 45-degree lines	To draw perfect shapes such as circles or squares
Ctrl	To draw a line from the center point out	To draw a shape from the center point out
Shift-Ctrl	To draw vertical, horizontal, and 45-degree lines from the center out	To draw uniform shapes such as circles or squares from the center out

In this section, you have seen how to use the drawing tools to draw a number of special shapes. The following section explains how to draw a particularly useful shape: an arrow.

Drawing an Arrow

An arrow is one of the most useful objects you can draw; you can add an arrow to direct the audience's attention to the most important part of a slide. In a bulleted list, for example, an arrow can call attention to a particular point on the list. To draw arrows, you use the Arrowhead command on the Object menu; when you choose this command, the submenu shown in figure 5.6 appears.

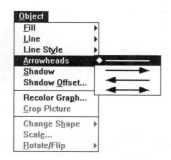

Fig. 5.6

The Arrowheads submenu.

The first choice on the submenu is a line with no arrowhead. This line is the default style and, unless you have changed it, the currently selected style (as indicated by the diamond on the left). The second choice is a line with an arrowhead on the right. The third choice is a line with an arrowhead on the left. The final choice is a line with arrowheads at both ends.

To draw an arrowhead, follow these steps:

1. On the tool palette, click the Line tool.

2. Choose Arrowheads from the Object menu. The Arrowheads submenu appears.

3. Click an arrowhead option. The submenu closes.

4. Position the mouse pointer where you want the arrow to begin.

5. Press the left mouse button and drag the mouse to draw the line with the arrowhead. Figure 5.7 illustrates a line with double arrowheads.

You might have drawn a line on a slide and decide later that you want the line to be an arrow. To convert the line to an arrow, select the line, choose Arrowhead from the Object menu, and select an arrowhead option from the Arrowhead submenu.

110

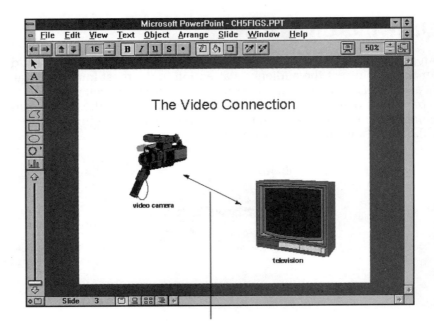

Fig. 5.7

A line with double arrow-heads.

Line with arrowheads

Editing Lines and Shapes

As you revise your slides, you might want to change or delete lines and shapes. This section shows you how to use the Delete key to delete a selected object. You also learn how to move and copy objects.

T I P Remember that after you have drawn an object, you cannot manipulate the object further until you select it by using the Selection tool.

Selecting Multiple Objects

You already know how to select a single object; just point to it and click. To select several objects at once, follow these steps:

1. Click the Selection tool, if it is not already selected.

2. Click the first object you want to select. A dotted line surrounding the object indicates that the object is selected.

3. Press and hold down the Shift key, and then click the next object you want to select. A dotted line surrounding the object indicates that the second object is selected.

4. Repeat step 3 for all objects you want to select.

Figure 5.8 shows several objects that were selected using these steps.

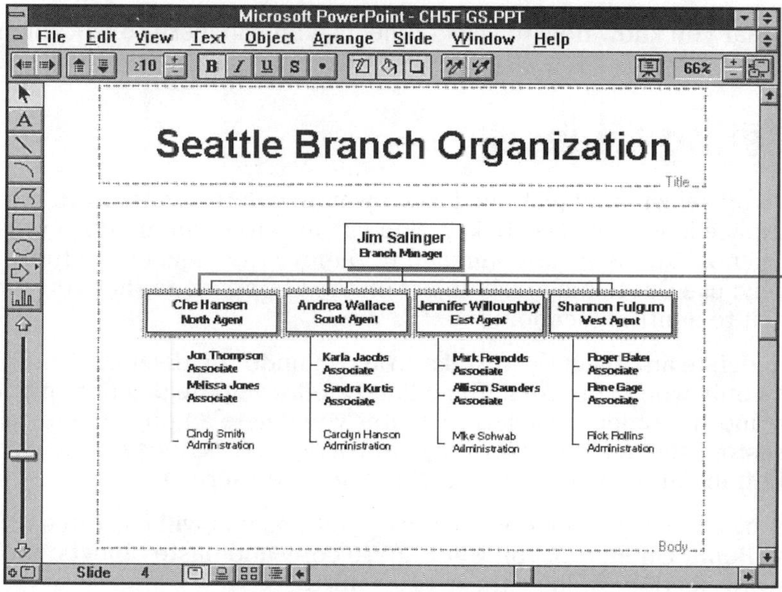

Selected objects

Fig. 5.8

Several objects selected on-screen.

T I P

To cancel a selection, click the Selection tool. To deselect a single object when multiple objects are currently selected, press and hold down the Shift key and click the object to be deselected.

You can also select a group of objects by dragging the mouse. Follow these steps:

1. Position the mouse pointer above and to the left of the leftmost object you want to select.

2. Hold down the left mouse button and drag toward the other objects to be selected. A dotted rectangle enclosing all the objects indicates the area being selected.

3. Completely enclose the objects to be selected, and then release the mouse button. The dotted rectangle disappears and each object is selected.

To use the dragging method to select objects, you must completely enclose all objects. Objects that are only partially enclosed are not selected.

To select all objects on the current slide—text objects as well as drawn objects—choose the Select All command from the Edit menu or press Ctrl-A. All objects on the slide become selected. (When you use this method, any tool can be selected; the result will be the same.)

Now that you know how to select objects, you can learn to edit them.

Deleting Objects

After you select an object, the fastest way to delete it is to press the Backspace key or the Delete key. You can also use commands on the Edit menu. Use the Clear command to remove the object from the slide entirely; use Cut to place the object on the Clipboard so that you can paste it to another location.

If you delete an object by mistake, you can undo the deletion. Undo works only when you use it immediately following the deletion. If you draw another object or insert text after you delete an object, you cannot restore the deleted object. To undo a deletion, choose Undo from the Edit menu. The deleted object reappears on-screen.

Deleting and undeleting objects are operations you will use often in PowerPoint. Often, too, you will want to copy and paste objects; the following section explains these procedures.

Copying and Pasting Objects

In the preceding section, you learned that one method of deleting an object is to cut it to the Clipboard. You use similar steps to make a copy of an object; that is, you place a copy of the object on the Clipboard while leaving the original intact. You then can paste the copy into another location in the drawing so that the object appears in two places: the original location and the new location.

Suppose that you have a slide that resembles figure 5.9, and you want a rectangle on the right of the slide that is the same size as the one currently in the center of the slide. Copying the center rectangle is much easier than trying to create a new one with the same dimensions.

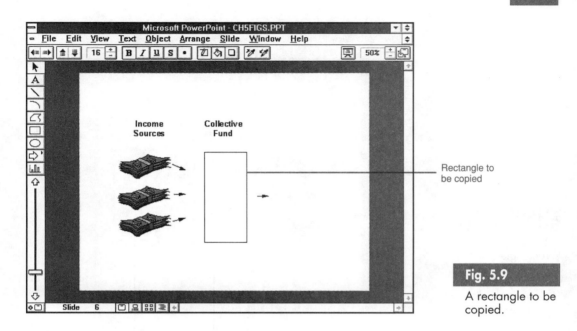

Fig. 5.9

A rectangle to be copied.

To copy an object to another location, follow these steps:

1. Select the object you want to copy.

2. From the Edit menu, choose Copy.

   The object on-screen does not change. By choosing Copy, you copy the object onto the Clipboard, where the copy remains until you copy another object onto the Clipboard. (*Be careful.* Remember that anything you copy to the Clipboard replaces anything that was previously on the Clipboard.) Now you can create as many copies of the original as you want.

3. Position the cursor where you want the copy to appear, and choose Paste from the Edit menu.

Figure 5.10 shows the drawing with both the original object and the copy. You can make as many copies as you like as long as the original remains on the Clipboard; just choose Paste from the Edit menu to insert another copy of the object.

You now know how to copy and paste objects; the next section explains how to move them.

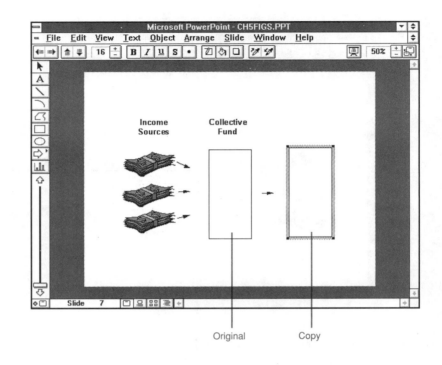

Fig. 5.10

The original
rectangle and the
copy made by
using the Edit
Copy and Edit
Paste commands.

Original   Copy

Moving Objects

Moving objects in PowerPoint is easy; simply select the object and drag
it to a new location. Follow these steps:

1. Move the mouse pointer to the object that you want to move;
   press and hold the left mouse button. A selection box surrounds
   the object.

2. Still holding down the mouse button, move the object to a new
   location by moving the mouse. As you move the mouse, a broken
   line traces the outline of the object's position on the screen.

3. When the object is positioned where you want it, release the
   mouse button.

T I P   When moving objects, be careful not to click the black handles at the
corners of the selection box. Clicking here will resize rather than
move the object. You learn about this technique in the next section.

You can also move more than one object at a time. Follow these steps:

1. Click the first object you want to move; a selection outline surrounds the object.

2. Press and hold the Shift key and click the next object you want to move. Both objects are now selected.

3. Repeat step 2 until all objects you want to move are selected. Release the Shift key and the mouse button.

4. Point to *any* one of the selected objects and press the left mouse button; while still holding down the mouse button, drag the objects to a new location.

5. Release the mouse button when the objects are repositioned where you want them.

You can force an object to move only horizontally or vertically—a useful feature when you want to keep a series of objects in alignment. Select the object, and then press and hold the Shift key as you drag the object. To keep the object aligned horizontally, drag the object to the right or left. To keep the object aligned vertically, drag the object up or down.

You now know how to move a single object or multiple objects. The next section shows how you use the resizing handles—the black squares in each corner of the selection box—to change the shape of objects.

Resizing Objects

At times, you might need to change the size or shape of an object you already have drawn. PowerPoint enables you to simply resize the object; you do not need to delete and redraw the object. Refer back to figure 5.10. The figure contains two identically sized rectangles; suppose that you want to increase the size of the right rectangle. Follow these steps:

1. Click the object you want to resize. The selection box surrounds the object. Notice the black handles (squares) in each corner of the selection box. You use these handles to resize the object.

 When you select a line object, there are only two resizing handles—one at each end of the line.

2. Point to one of the resizing handles, press the left mouse button, and drag the handle. The shape expands (or contracts) in the direction you drag the mouse.

3. Release the mouse button when the object is sized as you want it.

4. Click anywhere on-screen, except on the object, to deselect the object.

As you learned earlier in this chapter, the Shift and Ctrl keys perform special functions when you draw objects. When resizing objects, these keys also have special functions. To maintain an object's height-to-width ratio, press the Shift key while resizing, and then drag the object diagonally. If you drag the object horizontally, the object changes only in width. If you drag the object vertically, the object changes only in height. To resize an object from the center point, hold down the Ctrl key as you resize the object. To maintain the height-to-width ratio *and* resize from the object's center point, press Shift-Ctrl as you drag the object diagonally. In figure 5.11 the rectangle on the right was resized using Shift-Ctrl so that its height-to-width ratio was maintained and its center point didn't move.

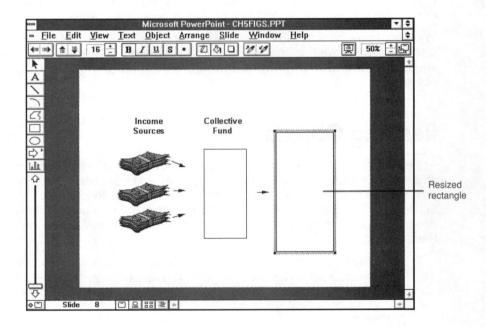

Fig. 5.11

The rectangle on the right was resized using the Shift-Ctrl constraint key combination.

The functions of the constraint keys are summarized in table 5.2.

Table 5.2 Resizing Guide

Use	To Resize a Line...	To Resize a Shape...
Shift	...without changing the angle of the line.	...vertically only or horizontally only. To maintain the height-to-width ratio as you resize, drag the handle diagonally.
Ctrl	...and change the angle while keeping the center fixed.	...while keeping the center point fixed.
Ctrl-Shift	...from the center point without changing the angle of the line.	...vertically only from the center point, or horizontally only from the center point. To resize from the center point while maintaining the height-to-width ratio, drag horizontally.

You now have seen how to resize objects. In the following sections, you learn more advanced techniques for improving or manipulating objects.

Enhancing Objects

All the objects you have drawn in this chapter are surrounded by *frames* that define the outer boundary of an object. In this section, you learn how to turn on and off a frame and how to add a shadowed effect to objects. You also discover how to change the design of frames.

NOTE PowerPoint refers to object boundaries as *lines*. This terminology can be confusing, however, because *line* also refers to a type of object. To avoid confusion, this book refers to object boundaries as frames.

Framing and Shadowing Objects

By default, PowerPoint makes the frame of any object you draw visible. You can tell that the frame feature is turned on because the Line tool on the Toolbar is selected whenever you create a new file using the default settings (see fig. 5.12).

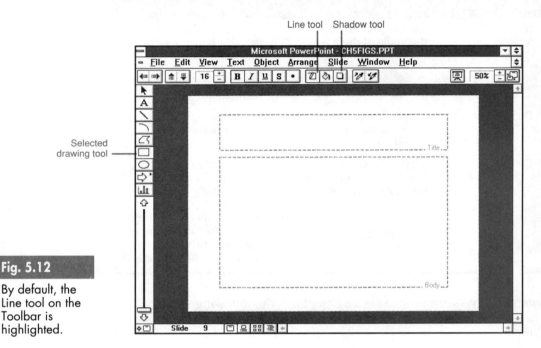

Fig. 5.12

By default, the Line tool on the Toolbar is highlighted.

You can also verify this default setting by choosing the Line command from the Object menu. The Line submenu displays a diamond next to the black color, meaning that whenever you draw an object, it is automatically framed in black.

To remove a frame from an object, select the object; then click the Line tool on the Toolbar. The tool is deselected and the frame around the object immediately disappears. To use the menus to remove a frame, select the object, and then choose the Line command from the Object menu. When the Line submenu appears, choose None to turn off the frame feature.

If an object does not contain text and you remove the frame, you will be unable to see the object on-screen because the screen background and the object are both white. If the object contains text or is filled with a color other than white, however, removing the frame can produce attractive results in your slides. For more information, see the section "Filling Objects and Adding Patterns" later in this chapter.

You can shadow an object in the same way that you frame one, except that shadowing is not a default option; you must switch it on.

Shadows are a type of special enhancement. When not overused, shadows make objects look finished and attractive. You can add shadows easily by clicking the Shadow tool on the Toolbar.

To shadow an object, follow these steps:

1. Draw a new object or select an existing object.

2. Click the Shadow tool on the Toolbar. PowerPoint immediately adds a shadow to the object using the default shadow color.

   If you choose the Shadow command from the Object menu rather than the Shadow tool, PowerPoint displays a shadow submenu showing a list of colors. Click the color you want to use for the shadow. PowerPoint immediately adds a shadow to the object in the color you choose.

The title object in figure 5.13 is shadowed.

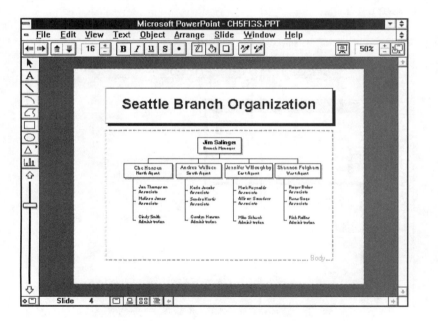

PowerPoint automatically positions the shadow six points to the right and six points below the object. This positioning is called the shadow *offset*. You can change the depth and position of the shadow; follow these steps:

1. Select the shadowed object you want to change.

2. Choose Shadow Offset from the Object menu. PowerPoint displays the Shadow Offset dialog box (see fig. 5.14). If the dialog box covers the selected object, drag the title bar to move it to another part of the screen.

3. To move the shadow up or down, click the Up or Down option button. To change the depth of the shadow, click the arrows in the Points box. The shadow is repositioned as you change the settings.

4. To move the shadow right or left, click the Right or Left option button. To change the depth of the shadow, click the arrows in the Points box. The shadow is repositioned as you change the settings.

5. When the shadow is positioned where you want it, click OK.

Figure 5.14 shows a shadowed object and the shadow offset settings that were used.

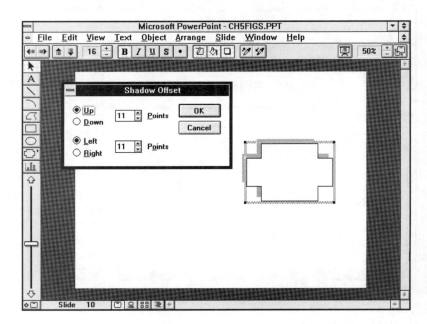

Fig. 5.14

The shadow was moved up and to the left.

In the next section, you learn how to enhance an object's frame by changing the line style.

Changing Line Styles

After an object is framed, you can enhance the lines of the frame by changing the line style. A *line style* refers to the formatting of a line; by default, PowerPoint makes lines black with a width of 2 points. You can apply different line styles to object frames or to individual lines on the slides. Using a line style is often a useful way to draw attention to certain parts of your slide or to distinguish between different objects.

To apply a line style to a line or an object, follow these steps:

1. Select a line or object.

2. Choose Line Style from the Object menu. PowerPoint displays the Line Style submenu (see fig. 5.15). The dot next to the first option indicates that this style is active.

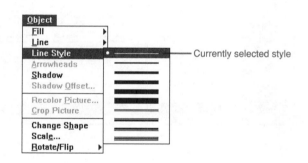

— Currently selected style

Fig. 5.15

The Line Style submenu.

3. Click the line style to apply to the selected object or line. PowerPoint applies the style.

Use different line styles for different emphasis. A heavy line, for example, makes an object stand out. In figure 5.16, the shadow was removed from the title object and replaced with a heavy line style.

As you learned earlier, you can remove the frame from an object, making that object invisible. This capability is of little use unless you are dealing with filled objects that remain visible without the frame. The next section explains how to change the colors and patterns inside your objects.

Filling, Shading, and Patterning Objects

Objects that contain a color or a pattern are more interesting than plain white objects. With PowerPoint, you can fill an object with a solid color, shaded color, or a two-color pattern. This section explains how to apply each of these attributes to objects. To add a fill color or pattern to an object, choose the Fill command from the Object menu. The Fill submenu appears (see fig. 5.17).

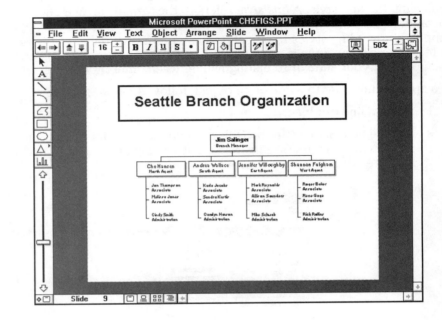

Fig. 5.16

A heavy line style was used to outline the title object.

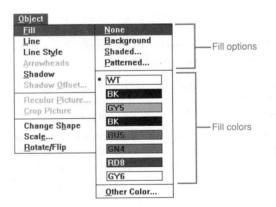

Fig. 5.17

The Fill submenu.

The fill options appear in the upper half of the submenu. The fill colors available with the current color scheme appear in the lower half of the menu. (For steps on choosing another color, refer to Chapter 7.)

To fill an object with a solid color, follow these steps:

1. Draw a new object or select an existing object.

2. Choose Fill from the Object menu. The Fill submenu appears.

3. From the Fill submenu, select a color. The submenu closes and the object is colored.

In figure 5.18, a title object was added and filled with a solid color; these enhancements make the title object more prominent.

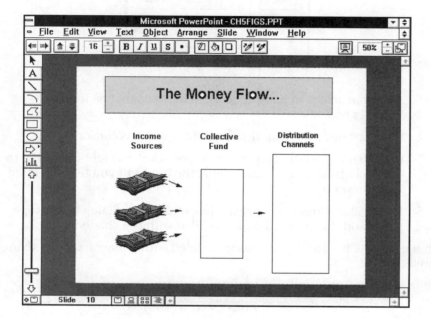

Fig. 5.18

The title object is filled with a solid color.

A variation on the Fill command enables you to fill an object with a shaded color. Using a shaded color enables you to include light-to-dark or dark-to-light variations in the color. Using the following steps, you choose a shade style, color, and intensity:

1. Draw a new object or select an existing object.

2. Choose Fill from the Object menu. The Fill submenu appears.

3. From the Fill submenu, choose the Shaded option. PowerPoint displays the Shaded Fill dialog box (see fig. 5.19). The dialog box contains six options for shade styles, a drop-down box from which you can choose a color, and a Dark/Light scale.

4. Click on several shade styles until you find one you like. The Variants box displays variants of each style you select.

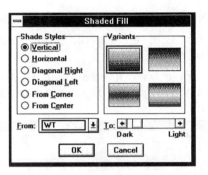

Fig. 5.19

The Shaded Fill
dialog box.

5. After you select a shade style, select a variant style from the Variants box.

6. Click on the From drop-down box to select a color for the fill.

7. In the To box, slide the scroll box from Dark to Light, releasing the mouse button several times along the bar until you find the intensity you want.

8. When all settings are correct, choose OK. The dialog box disappears and the selected object is filled with the shaded color.

In figure 5.20, the two rectangles were filled with a diagonal right shade style.

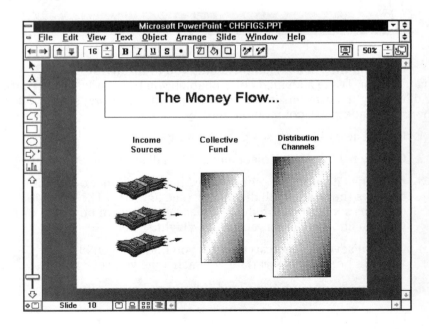

Fig. 5.20

The two rectangles with a shaded fill.

Patterning is another variant of the fill command. PowerPoint enables you to select a pattern style and two colors: one for the pattern foreground and one for the background. Follow these steps:

1. Draw a new object or select an existing one.

2. Choose Fill from the Object menu. The Object Fill submenu appears.

3. From the submenu, choose Patterned. The Patterned Fill dialog box appears (see fig. 5.21). The dialog box contains 36 pattern styles, and drop-down boxes from which you choose a foreground and a background color.

The Patterned Fill dialog box.

4. Click a pattern in the Pattern box.

5. From the Foreground drop-down list box, select a color. (The *foreground color* corresponds to the black part of the pattern, as shown in the dialog box.)

6. From the Background drop-down list box, select a color. (The *background color* corresponds to the white part of the pattern, as shown in the dialog box.)

7. When all settings are correct, click OK.

In figure 5.22, two rectangles in the figure are filled with a dot pattern.

Making Objects Opaque

All filled and patterned objects are *opaque*, which means that you cannot see other objects or text through them. All unfilled objects are *transparent*, which means that you can see other objects or text through them. In some cases—usually as a design technique—you might want to make an object opaque without filling it with a color. The examples in figure 5.23 and 5.24 illustrate this technique.

I — POWERPOINT BASICS

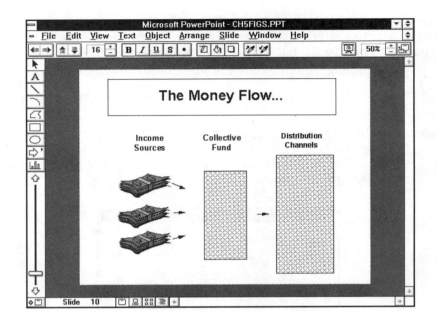

Fig. 5.22

The two rectangles filled with a dot pattern.

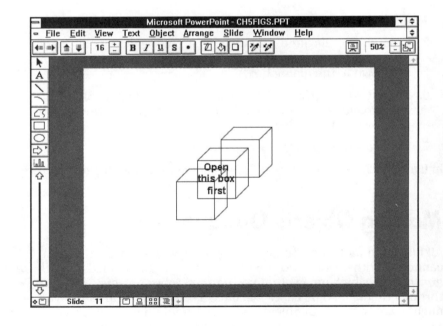

Fig. 5.23

Three transparent objects.

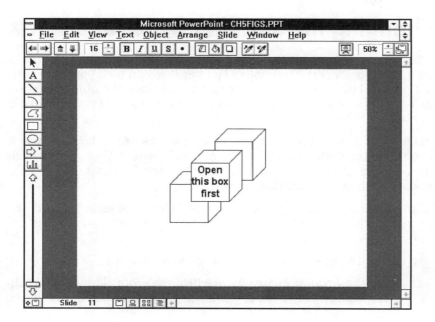

Fig. 5.24

Three opaque
objects.

In figure 5.23, the unfilled objects overlap one another and make the slide look messy. By making the objects opaque, you achieve the results shown in figure 5.24.

To make an object opaque without giving it a new color, simply fill it with the same color as the background color. In this case, the background of the slide is white, so the fill "color" is white. Because each box in figure 5.24 now has "color," you cannot see through any of the boxes.

Be default, PowerPoint makes all objects opaque. To make a transparent object opaque, follow these steps:

1. Click the transparent object to select it.

2. Click the Fill tool on the Toolbar. PowerPoint fills the object with the default fill color: white.

   If you choose the Fill command from the Object menu instead of clicking the Fill tool, PowerPoint displays a submenu listing colors. Click white; PowerPoint fills the object with white.

Now that you know how to make an object opaque, you will learn how to change the stacking order—an important feature for arranging opaque objects.

Changing the Stacking Order of Objects

When you create several opaque objects on top of one another, the last object you draw is the top object (just as it would be if you were stacking physical objects). In many cases, you will want the objects stacked in a different order. You must know how to change the stacking order of objects if you want to rearrange them.

In figure 5.23, you know that the center box was drawn last because it is on top of the other two boxes. Suppose, however, that you want the boxes to be stacked in order from front to back. To create this effect, you must change the stacking order.

You can change stacking order by bringing lower objects forward or by sending forward objects backward. Follow these steps to bring an object to the top of the stack:

1. Select the object that you want to move forward.

2. From the Arrange menu, choose Bring to Front. The selected object is placed at the top of the stack of objects. The newly placed object is still selected.

3. Click anywhere other than on the object to deselect the object.

The Arrange menu also contains the Send to Back command. When you choose this command, the selected object goes to the bottom of the stack.

PowerPoint also enables you to move an object forward in a stack one step at a time instead of directly to the top of the stack. Follow these steps:

1. Select the object you want to move forward.

2. From the Arrange menu, choose Bring Forward. The selected object is moved forward one step in the stack. The object remains selected.

3. To continue moving the object forward one step at a time, repeat step 2.

4. When the object is positioned in the stack where you want it, click anywhere outside the group of objects. This step deselects the object.

You can also use the Send Backward option on the Arrange menu to send an object further down the stack one step at a time.

In figure 5.25, the three boxes were stacked from front to back by using the Send to Back option on the second and third boxes until they were positioned properly.

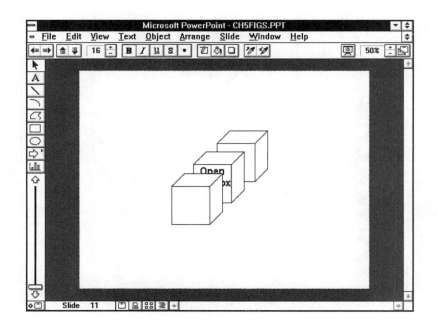

Fig. 5.25

The boxes were rearranged by using the Send to Back option on the second and third boxes.

Using Guides, Grids, and Edges

At the bottom of the Arrange menu are three helpful commands: Snap to Grid, Show Guides, and Show Edges. When you choose any of these commands, a check mark appears to the left of the command to indicate that it is selected. Use these three commands to align, move, and display objects.

Using the Guides To Align Objects

You might need to align objects to make your slides look neater. The guide lines available from the Arrange menu help you align objects along the vertical or horizontal axis. Suppose that you have an oval in the upper left portion of the screen and an arrow on the right. You want the two objects to align exactly one-half inch above the horizontal center of the slide. Follow these steps to align the objects:

1. From the Arrange menu, choose Show Guides. A pair of dotted lines—one vertical and one horizontal—appears on the slide (see fig. 5.26). The lines are placed at the horizontal and vertical center of the slide.

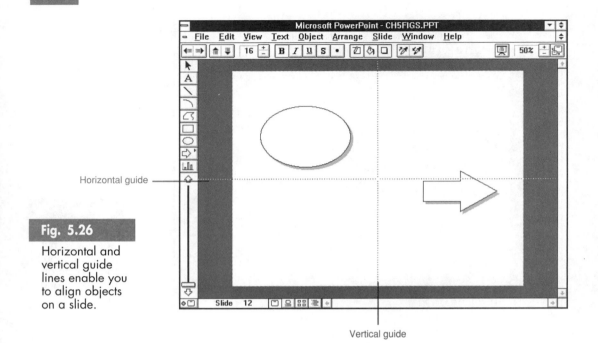

Horizontal guide ⎯⎯

Fig. 5.26

Horizontal and
vertical guide
lines enable you
to align objects
on a slide.

Vertical guide

2. Click the Selection tool if it is not already selected.

3. Click the horizontal guide line and drag the line upward. As you drag the line, 0.00 appears when you first press the mouse button; this number increases as you drag the line upward. The number represents inches (or centimeters, if you selected centimeters as the default unit when you installed PowerPoint) from the center of the slide, as measured on the printed output, not on the screen slide.

4. Release the mouse button when you reach the point where you want to align the objects. In the example, stop at one-half inch (0.50).

5. Move the object to the guide line. In this example, move the oval upward until its bottom edge touches the guide.

   The guide has a magnet-like attraction to the objects, which helps you align objects easily. Objects "jump" to a guide line when you move them close to the line. When you move the guide line, however, objects do not jump to the guide line's new position. If you want to align objects, therefore, you must move the objects to the guide and not the guide to the objects.

   Now you can align the arrow.

6. Click and drag the arrow to align it to the guide line. In this instance, move the arrow upward until its bottom edge jumps to the guide (see fig. 5.27). The arrow remains selected.

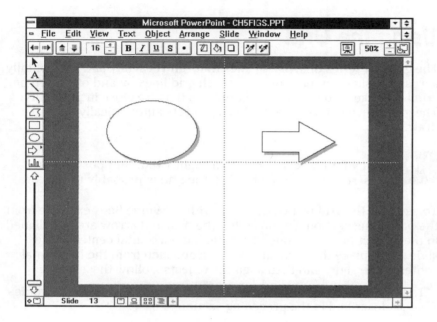

Fig. 5.27

The bottom edges of the two objects are horizontally aligned.

7. Click anywhere on the screen, except on the arrow, to deselect the arrow.

8. To hide the guides, choose Show Guides from the Arrange menu; this step deselects the command. The check mark disappears from the command and the menu closes.

> If you have trouble seeing clearly when aligning objects, use the View menu to switch from the 50% Size default to Full Size.

T I P

You can use the guides with the Ctrl and Shift keys to align objects. You can, for example, draw a square centered on a specific point. First, move the guide lines so that they intersect on the point you have chosen to be the center point of the square. Next, position the cursor on the point of intersection and draw the square while holding down the Ctrl and Shift keys.

Use the guide lines as shown in the preceding steps to place objects with precision. You can use an additional tool—the grid—to place objects on slides.

Using the Grid

The *grid* is a series of invisible lines that run vertically and horizontally across the slide screen. You can switch grid lines on and off. When on, grid lines, like guide lines, attract objects that are close in proximity. The grid is useful if you want to align objects automatically as you draw.

 NOTE If your objects "snap" to a slightly different position on-screen than you intended, the grid is probably turned on.

To see how the grid works, continue with the guide lines example from the preceding section. Suppose that the oval and arrow are not aligned in their exact positions, one inch from the horizontal center of the slide. First, place the vertical guide line one inch from the horizontal center of the slide, and then align the objects. Follow these steps:

1. Choose Actual Size from the View menu and switch on the guides, as described in the preceding section.

2. Open the Arrange menu. If the Snap to Grid command is not selected, choose it. The option is selected if a check mark appears to the left of the command.

3. Move any object on the slide; you will notice that the object moves in a jerky motion.

   When the Snap to Grid option is on, all objects move by jumping from grid line to grid line; the grid lines are invisible.

4. Move one of the guides and watch the numbers change. For example, move the vertical line to the left until the number reads 1.00.

   The numbers always increase or decrease in units of 0.08 or 0.09—the distance between each grid line.

5. Move the object to the guide line. For the example, move the oval and arrow to the new guide line position to realign them.

Now see how moving objects works without the grids; follow these steps:

1. Open the Arrange menu and choose Snap to Grid to turn off the option.

2. Move a guide line; notice that the increments can be as low
as 0.01.

PowerPoint leaves the grid turned on by default. You can turn off the
grid if you need to position objects with greater precision than the grid
allows.

Showing the Edges of Objects

In the section "Framing and Shadowing," you saw that you can make an
unfilled object invisible by clicking the Line tool on the Toolbar or by
selecting None for the Line Style option on the Object menu. The object
remains and can be manipulated and filled as usual, but you cannot see
it. If you have many such objects on your slide, you might want to make
them visible, at least while you're working with them, so that you can
decide which objects to keep and which to delete.

To make unframed objects visible, choose Show Edges from the
Arrange menu. When you return to the slide, all invisible objects are
surrounded by a broken line. A slide with many unframed objects and a
few framed objects might resemble figure 5.28.

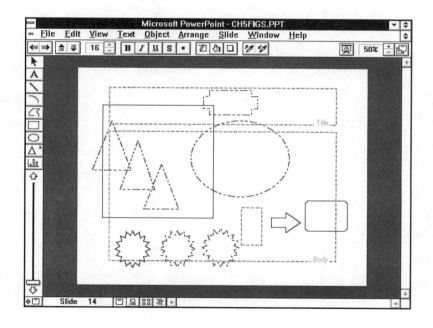

Fig. 5.28

The edges of
unframed objects
are visible when
you choose the
Show Edges
option.

The line produced by the Show Edges option, unlike the selection outline, follows the exact shape of the object (oval, for example). To make the edges invisible again, go back to the Arrange menu and choose Show Edges again to deselect the option. The check mark disappears from the menu option and all unframed objects become invisible again.

Chapter Summary

In this chapter, you learned to draw a variety of shapes, including lines, circles, squares, and special shapes and lines with arrowheads. You learned how to move, resize, fill, frame, and shadow objects, as well as how to change their line styling. Finally, you discovered how to use guides, grids, and edges to help you arrange and align objects.

In the next chapter, a quick start, you learn how to work with color.

Quick Start: Choosing Color Schemes and Creating Graphs

This Quick Start prepares you for the two following chapters: "Using Basic Color" and "Creating Basic Graphs." In this chapter, you learn how to choose an existing color scheme and apply it to a presentation. You then go into the PowerPoint Graph window—the window you use to produce charts and graphs—and enter data for creating a graph. You choose the type of graph that best suits the data, place the graph on a slide in a presentation, and then recolor the graph to make it stand out on the slide.

Choosing a Color Scheme

You might not feel comfortable working with color, but you don't have to be a professional artist to effectively use color in PowerPoint. The color schemes in PowerPoint are designed by color experts. Each color

scheme consists of a set of colors that are designed to work well together. Each scheme includes colors for the screen background, title
text, lines and text, object fills, shadows, and accent colors, as shown
in figure 6.1.

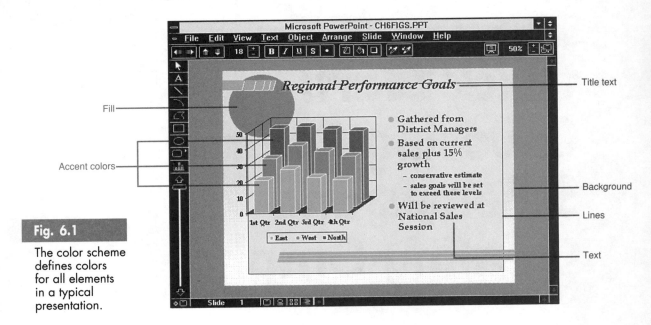

Fig. 6.1

The color scheme
defines colors
for all elements
in a typical
presentation.

To choose a color scheme, you use the Choose a Scheme dialog box.
PowerPoint gives you some control and flexibility in defining the
scheme. First choose a color for background, and then choose a color
for text and lines. PowerPoint then presents sets of additional colors
that work well with your choices of background and text colors.

To choose a color scheme, follow these steps:

1. Open the new presentation.

2. From the Slide menu, choose Color Scheme. The Color Scheme
   dialog box appears, displaying the current color scheme.

3. Click the Choose a Scheme button in the upper right corner of the
   dialog box. The Choose a Scheme dialog box appears (see fig. 6.2).

4. From the Background list, click a background color for your color
   screen. For additional color choices, you can scroll through the
   list. When you choose a color, a list of complimentary colors
   appears in the Text list.

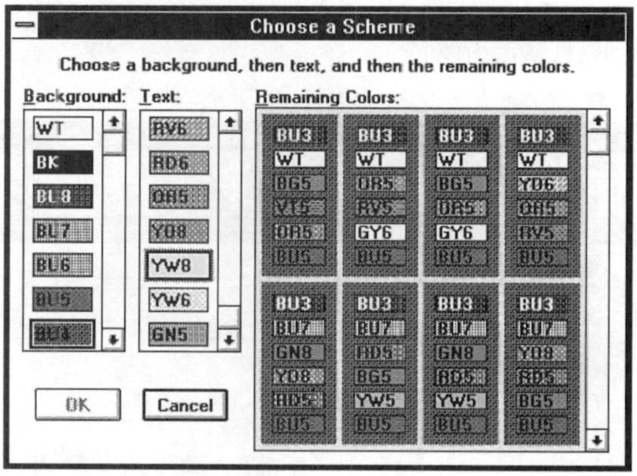

Fig. 6.2

The Choose a Scheme dialog box.

5. From the Text list, click a color. Scroll through the list if you want additional color choices.

6. From the Remaining Colors box, choose one set of colors, and then click OK. The Color Scheme dialog box reappears, displaying the new color scheme.

7. Click the All Slides option in the Apply To box.

8. Click OK. PowerPoint returns to the active presentation and applies the new colors to all slides in the existing presentation.

Two other options in the Color Scheme dialog box are Change a Color and Shade Background. You learn about these options in Chapter 7.

Figure 6.3 shows an unenhanced presentation. Figure 6.4 shows the same presentation after PowerPoint applies a color scheme. Experiment with different color schemes to find combinations that you like.

Creating a Graph

PowerPoint enables you to easily create graphs and incorporate them into your slides. Using Microsoft Graph, an embedded application within PowerPoint, you can create graphs without leaving PowerPoint. In Chapter 8, "Creating Basic Graphs," you learn the details of using Microsoft Graph. In this section, however, you learn enough to start using Microsoft Graph.

When you click the Graph tool on the tool palette, Microsoft Graph starts and opens a new window on-screen like the one shown in figure 6.5. The Graph window contains two smaller windows: the datasheet window and the chart window. You enter the data for the graph into the datasheet window, and the graph created from the data appears in the chart window.

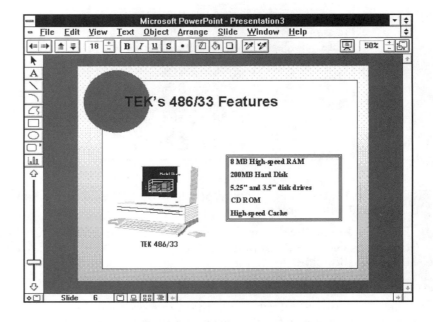

Fig. 6.3

A slide that uses the default color settings in PowerPoint.

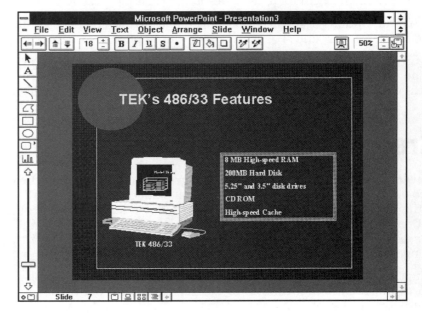

Fig 6.4

A slide that uses a PowerPoint color scheme.

NOTE The terms *graph* and *chart* are often used interchangeably. In this book, all graphic representations created with Microsoft Graph are referred to as graphs rather than charts. (The word *Graph*, when capitalized, refers specifically to the embedded application, Microsoft Graph.)

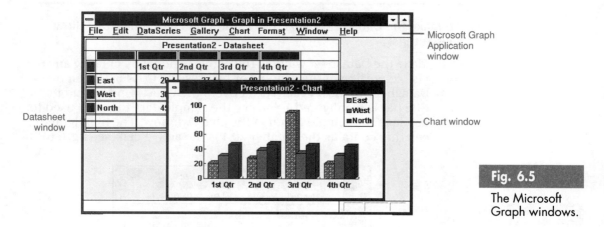

Datasheet window

Microsoft Graph Application window

Chart window

Fig. 6.5

The Microsoft Graph windows.

When you first open Graph, the datasheet and chart windows contain sample data and a sample graph. You replace the sample data with your own data.

Before creating a graph to embed, you select a location for the graph on the slide. To prepare the slide for the graph and to open Graph, follow these steps:

1. Display Slide #1 in the current presentation.

2. Click the Graph tool on the tool palette. The mouse pointer changes to a crosshair.

3. Place the crosshair where you want to embed the graph. Click and drag the mouse, drawing a box—a graph object—about the size you want the graph to be. After a few seconds, the Graph window opens.

Entering and Deleting Data

Microsoft Graph is easy to use—even if you have never used a spreadsheet product. You enter data in the Datasheet window "on top of" the existing sample data. In the following steps, you change the sample data to the data shown in table 6.1. This data represents the number of cars and trucks sold by a salesperson in January through April.

Table 6.1 New Data for the Datasheet Window

	January	February	March	April
Cars	4	8	6	4
Trucks	1	1	3	1

To make the Datasheet the active window and to enter data, follow these steps:

1. Make the Datasheet window the active window by clicking any visible portion of the window or by pressing Ctrl-F6. (When the Datasheet window is active, it covers the Chart window and its title bar is highlighted.) You see the sample data that was used to produce the sample graph in the chart window. The highlighted cell that contains the number 20.4 is the active cell (see fig. 6.6).

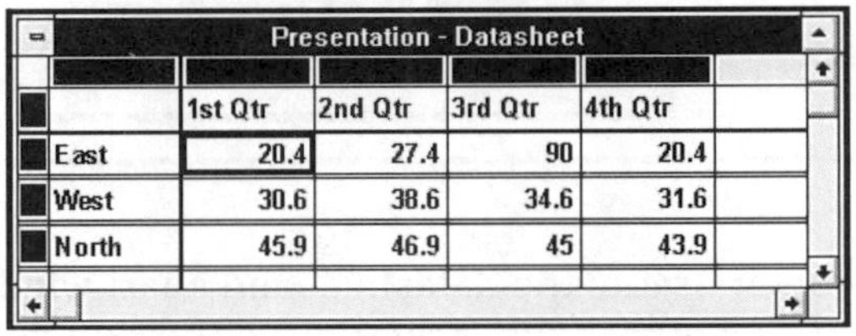

Fig. 6.6

Sample data in the Datasheet window.

Presentation - Datasheet

	1st Qtr	2nd Qtr	3rd Qtr	4th Qtr
East	20.4	27.4	90	20.4
West	30.6	38.6	34.6	31.6
North	45.9	46.9	45	43.9

T I P Using either the Maximize button or the window borders, resize the datasheet window to display more rows and columns in the window.

2. Using the arrow keys, move to the cell labeled *1st Qtr*. Type *January*, and then press the Tab or the right arrow key to move to the cell labeled *2nd Qtr. January* replaces *1st Qtr.*

3. Type *February*, and then press the right-arrow key.

4. Continue filling in the datasheet with the data shown in Table 6.1. Use the arrow keys to move to any cell in the datasheet.

T I P Pressing an arrow key after typing an entry enters the data into the current cell and moves the cursor to the next cell. This tip saves you the trouble of pressing Enter after each entry and then pressing an arrow key.

As you change the data, watch the visible portion of the Chart window; the graph reflects the data changes. At this point, you are not ready yet to display the Chart window; you need to delete the third row of sample data first. To delete an entire row, follow these steps:

1. Click the black square to the left of the word *North* in the third row of data. PowerPoint highlights the entire row.
2. From the Edit menu, choose Delete Row/Col. The selected row disappears.

You can delete unwanted columns from the datasheet using the same basic steps. Click the black square above the column you want to delete. PowerPoint highlights the entire column. Then choose the Delete Row/Col command from the Edit menu.

Your datasheet window should now look like the one shown in figure 6.7.

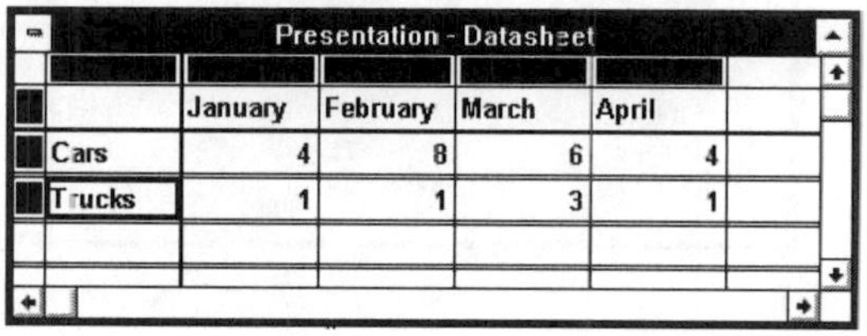

Presentation - Datasheet
January
February
March
April
Cars
4
8
6
4
Trucks
1
1
3
1

Fig. 6.7

The Datasheet window containing the new data.

Changing the Graph Type

After creating the data for your graph in the Datasheet window, you can manipulate the resulting graph using the Chart window and its options. To move to the Chart window, click any visible portion of the window or press Ctrl-F6. Your graph should look like the one shown in figure 6.8.

Presentation - Chart
8
7
6
5
4
3
2
1
0
Cars
Trucks
January
February
March
April

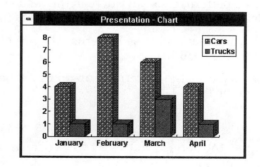

Fig. 6.8

A 3-D column graph displaying the sales data you entered.

This type of graph, called a 3-D column graph, is the default graph type. You can change the graph type by choosing a different type from the Gallery menu. To change the graph type, follow these steps:

1. Make sure the Chart window is active.

2. From the Gallery menu, choose 3-D Line. The Chart Gallery dialog box displays a variety of styles for the 3-D line graph type.

3. Choose style #2, and then click OK. PowerPoint reformats the graph to the new graph type and style.

Figure 6.9 shows the data as a 3-D line graph.

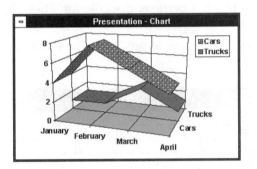

Fig. 6.9

A 3-D line graph displaying the sales data you entered.

Changing Graph Patterns

In figure 6.9, each data area of the graph is filled not only with color, but also with a pattern. (The data areas are the parts of the graph that represent categories. In this example, the lines that represent the Cars and Trucks data are data areas.) To change the pattern of a data area, follow these steps:

1. Make the Chart window the active window.

2. To change its pattern, click anywhere in the data area. In this example, click anywhere on the line that represents the Cars data.

3. From the Format menu, choose Patterns. The Area Patterns dialog box appears (see fig. 6.10).

4. In the Area box, click the Patterns drop-down list box. Choose a pattern from the list.

T I P If you want to apply the pattern you select to all data areas on the graph, click the Apply to All check box (located just below the OK button).

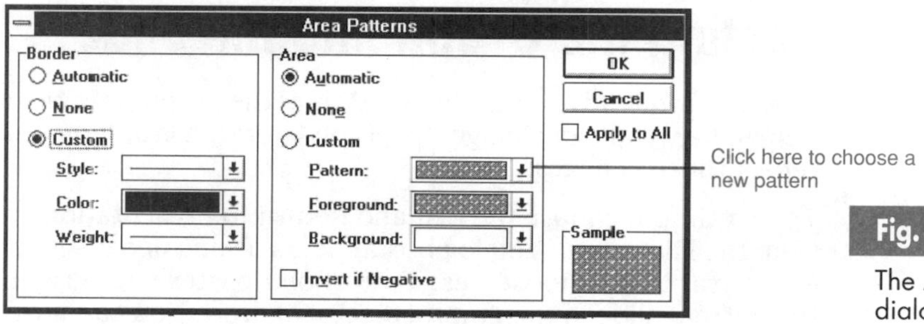

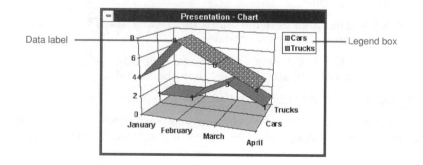

Fig. 6.10

The Area Patterns dialog box.

5. Click OK. PowerPoint applies the new pattern to the selected data area.

Adding Data Labels

The legend box in the upper right portion of the Chart window identifies the categories of data represented by each pattern in the graph—in this case, cars and trucks. Suppose that you want the graph to show the exact number of cars and trucks sold. You can label each data point by following these steps:

1. Make sure the Chart window is active.

2. From the Chart menu, choose Data Labels. The Data Labels dialog box appears.

3. In the dialog box, choose the Show Values option, and then click OK. Data labels are added to the graph.

The graph now looks like the one shown in figure 6.11.

Fig. 6.11

Data labels are added to the 3-D line graph.

Pasting the Graph into the Slide

Now you are ready to put this version of the graph onto the slide. Remember, you can change the graph later; the graph on the slide will reflect those changes.

To exit Graph, choose the Exit and Return to Presentation command from the File menu. A dialog box appears asking Update Graph in Presentation? Choose Yes. PowerPoint pastes your graph into the current slide in the graph object you drew. You can move, resize, copy, or delete the graph object just as you can any other object in your presentation.

Recoloring a Graph

PowerPoint applies the fill and accent colors from the current color scheme to the categories of data represented in your graph. Suppose that, after you paste the final graph into your slide, you decide you want to change the colors of each data category.

The graph is still selected after you paste it from Graph. To recolor the graph, follow these steps:

1. From the Slide menu, choose Color Scheme. The Color Scheme dialog box appears (see fig. 6.12). PowerPoint applies the fill color to the first data category, Cars, and the first accent color to the second data category, Trucks.

2. Click the Fills color, and then click the Change a Color button. The Change a Color dialog box appears (see fig. 6.13).

3. In the color grid, click the color with which you want to replace the selected color.

4. Click OK. The Color Scheme dialog box reappears. This box shows the replacement color you chose.

5. To change the first accent color, repeat steps 2-4, selecting the first accent color in step 2 rather than the fill color.

6. Click the This Slide option in the Apply To box.

7. When you have set all the colors as you want them, click OK in the Color Scheme dialog box. The colors in your graph are updated.

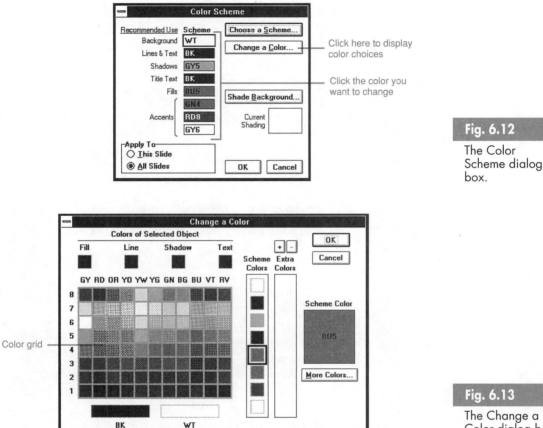

Fig. 6.12

The Color Scheme dialog box.

Fig. 6.13

The Change a Color dialog box.

Chapter Summary

In this chapter, you learned some basics steps for choosing a color scheme and creating a graph. First, you changed a color scheme in the active presentation. You created a graph by using Microsoft Graph. You replaced the sample data in the Datasheet window with your own data, and then you displayed the graph in the Chart window. From the Chart window, you added data labels and changed the patterns on the graph. You then pasted the new graph onto the slide and changed the colors used in the graph.

Now that you have worked with PowerPoint tools for defining color schemes and creating graphs, you are ready to learn about these tools in detail. Chapter 7 explains how to use colors in PowerPoint, and Chapter 8 discusses creating graphs.

Working with Color

For graphics such as handouts or overheads, color is not always available or essential. You can create these types of graphics effectively with little or no knowledge of color. Color is important, however, when you create slides. Coloring your slides can make the difference between a striking presentation and a dull one.

In PowerPoint, you do not have to learn all the nuances of color theory in order to use color well. PowerPoint provides default colors; you can simply start drawing and typing to use them. Better yet, you can apply one of PowerPoint's many color schemes without being a color expert. As you discovered in Chapter 3, you can copy the templates prepared by Genigraphics artists and instantly have well-developed color schemes for your slide shows.

PowerPoint's full range of color features is extensive. Because the topic of color is so broad, however, it is split into two chapters in this book. This chapter covers the basic techniques for setting and changing color. Chapter 14 deals with the more advanced color features.

This chapter first takes you through the color schemes in PowerPoint's template files, showing you how to choose one and apply it to your presentation. Then it provides instructions for creating new color schemes using the Color Scheme dialog box. Finally, because you don't always want to change an entire color scheme, it gives you instructions for changing the color of individual objects.

Reviewing Some Color Guidelines

Color is often considered the most advanced feature in a graphics program because of the endless variety of colors and color combinations. Unfortunately, few people have the background and knowledge to take full advantage of a program's color capabilities. Some basic guidelines for using color might prove helpful:

■ *Limit the number of colors you use.* You can, of course, use PowerPoint default color schemes. Designed by professional artists, these color schemes apply established rules about which colors work well together, which background colors enhance text and lines, and so on. When you create color schemes of your own, tread lightly at first.

■ *Use bright colors for slides.* Bright colors are often used in slides to draw attention and to improve viewer retention. Use bright colors to call attention to important objects on the slide; use subdued colors to highlight thin lines and create shadows.

■ *Maintain high contrast between text and backgrounds.* Whether text is dark or light, the background color should present enough contrast to make the text readable.

■ *Choose color combinations carefully.* Choose thematic color combinations; warm colors complement one another and cool colors complement one another, but the two themes don't mix well.

Using the Color Scheme from Another Presentation

When creating a presentation, you have many choices for working with color. You can use the default color scheme, create a completely new color scheme, or change individual colors. When not using the default color scheme, your safest option, however, is to copy a color scheme from one of PowerPoint's professionally designed templates.

Chapters 2 and 3 explain how to apply a template to a presentation. Use the following steps to copy the color scheme from a template to the active presentation:

1. Open or create the presentation to which you want to apply a template color scheme.

2. From the File menu, choose Open. The Open dialog box appears (see fig. 7.1).

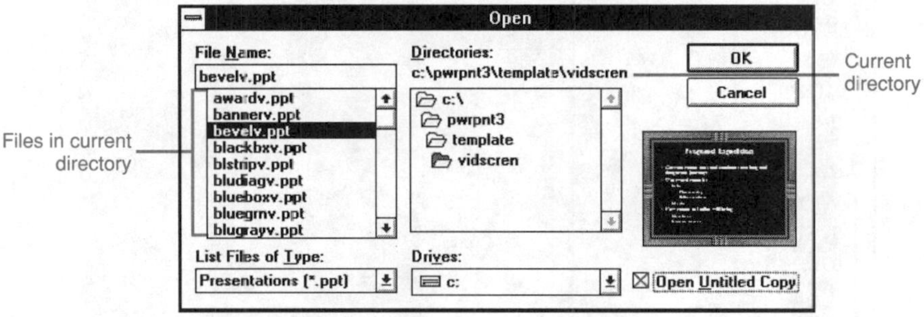

Files in current directory

Current directory

Fig. 7.1

The Open dialog box.

3. Choose the template directory, then choose the 35mslide, b&wovrhd, clrovrhd, or vidscren subdirectory. The Files box shows a list of the templates in the subdirectory you choose.

4. Select one of the files in the Files box. (Remember that when you click or select a file name, you can preview that particular template in the lower right corner of the dialog box.) Repeat this step until you find a template with a color scheme you like.

5. To ensure that you don't inadvertently change the template file, click the Open Untitled Copy check box at the lower right corner of the dialog box; then click OK. PowerPoint opens an untitled copy. Figure 7.2 shows an example of a slide that uses the bevelv.ppt template.

6. From the Slide menu, choose Color Scheme. The Color Scheme dialog box appears (see fig. 7.3). This dialog box lists every color in the color scheme and identifies the objects to which each color is applied. Verify that the color scheme shown is the one you want. Click OK to close the dialog box.

NOTE Step 6 is optional; it simply enables you to view all the colors in the color scheme. (The sample template slide might not use them all.)

7. Click the Pick Up Scheme tool on the Toolbar (see fig. 7.4), or choose Pick Up Style/Scheme from the Edit menu.

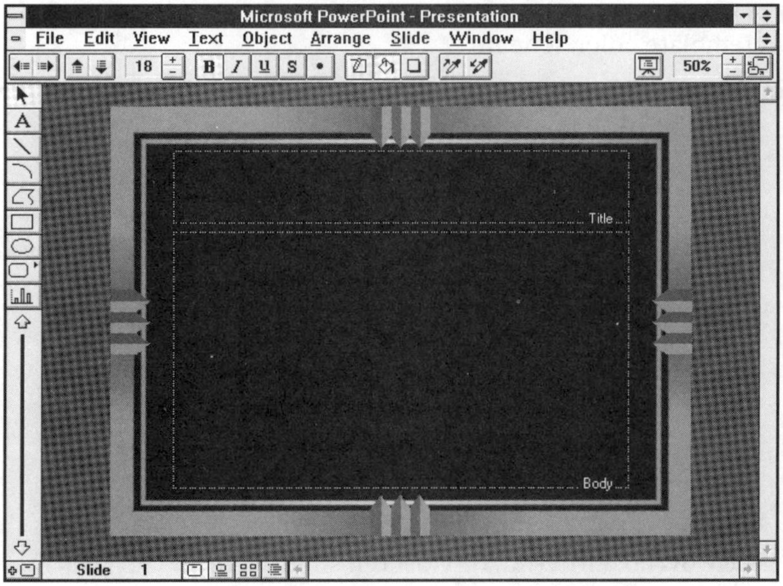

Fig. 7.2

A sample slide that uses a professionally designed color scheme.

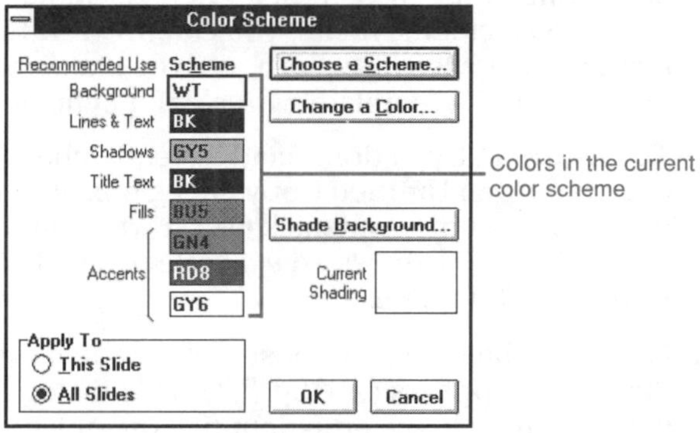

Fig. 7.3

The Color Scheme dialog box.

Colors in the current color scheme

8. From the Window menu, choose the presentation to which you want to apply the color scheme (the presentation you opened in step 1).

9. Click the Slide Sorter View button.

10. Select the slide or slides to which you want to apply the color scheme.

11. Click the Apply Color Scheme tool on the Toolbar or choose Apply Scheme from the Edit menu. The color scheme is applied only to the slides you select.

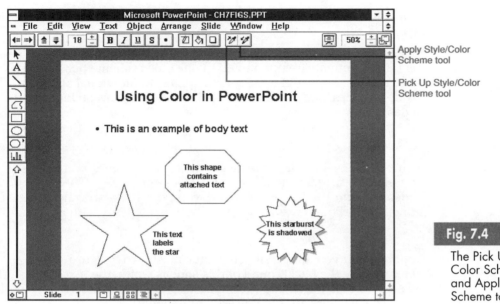

Apply Style/Color
Scheme tool

Pick Up Style/Color
Scheme tool

Fig. 7.4

The Pick Up
Color Scheme
and Apply Color
Scheme tools.

NOTE Because in this example you are working with a new presentation that contains only one slide, steps 9 and 10 might seem unnecessary. If you are applying a color scheme to an existing presentation that contains multiple slides, however, steps 9 and 10 enable you to apply the color scheme *only to selected slides*. This technique gives you more control over the use of color in a presentation. In a presentation that contains only one slide, the color scheme is applied to that single slide. If you add slides later, you can simply pick up the scheme from the first slide and copy it to the others.

At some point, you might want to create your own color schemes to supplement those supplied with PowerPoint. The following sections provide instructions for doing so.

Creating and Applying a Color Scheme

Every color scheme consists of a set of colors that are designed to work well together. Each scheme includes a total of eight colors—one each for the screen background, lines and text, shadows, title text, and object fills, and three for accents. (To see these categories, refer back to fig. 7.3.)

In most cases, the same color scheme is employed throughout a presentation, but you are not limited to one color scheme per presentation. You can apply different color schemes to individual slides or group of slides, and you can change individual colors on individual slides.

T I P   You can change a color scheme at any time, even after you have completed a presentation. You can also use one color scheme for slides and another (often black and white) for handouts and pages of notes. PowerPoint gives you a great deal of flexibility with coloring.

Suppose that you have a slide like the one shown in figure 7.5. On a color screen, the background of this slide is white, the text is black, the oval fill color is white, and the shadow color around the oval is a dark gray. These colors are the PowerPoint defaults.

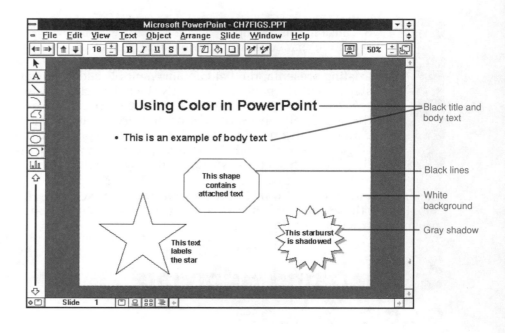

Fig. 7.5

A slide that uses PowerPoint's default color scheme.

The following sections of this chapter show you how to change a color scheme and how to apply the new scheme to one slide, several slides, or all slides. In each case, the first step is to choose Color Scheme from the Slide menu. The Color Scheme dialog box appears (see again fig. 7.3).

The left side of the box displays the eight colors in the default color scheme and their respective uses. PowerPoint automatically applies the first color, white, to the slide background. It applies the second color, black, to lines and text. It uses the third color, gray, to create shadows. The fourth color is used for title text, and the fifth color is used to fill objects. The last three colors are accent colors, used to enhance special items on a slide or on a graph.

All the colors have unique identifying labels—*WT* for white, *BK* for black, *RD8* for a specific shade of red, and so on. (See the section "Changing a Color" later in this chapter for an explanation of the color numbering system.) These identifying labels enable you to more easily choose the same color when you want to apply it in another presentation.

On the right side of the Color Scheme dialog box are four command buttons: Choose a Scheme, Change a Color, Rearrange Colors, and Shade Background. The next three sections discuss the use of these buttons.

Creating a New Color Scheme

To create a new color scheme, follow these steps:

1. In the Color Scheme dialog box, click the Choose a Scheme button. The Choose a Scheme dialog box appears (see fig. 7.6).

The Choose
a Scheme
dialog box.

The Choose a Scheme dialog box contains three scroll boxes: Background, Text, and Remaining Colors. As the instruction line along the top of the box states, these boxes should be used in their order of appearance. When you first open the Choose a Scheme dialog box, only background colors are displayed.

2. In the Background box, choose the color you want to use for slide backgrounds by clicking once on the color. You can use the scroll bars to view as many of the available colors as you like. After you choose a background color, the Text box immediately fills with color choices (see fig. 7.7).

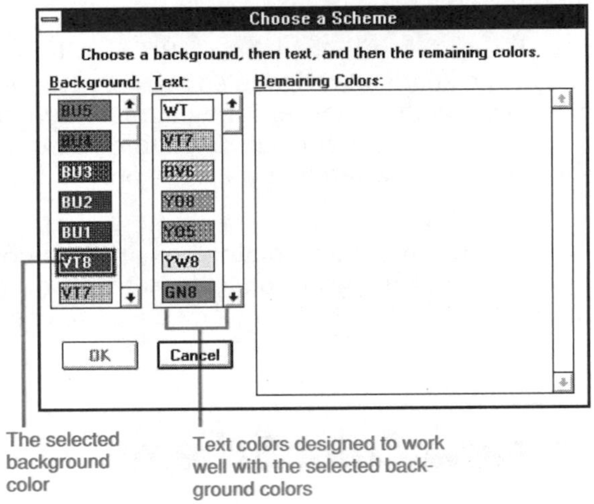

Fig. 7.7

The Text color choices appear after you choose a background color.

The text color is used for all text (other than the slide title) and for lines. PowerPoint displays a set of text colors suited for the background color you choose.

3. In the Text box, choose the color you want to use for text and lines by clicking that color. As in the previous step, you can use the scroll bars to view as many of the available colors as you like. After you choose a text color, the Remaining Colors box immediately fills with color sets (see fig. 7.8).

4. Click one of the color sets in the Remaining Colors box. Instead of choosing individual colors here, you choose one *color set* containing six colors. The first color in each set is used for shadows, the second color for title text, the third color for fills, and the fourth, fifth, and sixth colors for accents.

The background color you chose in step 2 is displayed behind the six color boxes in each set. The text color you chose in step 3 is displayed in the borders between sets of colors.

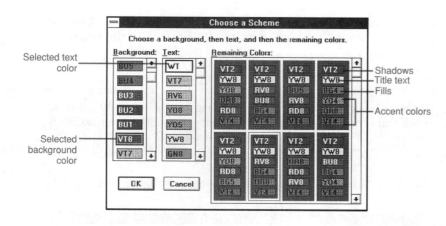

Fig. 7.8

When Background and Text colors are chosen, the Remaining Colors box fills with color choices.

If you're not happy with the results at this point, you can go back to the Background list and start the process over again.

5. When you're satisfied with the color scheme, click OK to return to the Color Scheme dialog box. (Clicking Cancel cancels all the choices you made in the Choose a Scheme dialog box and returns you to the Color Scheme dialog box.)

The eight new colors you chose appear in the Color Scheme dialog box (see fig. 7.9).

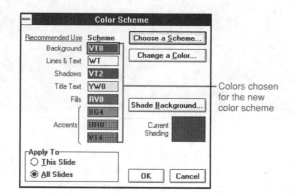

Fig. 7.9

The Color Scheme dialog box displays the new color scheme.

6. Choose one of the two options—This Slide or All Slides—shown in the Apply To box in the lower left corner of the Color Scheme dialog box.

At this stage, you have set up the new scheme but not actually applied it to the presentation. The This Slide option applies the color scheme you just defined to the current slide only. Use the All Slides option to apply the new color scheme to the entire presentation.

7. Click the OK button to apply the new color scheme (see fig. 7.10).

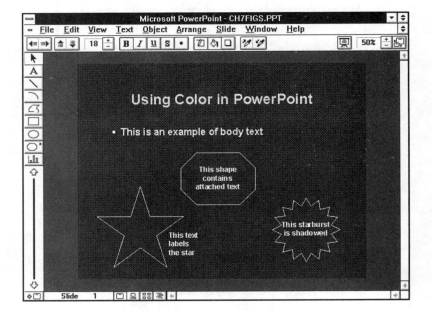

Fig. 7.10

The new color scheme applied to the slide.

In the figure, the background color is violet (VT8), the fill color is red-violet (RV8), the text and the frames of each object are white, the title text is bright yellow (YW8). Finally, the shadow color is a dark violet (VT2) that is similar to the background color.

When you change the color scheme for an existing presentation and use the All Slides option, all the slides *except ones that have been colored individually* are altered accordingly. The slides that have been colored individually remain unchanged.

You might be satisfied with a particular color scheme except for one color. The next section explains how to change individual colors.

Changing a Color

You can change one color in your color scheme without affecting all the other colors. To do so, use the Change a Color dialog box shown in figure 7.11.

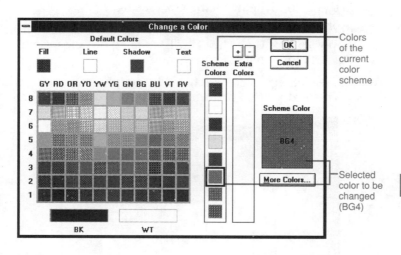

Fig. 7.11

The Change a Color dialog box.

The colors that the current color scheme uses for fill, line, shadow, and text are shown at the top of the dialog box.

The color table displays 88 colors from which you can choose. You can also create a custom color using the More Colors button (more about this in Chapter 14). Each column in the table is labeled with a code that corresponds to a color group; *RD* indicates red, for example, and *RV* indicates red-violet. Each row in the table is numbered. Each color can be identified individually by the appropriate label and number (BU5, for example). Entries for black and white are located below the color table.

The colors shown in the Color Scheme column (to the right of the table) are the eight colors of your current scheme.

To change a color, follow these steps:

1. From the Slide menu, choose Color Scheme. The Color Scheme dialog box appears.

2. Select the color you want to change, and then choose Change a Color, or double-click the color. The Change a Color dialog box appears (see again fig. 7.11).

3. Click any color in the color table. The color is displayed in the preview box (labeled Scheme Color) to enable you to see the

color more clearly. Repeat this step until you find a color you want to use.

4. When you are satisfied with a color, click OK, or click Cancel to revert to the old color. The Color Scheme dialog box returns to the screen. If you clicked OK, the new color replaces the old color in the Color Scheme dialog box (see fig. 7.12).

5. Choose one of the options—This Slide or All Slides—from the Apply To box; then click OK. The dialog box closes and PowerPoint applies the new color.

You can also change a color scheme by simply rearranging the existing colors. The next section provides instructions for doing so.

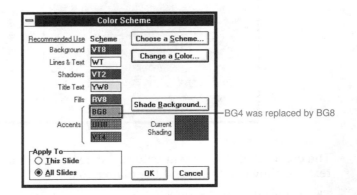

Fig. 7.12

The new color has replaced the previous color in the color scheme.

BG4 was replaced by BG8

Rearranging Colors

If you like the colors included in a color scheme but want to apply them differently, you can change the order of the colors. You could replace the shadow color, for example, with one of the accent colors. To rearrange colors, follow these steps:

1. From the Slide menu, choose Color Scheme. The Color Scheme dialog box appears.

2. Use your mouse to point to one of the colors you want to switch, and then click and drag the color to the desired new position. For the sample rearrangement mentioned previously, choose one of the accent colors and drag it to the Shadow position.

3. Release the mouse button; the two colors switch positions. If the accent color was orange and you dragged it to the gray shadow position, the shadow is now orange and the accent is now gray. Double-check the colors in all slots to make sure they are positioned correctly.

4. Choose one of the options—This Slide or All Slides—in the Apply To box; then click OK. The colors you rearranged are applied to the appropriate elements on the slide.

The next section provides instructions for using Shade Background, the last button in the dialog box.

Shading a Slide Background

A shaded background adds visual interest to a slide—it provides an alternative to a solid white or other solid-colored background. When a background is shaded, the background color moves gradually from dark to light, or vice versa. PowerPoint offers a variety of shading styles, including vertical, horizontal, and diagonal. To apply a shaded background to slides, follow these steps:

1. Display the slide for which you want to shade the background.

2. From the Slide menu, choose Color Scheme. The Color Scheme dialog box appears.

3. Click the Shade Background button. The Shade Background dialog box appears (see fig. 7.13).

   On the left side of the box, a column titled Shade Styles lists the various styles: None, Vertical, Horizontal, Diagonal Right, Diagonal Left, From Corner, and From Title. The first style listed, None, is the default value, as indicated by the black circle to the left of the option. Because None is selected, the Variants section of the Shade Background box shows a single choice that contains no shading. Other styles offer up to four variants, as the following steps show.

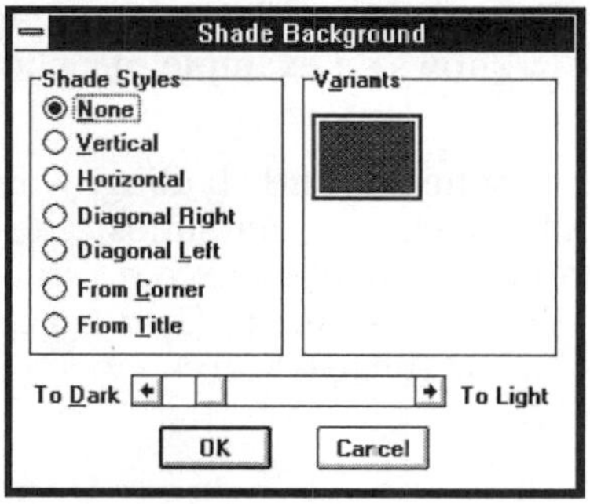

Fig. 7.13

The Shade Background dialog box.

4. Click any of the Shade Styles to see the variants available with that style. Figure 7.14 shows the four variants for the Diagonal Right option.

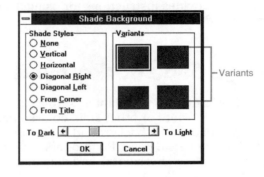

Fig. 7.14

The variants for the Diagonal Right shade style.

5. When you're ready to choose a style, click the style option, and then click the variant you want to use.

6. To control the intensity of the shade, use the Dark/Light scroll bar just below the Shade Styles and Variants boxes. Simply click and drag the scroll box to the right or the left to make a change quickly; click the right and left arrows to change the intensity one step at a time. As you change the intensity using the scroll bar, the shading of the variant you have selected changes accordingly.

7. When you're satisfied with the shade style, variant, and intensity, click OK. (You can, of course, click Cancel at this point to return to the original shading.) PowerPoint returns you to the Color Scheme dialog box. The Current Shading box displays the shading choices you made.

8. Choose This Slide or All Slides from the Apply To box, and then click OK. PowerPoint applies the new shading to the selected slides. Figure 7.15 shows an example of a slide that uses Diagonal Right shading.

After deciding on color schemes and shading, you might want to alter the color of individual objects on your slides. The Object and Text menus have commands that enable you to do so without having a permanent effect on the color scheme. The next few sections of this chapter explain how to use these features.

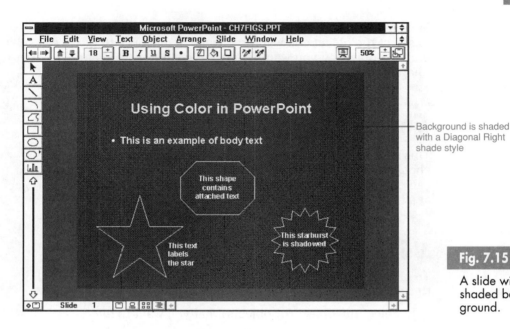

Background is shaded with a Diagonal Right shade style

Fig. 7.15

A slide with a shaded background.

Coloring Individual Objects

You can color individual objects by using the Fill, Line, or Shadow commands from the Object menu. In similar fashion, you can color text (in a Text object or attached to drawn objects) by using the Color command from the Text menu. Using these commands does not change the current color scheme; only the selected objects are changed. Table 7.1 summarizes the use of these commands.

Table 7.1 Object Menu Commands

Menu/Command	Use
Object/Fill	Fills the inside of the drawn objects, text blocks, pictures, and so on with the selected color. The fill can be shaded or patterned.
Object/Line	Frames drawn objects and text boxes with the selected color. Changes individual lines (including lines with arrowheads) to the selected color.
Object/Shadow	Adds a shadow to objects by using the selected color.
Text/Color	Changes text in an object to the selected color.

Most of the steps outlined in the following sections begin by telling you to select the object you want to change. Remember that you can select multiple objects if you want to change several objects at once. Refer to Chapters 4 and 5 for instructions on selecting multiple objects.

Changing the Color of an Object

This section explains how to change the color of an object without changing the default fill color. In addition to changing the color, you can choose a shaded fill or a patterned fill. You can change one object at a time or multiple objects simultaneously.

Using Only Color

To change only the fill color of one or more selected objects, follow these steps:

1. Select the object (or objects) that you want to fill.

2. From the Object menu, choose Fill. A submenu that lists the eight colors of the current color scheme appears (see fig. 7.16).

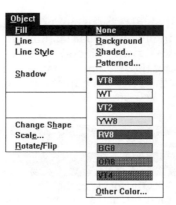

Fig. 7.16

The Fill submenu.

3. Click one of the eight colors shown on the submenu. The new color fills the selected object or objects immediately.

Figure 7.16 shows the four choices on the Fill submenu: None, Background, Shaded, and Patterned. When you choose None, the selected objects are not filled. When you choose Background, the selected objects are filled with the same color as the slide background. The Shaded option enables you to fill selected objects with a light-to-dark (or dark-to-light) version of the color you choose. (There are a variety of shade patterns from which to choose.) The Pattern option lets you choose a pattern (one of 36 styles) and define the foreground and background colors used in the pattern. The steps for filling an object with a shade or a pattern are slightly different from those used to fill an object with a color. Each is described separately in the following sections.

Using Shaded Color

To change the fill of an object to a shaded color, follow these steps:

1. Select the object (or objects) that you want to fill.

2. From the Object menu, choose Fill. The Fill submenu appears.

3. Click the Shaded option. The Shaded Fill dialog box appears (see fig. 7.17).

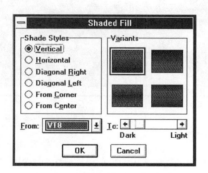

Fig. 7.17

The Shaded Fill dialog box.

4. Choose a shade style from the Shade Styles section of the dialog box, and then choose the variant of that style that you want to apply.

5. Use the From box to choose the color you want to use for the fill.

6. Slide the scroll box (or click the right and left arrow buttons) on the Dark/Light scroll bar to adjust the intensity of the shaded fill.

7. Click OK. PowerPoint returns to your presentation and fills the selected object or objects with the color and shade style you chose.

For detailed information on shading options, refer to the section "Shading the Background" earlier in this chapter.

T I P

Figure 7.18 shows a screen in which a single object has been filled with shaded color.

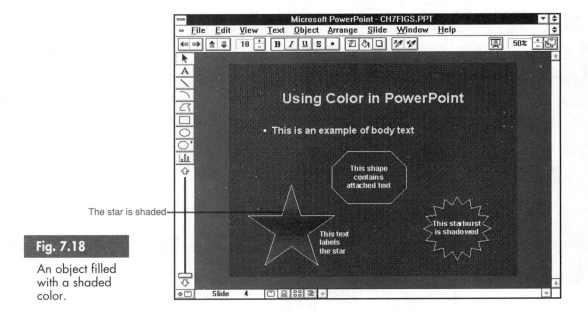

The star is shaded

Fig. 7.18

An object filled with a shaded color.

Using a Pattern

The steps for filling an object with a pattern are similar to those covered in the preceding section. In this case, however, you use the Patterned Fill dialog box. Follow these steps:

1. Select the object (or objects) that you want to fill.

2. From the Object menu, choose Fill. The Fill submenu appears.

3. Click the Patterned option. The Patterned Fill dialog box appears (see fig. 7.19).

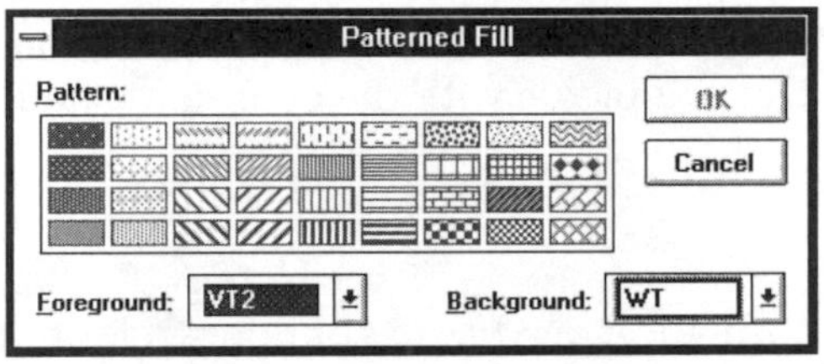

Fig. 7.19

The Patterned Fill dialog box.

4. Choose a pattern style from the Pattern section of the dialog box.

5. In the Foreground box, choose the color you want to use for the pattern foreground.

6. In the Background box, choose the color you want to use for the pattern background.

7. Click OK. PowerPoint returns to your presentation and fills the selected object or objects with the fill color and pattern you selected.

Figure 7.20 shows an object that has been filled with a pattern.

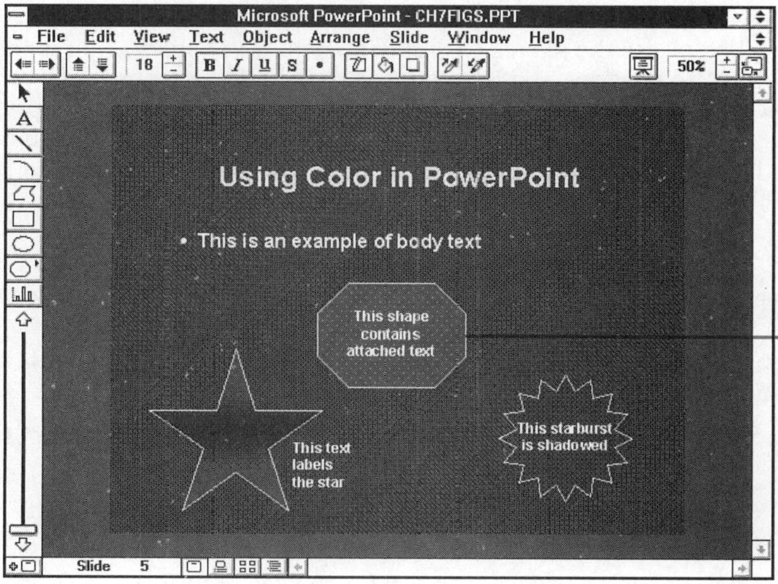

The hexagon is filled with a two-color pattern

Fig. 7.20

An object filled with a pattern.

Changing Line Color

To change the color of a selected line or lines, use the same basic steps you learned for changing the fill color of an object. Select the lines or framed objects that you want to change, and then choose the Line command from the Object menu. A submenu similar to the Fill submenu appears; it displays the eight colors in the current color scheme. Simply choose a color from the list to change the selected object—whether it is a line or a frame around a shape—to that color.

Changing Shadow Color

The steps for changing a shadow color are similar to those used to change fill or line colors. Just select the object with the shadow you want to change, choose the Shadow command from the Object menu, and then choose a new color from the submenu. The shadow of the selected object changes to the color of your choice.

The Shadow command, however, includes one style variation. Shadows can be *embossed*, making the associated object appear to stand out from the page. This technique is what gives the tools on the PowerPoint Toolbar and tool palette an appearance of depth.

Embossed shadows work best when the object fill color and the background color are the same. To create an embossed shadow, first select the object to shadow, and then choose the Shadow command from the Object menu. When the submenu appears, click the Embossed option. Embossed shadows use their own color (two shades of gray); you do not choose a color for an embossed shadow. If you choose a color by mistake, PowerPoint creates a standard colored shadow.

Changing Text Color

To change the color of text in Text objects and drawn objects, follow these steps:

1. Select the object (or objects) that contains the text you want to change.

2. From the Text menu, choose Color. A submenu appears that displays the eight colors in the current color scheme.

3. Click the color you want to use for the selected text. The text immediately changes to the color of your choice.

Changing Default Colors

The previous section showed you how to use the Fill, Line, and Shadow commands on the Object menu and the Color command on the Text menu to change the color, shading, and pattern of individual objects. In each case, these features were used on *selected objects*. You can use the same procedures and commands to change the *default* color settings quickly by simply omitting the first step of selecting objects. Just click any blank area of a slide to ensure that no objects are selected; then use the same steps to change the default fill, line, shadow, or text color. You can use shading or patterns as defaults, as well.

NOTE When no objects are selected, the settings you choose become the default settings.

Remember that after you change the default settings, any new text or objects entered on the screen conform to the new settings. If you select no objects and change the text color to blue, for example, all text you type in the future appears on the slide in blue (until you change the default text color again). If you select no objects and change the fill color for objects to red, all objects that you draw in the future are automatically filled with red (until you change the default fill color again).

Chapter Summary

This chapter showed you how you can use PowerPoint templates to use professional-looking color schemes. It also outlined the basics of creating completely new color schemes.

You learned to change your eight-color color scheme, change an individual color within that scheme, and reposition colors in that scheme. The chapter also showed you how to shade your background color so that different parts of the screen are lightened and darkened. In addition, you learned how to change the colors of individual items on your slide, such as text, lines, or objects. Finally, you learned how to change default colors for the Fill, Line, Shadow, Pattern Contrast, and Text features.

Now you know the basics of manipulating color in PowerPoint. Chapter 14 offers you helpful information about the more advanced capabilities of color. The next chapter, however, provides the basic information needed to use another PowerPoint capability—creating graphs.

Creating Basic Graphs

A s spreadsheet users know, a graph consists of two components: data, which you enter into the spreadsheet, and the graph form itself, which you select as a way to display the data. PowerPoint reduces graphing to these two basic components and enables you to present your data in just about any graph form you like. (Note that this book uses the term *graph* to indicate what PowerPoint documentation often refers to as a *chart*.)

Microsoft Graph, a graphics application embedded in PowerPoint, provides excellent graphing capabilities. Graph contains a *Datasheet* window with rows and columns for data entry and a *Chart* window that displays your data in one of many chart or graph forms. You devote your energy to the content—entering the data. In order to express the data, you just click the graph window to display your chart automatically. The Datasheet and Chart windows work together simultaneously; whenever you change the data, the graph in the Chart window changes automatically to reflect the new data.

This chapter shows you how to access PowerPoint's Graph menu. It shows you how to insert data into a sample datasheet; how to organize the data into rows or columns; how to select, cut, copy, paste, and clear cells; and how to manipulate columns and rows. It also provides instructions for changing the appearance of your data and labels by formatting numbers, altering text, and changing column widths.

After you have mastered the datasheet, you can use the rest of this chapter to learn to work with graphs (or *charts*, in PowerPoint terminology). You will find instructions for displaying the default graph and changing the graph to a different type. (PowerPoint offers 12 primary graph types with variations of each.) In this chapter, you will also find the steps required for changing line styles, fonts, and fill attributes, as well as instructions for adding legends and data labels. And finally, this chapter shows you how to take the graph with you when you return to the slide you're working on.

Accessing the Graph Window

Because Microsoft Graph is an embedded application, it is displayed in its own window right on top of PowerPoint. You can access Graph by clicking the Graph tool on the tool palette. In order to use PowerPoint menus or tools, you must exit Graph and return to PowerPoint.

To access Graph, you must first create an object on your slide in which to insert the graph you generate. To prepare your slide and open Graph, follow these steps:

1. Open the presentation in which you want to embed a graph.

2. Select the slide on which you want to place the graph.

3. Click the Graph tool on the tool palette. The mouse pointer changes to a crosshair.

4. By clicking and dragging your mouse, draw a box that is approximately the size you want your graph to be in the approximate location for the graph on your slide. Figure 8.1 shows the graph window that appears after you execute these steps and Microsoft Graph is up and running.

As figure 8.1 shows, Microsoft Graph consists of three windows. The Graph window is the application window itself, the Datasheet window is used to enter data for the graph, and the Chart window displays the graph you create. The title of the current presentation—the default name *Presentation* is used in the example shown—appears in the title bars of both the Datasheet and Chart windows. The sample graph in the Chart window displays the sample data in the Datasheet window. PowerPoint provides this sample so that you can easily create a new graph. The next section of this chapter shows you how to move between the two windows.

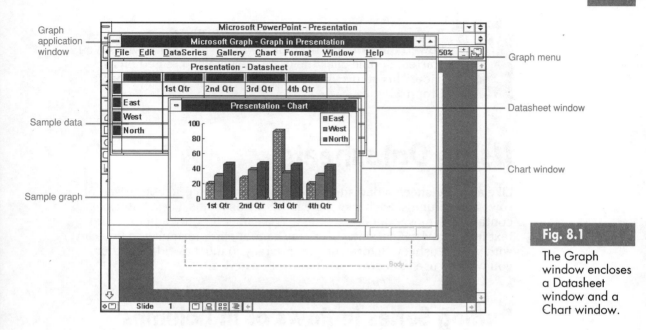

Graph application window

Sample data

Sample graph

Graph menu

Datasheet window

Chart window

The Graph window encloses a Datasheet window and a Chart window.

Moving between Datasheet and Chart Windows

When you first enter Graph, the Chart window is active and appears on top of the Datasheet window on-screen. The quickest way to switch between the two windows is to click any visible portion of the window you want to activate. You can also select the window you want from the list at the bottom of the Window menu. Just open the Window menu and click Chart or Datasheet.

To switch between windows quickly, press Ctrl-F6.

T I P

The Datasheet and Chart windows can be resized. Use the same principles you use to resize other windows; simply click and drag the window borders. If one window completely covers the other when you resize it, the easiest way to switch back and forth between windows is to press Ctrl-F6.

NOTE If you inadvertently click PowerPoint's Window menu, the PowerPoint window becomes active. To get back where you started, double-click the graph object you created on the slide. This step switches the screen back to the Microsoft Graph window.

Using Datasheets

Like a spreadsheet, a datasheet holds your data in a grid comprised of rows and columns. Each rectangle in the datasheet is a *cell*. Some cells contain text; most contain numbers. You can enter only numbers and text into a PowerPoint datasheet; you cannot enter formulas as you can with a spreadsheet. Before you enter data, you must decide whether you want to use your rows or columns as a series.

Putting Series in Rows or in Columns

Graphs give data a meaningful visual representation. In most cases, graphs plot the occurrence of *data points* along some type of *measurement scale* or *timeline*. Several *categories* of data are often combined on a single graph for purposes of comparison. A simple graph depicting sales performance, for example, might plot the number of products sold each day over a three-month period. In this example, the number of products sold each day is plotted as a data point along the three-month timeline. If more than one type of product is represented on the graph, each product type forms a unique data category.

In the datasheet, a category is referred to as a *data series*. When entering data into the datasheet, you choose whether to arrange each data series in rows or in columns.

Assume, for example, that the sample data that appears in the datasheet window represents sales by region for the four quarters of a given year. In figure 8.2, the data series—sales—for each region are arranged in rows. The columns form a timeline for the data, with each column representing one quarter of the year. On the chart, each data series is represented by a column; each quarter contains three columns representing sales for each region.

Each data series translates to
a column style in the graph

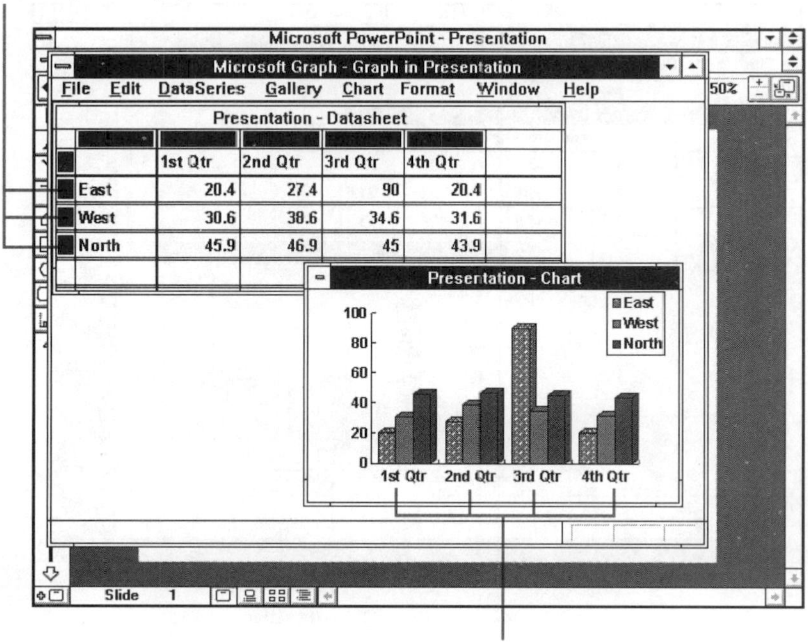

Fig. 8.2

Data series
arranged in rows.

The East data series

Placing data series in rows—the PowerPoint default setting—creates
the best data presentation in many cases. But the choice of data arrangement depends on what data you want to emphasize. In figure 8.2,
for example, the presentation of data emphasizes the timeline. The
chart's format lets you see instantly that sales for the year were fairly
constant except for a sharp rise in the third quarter.

Suppose, however, that you want to define the quarters (rather than
the regions) to be the data series. Quarterly data is broken down by
column in the datasheet, so you need to redefine your data series in
columns.

Follow these steps to redefine data from series in rows to series in
columns:

1. Open the DataSeries menu on the Graph menu bar. Note that the
   Series in Rows option is checked because it is the default setting.

2. Click the Series in Columns option. PowerPoint reformats the
   graph in the Chart window automatically.

Figure 8.3 shows how this change affects the chart. In the new graph,
each bar represents a quarter and each grouping of bars represents a
sales region.

Each column is a data series that translates to a particular column style in the graph

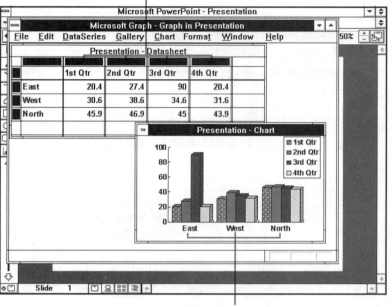

Fig. 8.3

Data series arranged in columns.

The 1st Qtr data series

Because the data series format was changed from rows to columns in figure 8.3, the new chart emphasizes the regions rather than the quarters. This chart enables you to see that the East region had one outstanding sales quarter while the other regions' sales quarters remained fairly constant.

T I P   No hard and fast rules exist about choosing the best arrangement for data series. Each arrangement simply emphasizes different data. Experiment with your data to determine the best arrangement. If you choose to define data series in rows, you don't need to do anything because that is the default format. If you choose to define data series in columns, be sure to change the setting on the DataSeries menu.

Now that you know how the data in the Datasheet window translates into the graph in the Chart window, the next section shows you how to enter your own data into the datasheet.

Inserting Data

PowerPoint displays sample data each time you use Graph, but you don't need to delete the sample data before you enter your own. You can simply type over the sample data.

The following steps offer an example that can help you learn how to enter new data. In this example, you plot the number of trips to three destinations—Europe, Asia, and the U.S.—arranged by a travel agency each month during a three month period: January, February, and March. Table 8.1 provides a summary of the data.

Table 8.1 New Data for the Datasheet Window			
	January	**February**	**March**
Asia	18	20	17
Europe	32	24	29
U.S.	88	69	73

To enter the data shown in table 8.1, follow these steps:

1. Click the cell labeled *1st Qtr*, or use the arrow keys to move to that cell.

2. Type *January*, and then press Tab or the right-arrow key to move to the cell labeled *2nd Qtr*. Your entry overwrites the contents of the first cell.

3. Repeat step 2, entering *Febuary* and *March* to replace *2nd Qtr* and *3rd Qtr*. The misspelled *Febuary* entry will be corrected later.

4. Click the cell labeled *East* and type *Asia*. Your entry overwrites the cell contents. Press the down-arrow key to move to the cell labeled *North*.

5. Repeat step 4, entering *Europe* and *U.S.* to replace *West* and *North*.

6. Use the arrow keys, or click the appropriate cell, to replace the data in the remaining cells with the data shown in table 8.1. When finished, your datasheet looks like the one shown in figure 8.4. Ignore the sample data in the last column for now; you will learn how to eliminate it later.

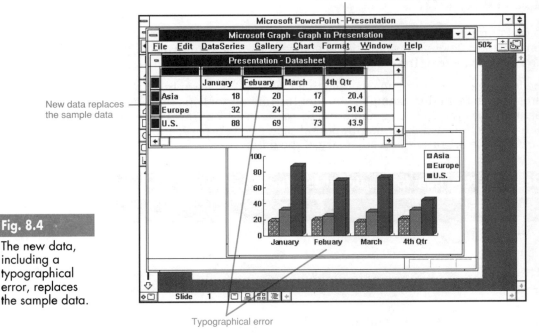

Old data will be eliminated later

New data replaces the sample data

Typographical error

Fig. 8.4

The new data, including a typographical error, replaces the sample data.

In the previous steps, you entered data by overwriting the existing data. You can also enter data by editing a cell. This method is often used instead of retyping an entire entry when you need to correct a simple error. To edit the cell containing the misspelled *Febuary* entry, follow these steps:

1. Double-click the cell you want to edit. The Cell Data dialog box appears (see fig. 8.5). The current cell entry is highlighted in the dialog box.

2. Use the arrow keys to move the cursor to the desired location; then make any necessary changes. If you begin typing while the current cell entry is highlighted, the contents of the cell are replaced by the new text you type. If you press an arrow key before beginning to type, however, the highlighting is removed and you can insert or delete characters within the entry.

3. After the cell entry has been corrected, click OK.

The next section shows you how to select and alter groups of cells rather than single cells.

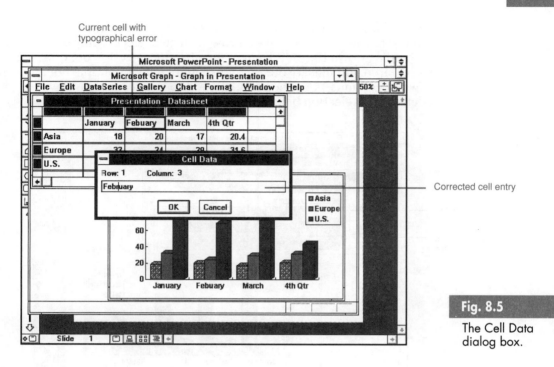

Current cell with
typographical error

Corrected cell entry

Fig. 8.5

The Cell Data
dialog box.

Selecting Cells, Rows, and Columns

In the Datasheet window, as in any spreadsheet application, there are times when you want to select and work with a group of cells rather than one particular cell. You might want to format an entire group of cells at once, for example. Or you might want to move, cut, or copy a group of cells together.

To select a group of cells, place the mouse pointer on the first cell to be selected (an end or corner cell), and then click and drag the mouse pointer over all the remaining cells to be included in the group. In figure 8.6, all the cells that contain numbers have been selected. The first cell selected remains the active cell. (In the figure, this cell is white with a black border.) The rest of the selected cells are also highlighted. (In this color scheme, they appear in black.)

You can also select a group of cells by selecting the first cell, and then holding down the Shift key while using the arrow keys to move to the last cell in the range.

Graph provides an easy way for you to select all the cells in a particular row or column. Above each column heading and to the left of each row heading are empty boxes called *selection boxes*. To select an entire column or row, click the selection box directly above the desired column or to the left of the desired row. You can select multiple columns by holding down the Shift key as you click the selection boxes above the desired columns. (Note that you cannot select multiple nonadjacent rows or columns.) Use the same method to select multiple rows by clicking the selection boxes to the left of the chosen rows.

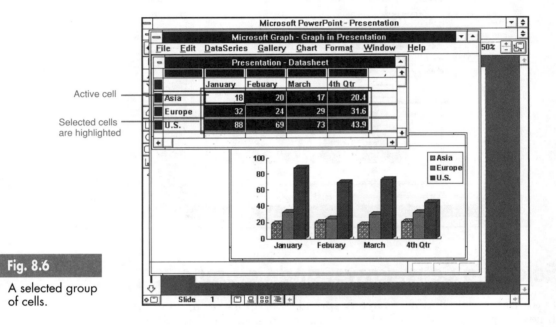

Active cell

Selected cells
are highlighted

Fig. 8.6

A selected group
of cells.

When you want to select all the cells in a datasheet, simply choose the Select All command from the Edit menu.

The next section provides instructions for editing the items you select.

Editing Cells

You can manipulate selected groups of cells, rows, or columns in PowerPoint the same way that you can in other spreadsheets. The Edit menu on the menu bar includes Cut, Copy, Paste, and Clear commands. The following sections discuss how to use each of these options.

Clearing Cells

When you clear cells, you do not delete them. The Clear command on the Edit menu gives you three different options. The Clear Data option clears the data from the selected cells but retains their existing format for future use. The *format* of a cell determines the way that it displays and uses data. You can format a cell, for example, so that each number entered is expressed as a two-decimal number. The Clear Format option leaves the data in the selected cells intact, but clears the format of the cells. The Clear Both option clears the data and formatting from the selected cells.

To clear the data contained in selected cells, follow these steps:

1. Select the cells, columns, or rows you want to clear.

2. Choose Clear from the Edit menu or press the Delete key. Graph displays the Clear dialog box.

3. Select one of the options (Clear Data, Clear Format, or Clear Both), and then click OK. PowerPoint Graph clears the selected cells according to your instructions.

As figure 8.4 shows, the last column of sample data still needs to be eliminated. Using these steps, the last column on the datasheet can be cleared (both data and formats). Now the sample chart shows the correct three groups of columns: January, February, March (see fig. 8.7).

If you prefer, you can use these steps to clear all sample data from the worksheet before entering new data.

T I P

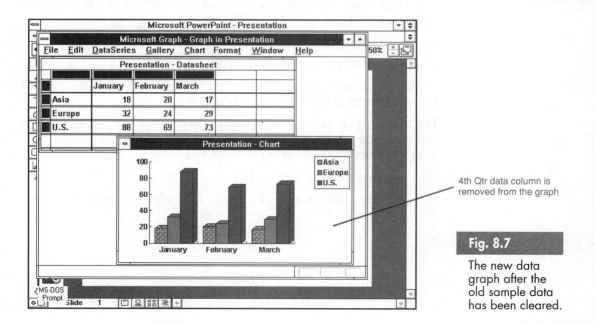

4th Qtr data column is removed from the graph

Fig. 8.7

The new data graph after the old sample data has been cleared.

If you accidentally clear data or cell formats that you don't want to lose, you can undo your mistake by choosing Undo Clear from the Edit menu. But remember that this technique only works if used *immediately* after the mistake; if you perform some other action (such as selecting a command or entering data) before attempting to use Undo Clear, your data and/or cell formats are lost for good.

Cutting and Copying Cells

When you use the Cut or Copy commands, PowerPoint places the selected data on the Windows Clipboard. The Cut command works best when you want to remove data from the datasheet. It removes data from a selected cell or group of cells and puts it on the Clipboard. You then have the choice of pasting the data at another location (or even the same location) in your datasheet or simply leaving it on the Clipboard. After the data is placed on the Clipboard, it remains available for pasting until you use Cut or Copy again.

The Copy option also copies the data in a selected cell or group of cells onto the Clipboard. But Copy does not delete the data from the original cell(s). As with Cut, after the data has been placed on the Clipboard you can paste it in other cells.

To copy and paste information in your datasheet, follow these steps:

1. Select the cells you want to copy.

2. From the Edit menu, choose Copy. PowerPoint places a copy of the selected data onto the Clipboard.

3. Select the starting cell to which you want to paste the data.

4. From the Edit menu, choose Paste.

When you paste to cells that already contain data, the data on the Clipboard overwrites the existing cell data.

The following steps tell you how to cut cells from the datasheet. You could also use these steps to remove the last column of sample data from the worksheet shown in figure 8.4.

1. Select the cells you want to cut.

2. From the Edit menu, choose Cut. The cells are removed to the Clipboard.

Inserting Columns and Rows

Sometimes it is necessary to insert a row or column between two exist-ing rows or columns in the datasheet. Graph enables you to insert a blank row or column by shifting the position of the adjacent rows or columns. When you insert a row, Graph moves down the selected row and places a new blank row above it. When you insert a column, Graph moves the selected column to the right and places a new blank column to the left of it.

Suppose that you want to insert an additional row of data between the rows labeled *Europe* and *U.S.* in the sample datasheet. Follow these steps:

1. Select the row or column where you want the new row or column to be located. In the sample datasheet, select the row labeled *U.S.*

2. From the Edit menu, choose Insert Row/Column. Graph inserts the new row or column immediately. In the sample datasheet, the new row appears above the *U.S.* row.

> If you do not select an entire row or column, the Insert Row/Col dialog box appears. Choose either Insert Row or Insert Column, and then click OK.

T I P

In figure 8.8, a new set of data for *Africa* has been entered in the new blank row between *Europe* and *U.S.*

You can also insert more than one row or column at a time by using steps similar to the preceding procedure. Suppose that you want to insert three new columns before the January column. To insert the new columns into the sample datasheet, follow these steps:

1. Click the selection box for the column where you want to begin inserting. Hold down the Shift key as you select additional adja-cent columns. In the sample datasheet, select the three columns labeled *January*, *February*, and *March*.

2. From the Edit menu, choose Insert Row/Col. Graph automatically inserts three new columns.

The selection boxes at the top of the new columns are gray, indicating that the columns are inactive. Inactive columns are not reflected on the graph in the Chart window. As soon as data is entered in a new column, however, the columns become active and the graph displays the new data.

New row ——

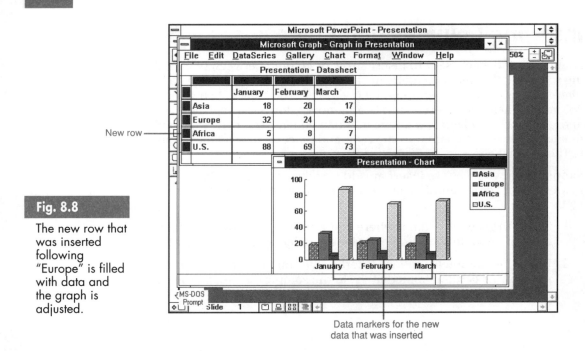

Fig. 8.8

The new row that was inserted following "Europe" is filled with data and the graph is adjusted.

Data markers for the new data that was inserted

To insert multiple rows into the datasheet, follow the same basic procedure. Simply select multiple rows beginning with the row where you want the new rows to be inserted. When you choose the Insert Row/Col command from the Edit menu, Graph inserts your new rows. These new rows are inactive until you start entering data into them.

NOTE You can insert multiple columns or rows without selecting entire columns or rows, but the procedure requires one extra step. Select just one cell in each of the rows or columns where you want to make the insertion, and then choose the Insert Row/Col command from the Edit menu. When the Insert Row/Col dialog box appears, choose either the Insert Columns or the Insert Rows option; then click OK.

Deleting Columns and Rows

You can delete columns or rows as easily as you can insert them. Follow these steps:

1. Select the row or column to delete. You can select multiple rows or columns.

2. From the Edit menu, choose Delete Row/Col. PowerPoint Graph deletes the selected rows or columns.

The Delete Row/Col dialog box only appears when you don't select entire rows or columns. If you delete the wrong rows or columns, choose the Edit Undo command immediately to restore them.

Formatting Data

The Format menu on the Graph menu bar provides a means for you to present the data in your datasheets in several different formats. The following sections show you how to change the format for numbers, how to change the font, and how to change the width of columns.

Changing a Number Format

Numbers that you enter in your datasheets can be displayed in many different ways. According to your instructions, PowerPoint can automatically add dollar signs or percentage signs to your entries, display entries in decimal notation, or alter the format of your numbers in other helpful ways. To take advantage of these capabilities, select the appropriate cells, and then apply the desired number format. Suppose, for example, that you want the numbers in the sample datasheet to be displayed with dollar signs. Follow these steps:

1. Select the cells to format.

2. From the Format menu, choose Number. The Number dialog box appears (see fig. 8.9).

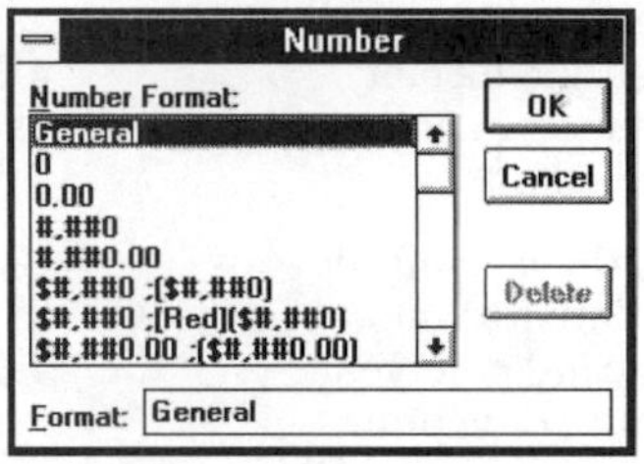

Fig. 8.9

The Number dialog box displays number format options.

The first choice—General—is the default option. See table 8.2 for an explanation of each format option.

3. Click a format option. An example of the format you choose is shown in the Format box.

4. Click OK. The cells you selected in the datasheet are immediately reformatted.

Table 8.2 Symbols Used for Number Formats

Symbol	Use	Examples
0 and #	These two symbols hold digits and place them where you indicate. 0 adds zeros. When used alone, it rounds to the nearest whole number.	*9* typed in a cell formatted with 00 appears as 09; *9.7* typed in a cell formatted with 0 appears as 10.
. (period)	Use the decimal point symbol to add the decimal point when it's not entered.	Use #.# to display *9* as 9.; use #.0 to display *9* as 9.0; use 0.00 to display *.9* as 0.90.
, (comma)	The comma is a useful format to use with large numbers.	Use #,##0 to display *9999* as 9,999.
$	This symbol adds a dollar sign.	Use $#0.00 to display *99* as $99.00.
%	This symbol adds the percentage symbol and multiplies the number in the cell by 00. Type decimal points in the cell, not fractions (not 2/4, for example).	Use 0% to display *.25* as 25%; use 0% to display *8* as 800%.
E	This symbol activates the scientific format. The menu choice is 0.00E+00.	Use E to display *7* as 7.00E+00, *.4* as 4.00E-01, and *6666* as 6.67E+03.
y m d h s AM/PM	Use these symbols for date formats. They indicate year, month, day, hour, second, AM, and PM.	Use h:mm AM/PM to display *7* as 7:00 AM.

Changing the Font

The Font option on the Format menu enables you to change the font style, size, and characteristics (bold, underline, and so on) in the current datasheet. You cannot change the font for just one cell; when you change the font for selected cells, the entire datasheet changes. These changes do not affect the font attributes of the current chart, however. (For instructions regarding changing the font of graphs, refer to the section "Creating the Graph" later in this chapter.)

To change the font of a datasheet, follow these steps:

1. Select any cell in the datasheet.

2. From the Format menu, choose Font. The Datasheet Font dialog box appears (see fig. 8.10).

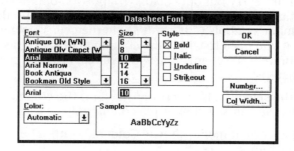

Fig. 8.10

The Datasheet Font dialog box.

3. Use the Font box scroll bar to view the available font styles, and click the font style of your choice.

4. Use the Size box scroll bar to view the available font sizes, and click the font size of your choice.

5. To add special characteristics to the font, choose one or more options from the Style box. To turn off an option, click the check box until it is clear.

6. To change the display color of the font, choose a color from the Color box.

NOTE As you make changes to the font, size, style, and color, the Sample box displays the changes.

7. When all font settings are correct, click OK.

T I P For convenience, the Number and Column Width buttons in the Font dialog box enable you to access the Number and Column Width dialog boxes directly. This addition saves you the extra step of returning to the Graph menu to access these boxes when you are using the Font dialog box.

Changing Column Width

Sometimes the standard column width—nine spaces—is not wide enough to display the complete entries that you make in the datasheet cells. If you enter too many text characters into a cell, PowerPoint stores the entire entry but only displays a portion of it. If you enter a number that is too large, PowerPoint stores the entry and displays a series of number symbols (##########) in the cell. This condition indicates that you need to widen the column in order to display the number accurately. To change the width of one or more columns, follow these steps:

1. Select the selection box of (or any cell in) the column you want to change. You can select multiple columns.

2. From the Format menu, choose Column Width. The Column Width dialog box appears (see fig. 8.11).

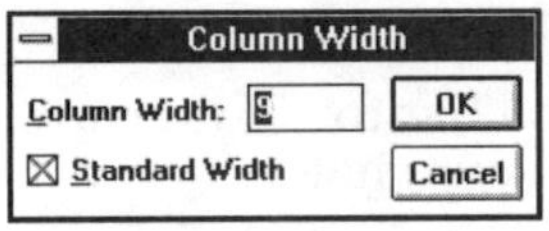

Fig. 8.11

The Column Width dialog box.

```
┌─────────────────────────────────┐
│ ▄  Column Width                 │
├─────────────────────────────────┤
│ Column Width: [9]      │  OK   │ │
│ ☒ Standard Width       │ Cancel│ │
└─────────────────────────────────┘
```

3. Enter the desired width in the Column Width box. The number entered must be between 1 and 255.

4. Click OK or press Enter. PowerPoint adjusts the width of the selected column or columns.

Clicking the Standard Width check box in the Column Width dialog box changes the selected column or columns back to the standard width of nine spaces.

To use a mouse to change column widths, follow these steps:

1. Place the mouse pointer on the right border of the selection box for the column you want to adjust. The mouse pointer changes to a black cross with arrows on the horizontal line (see fig. 8.12).

2. Drag the pointer right or left to adjust the column width.

3. Release the button when the column reaches the desired width.

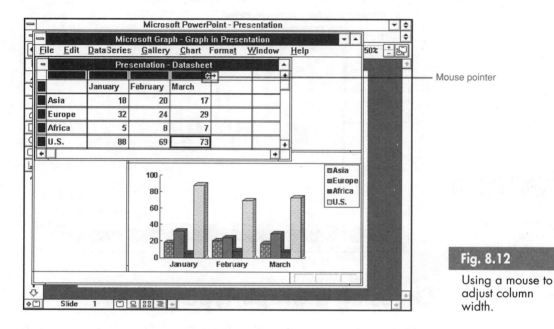

Mouse pointer

Fig. 8.12

Using a mouse to adjust column width.

Creating the Graph

The data you enter in the Datasheet window is used to produce the graph in the Chart window. The chart generated in the Chart window becomes part of your slide when you exit Graph and return to your presentation. You can change almost any attribute of a graph after it is created, but you can save time by setting the graph attributes correctly before starting to create the graph.

The following sections show you how to display datasheet information in different types of graphs, how to select objects on a graph, and how to use colors and patterns, line styles, fonts, and legends to modify graphs. And finally, you will learn how to insert the finished graph into your PowerPoint slide.

If you have been following along with the datasheet examples provided, switch over to the Chart window now by clicking any visible portion of it or by pressing Ctrl-F6. The data that was entered earlier in this chapter appears as a graph like the one in figure 8.13.

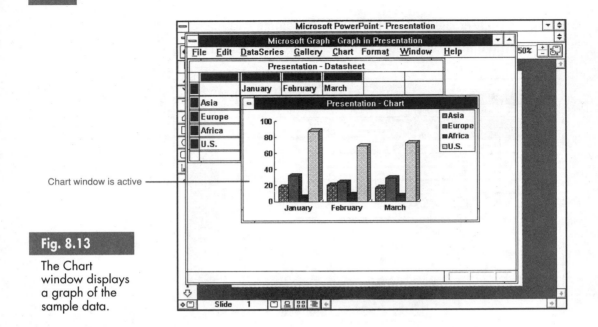

Chart window is active

Fig. 8.13

The Chart window displays a graph of the sample data.

Choosing a Graph Type

Graphs represent data in useful visual forms. They enable you to see trends in a set of data and relationships among different sets of data. The type of data being gathered determines the best type of graph to use. PowerPoint offers 12 different graph types, and each type offers a wide variety of variations (84 in all). The 12 basic types are Area, Bar, Column, Line, Pie, Scatter, Combination, 3-D Area, 3-D Bar, 3-D Column, 3-D Line, and 3-D Pie. Suppose that you don't know which kind of graph to use and you want to browse through the choices. To view a sample of each graph type and variation, follow these steps:

1. With the Chart window active, open the Gallery menu.

2. Click any of the 12 types of graphs. The Chart Gallery dialog box appears. The charts shown in the dialog box reflect the menu choice you made. In figure 8.14, for example, all variations of the 3-D pie chart style are shown in the Chart Gallery dialog box.

 NOTE When the More button is available, additional style variations exist. Click this button to display the additional styles.

3. To view other graph styles, click Cancel. Then repeat steps 1 and 2, selecting a different style from the menu.

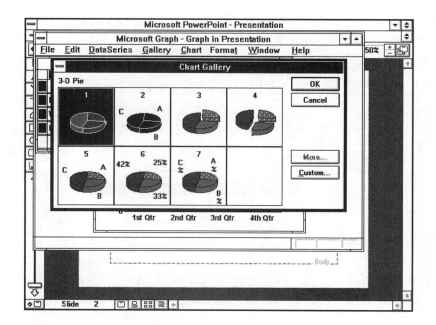

Fig. 8.14

The 3-D Pie chart style variations displayed in the Chart Gallery dialog box.

Each graph type and variation focuses attention on some significant aspect of your data. Refer back to figure 8.13, which shows a default 3-D column graph. Figures 8.15 through 8.18, all derived from the same datasheet that produced figure 8.13, illustrate the other 3-D graph types available in PowerPoint—Area, Bar, Line, and Pie.

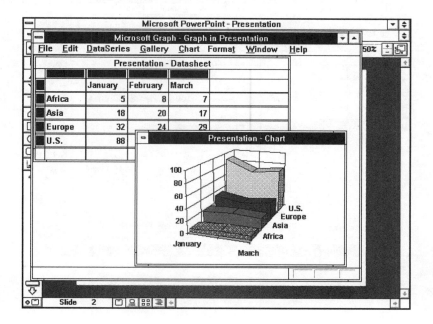

Fig. 8.15

A 3-D Area graph.

In figure 8.15 the data for Africa was moved to the first row so it would be visible in the area graph.

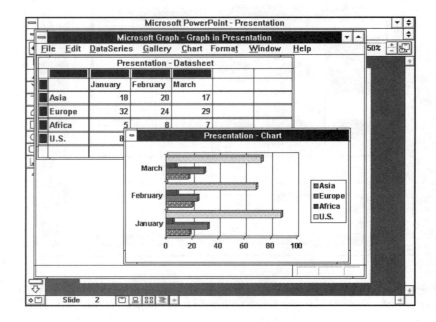

Fig. 8.16

A 3-D Bar graph.

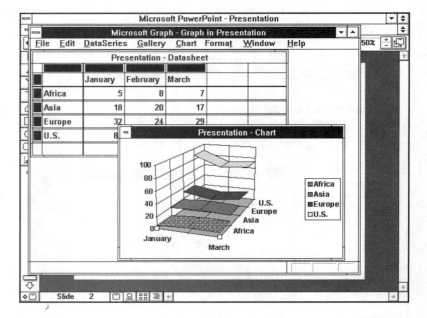

Fig. 8.17

A 3-D Line graph.

In figure 8.17 the data for Africa was moved to the first row so it would be visible in the line graph.

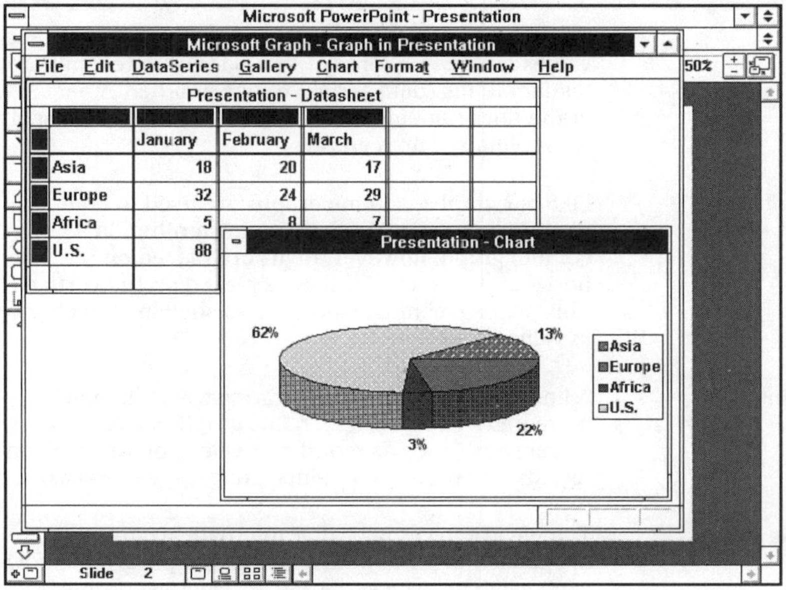

Fig. 8.18

A 3-D Pie graph.

This variation of the 3-D Pie chart in figure 8.18 notes percentages for each slice.

The best way to discover which graph type meets your particular needs is to experiment with different kinds of graph presentations for your data. Table 8.3 summarizes the advantages of each kind of graph. You can also customize each graph form by applying special 3-D options, formatting data markers and the axis scale, and so on. Chapter 14, "Using Advanced Graph Features," explains custom options.

Table 8.3 Choosing a Graph Type

Graph	Advantages
Area	An area graph is useful for showing the relative contribution that each item (data series) makes to the whole. Area graphs are often plotted against time on the horizontal axis to show a progression of values over time.

continues

Table 8.3 Continued

Graph	Advantages
Bar	A bar graph places categories on the vertical axis and values on the horizontal. Use a bar graph to compare distinct items (data series) to one another. A bar graph does not emphasize the flow of time as strongly as a column or area graph.
Column	Like bar graphs, column graphs are used to compare distinct items (data series) to one another. In a column graph, however, items are placed on the horizontal axis and values are placed on the vertical. This arrangement is conducive to showing the change in values over time.
Line	A line graph is best for illustrating trends in one or more items (data series). A line graph places even increments (such as months or years) on the horizontal axis and plots data points along the vertical axis.
Pie	The pie graph is the best graph to illustrate the proportion of parts to the whole. The pie graph shows each value in a single data series. In PowerPoint Graph, if you choose Series in Rows from the Datasheet window, the pie graph for that datasheet uses the data in the columns. If you choose Series in Columns, the pie graph uses the data in the rows. A pie graph does not show a measure of time.
Scatter	Also known as an XY graph, a scatter graph shows the relationship between values in two different data series, or it can be used to plot data pairs in XY coordinates. A scatter graph is a variation of a line graph in which time on the horizontal axis is replaced by a second data series.

Understanding the Elements of a Graph

Some of the elements that most graphs have in common include a vertical axis, a horizontal axis, a legend box, tick marks, tick mark labels, data markers, data points, data labels, gridlines, and a graph title.

Figure 8.19 shows the positions of these common elements in a column graph.

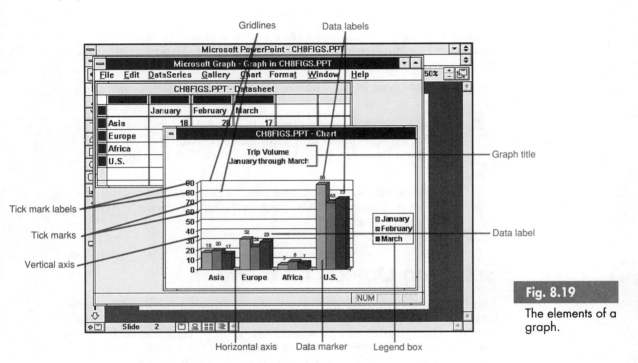

Fig. 8.19

The elements of a graph.

In this example, the datasheet is set up with data series in columns. The column headings—January, February, and March—appear in the legend box and the row headings—Asia, Europe, Africa, and U.S.—appear along the horizontal axis. If the data series were set up in rows instead of columns, these positions would be reversed.

The vertical axis is the measuring stick of the graph. In the example, the highest number of trips planned in a month was 88 and the lowest was 5; PowerPoint Graph draws the vertical axis with a scale of 0-90 to accommodate these numbers. The tick marks break that scale down into increments of 10; a tick mark label identifies the numeric value of each tick mark. Each data point (represented by the top of a column in this type of graph) corresponds to a number that appears in the datasheet. In the example, the data points for Asia are represented by column tops at 18, 20, and 17 for January, February, and March. The numeric values printed above each data point in this particular chart are data labels.

Adding a Title to a Graph

To add a title to a graph, follow these steps:

No graph is complete without a title. The title makes the numbers meaningful for those attending your presentation. To add a title, follow these steps:

1. From the Chart menu, choose Titles. The Chart Titles dialog box appears.

2. If it is not already chosen, choose the Chart option, and then click OK. PowerPoint Graph automatically inserts a Title object (containing the word *Title*) into your chart. The Title object is selected.

3. Type a new title in the box, and then click a location outside the Title object. The new title is displayed over the graph and the title box is unselected.

Selecting Objects on a Graph

You can change almost everything that you see on a graph: color, pattern, line style, and so on. In order to change an object, you must first select it. On a graph, you can select horizontal or vertical axis lines, data points, data markers, labels, gridlines, and the legend. Each graph type (except pie graphs) can contain all these features, although you must activate some of them (such as gridlines) yourself. The pie graph is an exception because it can represent only one series of numbers at a time. In order to select one of these objects on-screen, simply click it.

Figure 8.20 shows a selected data line in a line graph. The three open boxes at the ends and the midpoint of this line indicate that it is selected.

Objects in a graph are selected in the same way that you select objects in a PowerPoint slide. See Chapter 5, "Drawing Objects," for a helpful discussion of the process of selecting objects in PowerPoint. The next section shows you how to color and add a style to a selected object in a graph.

Choosing Line Styles

Choose the Patterns command from the Format menu to change the style, color, or thickness (weight) of a line in a line graph. The same option enables you to change the style or color of the line markers that represent the exact data points on a line. Square boxes show the position of line markers when you select a line.

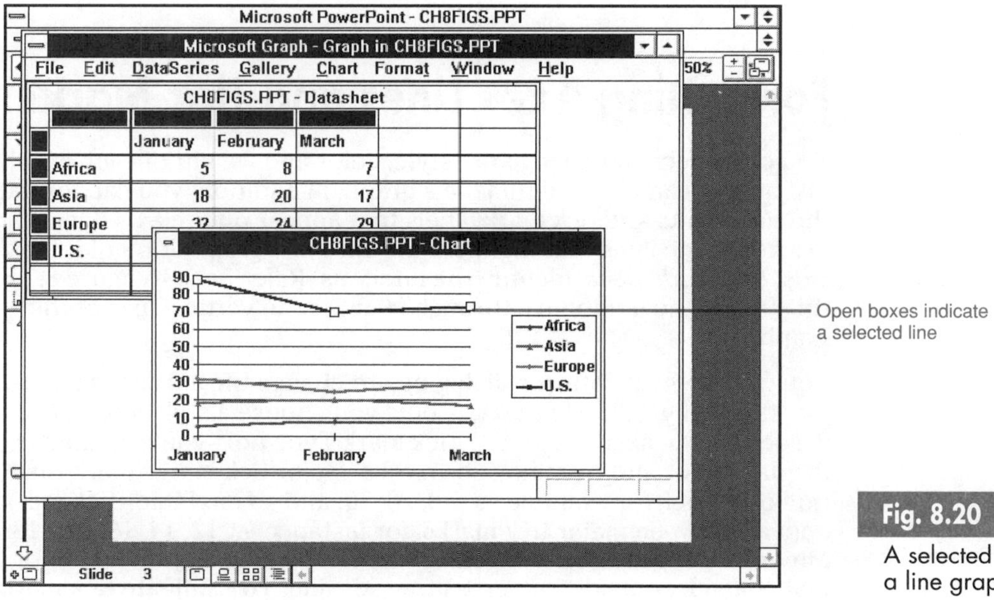

Open boxes indicate
a selected line

Fig. 8.20

A selected line in
a line graph.

To change the style of a line in a line graph, follow these steps:

1. Select a line.

2. From the Format menu, choose Patterns. The Line & Markers dialog box shown in figure 8.21 appears. (You can also display this box by double-clicking the line you want to change.)

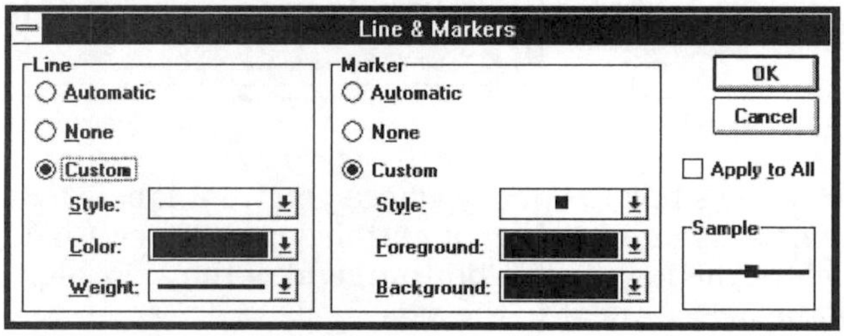

Fig. 8.21

The Line &
Markers dialog
box.

3. In the Line box, choose a style, color, and weight for the selected line.

4. In the Marker box, choose a style, foreground color (the fill for the marker), and background color (the frame for the marker) for the line markers.

5. Click OK.

Formatting Axes Lines and Tick Marks

You can select and change the style, color and weight of each axis line just as you can any other line in a graph. In addition, you can format the tick marks and tick mark labels that appear on the axis lines. *Tick marks* are the lines that intersect the axes of a graph at regular intervals; *tick mark labels* identify the intervals. Refer back to figure 8.19; in this figure, the numbers 0 through 90 mark the vertical axis of the graph.

You use the Axis Patterns dialog box to change the axis lines and tick marks (see fig. 8.22). In the Axis box, you choose a style, color, and weight for the axis line. In the Tick Mark Type box, you can choose to display major and/or minor tick marks. Major tick marks mark the location of a label, for example, at 10, 20, 30, and so on. Minor tick marks appear between major tick marks, for instance, at 12, 14, 16, and 18. Minor tick marks are not labeled. You can display major and minor tick marks inside, outside, or across the axis line. To eliminate tick marks, choose None.

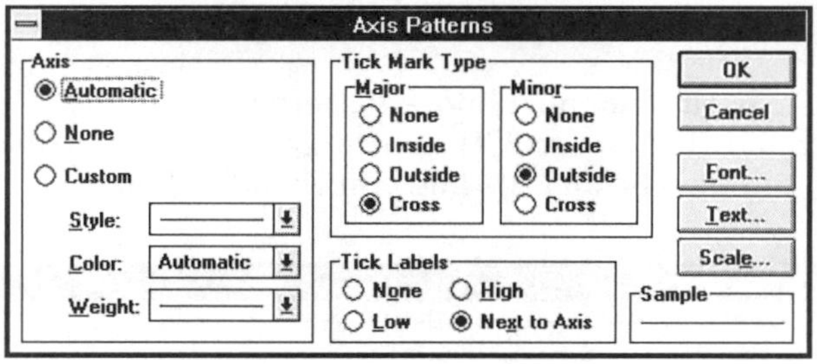

Fig. 8.22

The Axis Patterns dialog box.

Use the Tick Labels box to specify where you want labels to appear. (Some options are not available for certain graph types.) You can specify labels at the low (left or bottom) end of the axis, high (right or top) end of the axis, or next to the axis.

To change the axis line, tick marks, or tick mark labels, follow these steps:

1. Select the axis line you want to change.

2. From the Format menu, choose Patterns. The Axis Patterns dialog box appears.

3. In the Axis box, choose a style, color, and weight for the selected axis.

4. In the Tick Mark Type box, choose None, Inside, Outside, or Cross for Major and Minor tick marks.

5. In the Tick Labels box, choose None, Low, High, or Next to Axis.

6. Click OK to close the Axis Patterns dialog box and return to the Chart window.

Choosing Fill Colors and Patterns

Fill colors can provide strong contrast between the data markers in a graph. As mentioned earlier, a data marker—a bar in a bar graph, a column in a column graph, or a slice in a pie graph, for example—represents a single data point. You can change the style, color, and weight of the borders of these data markers, as well as the pattern, foreground color, and background color with which they are filled. Follow these steps:

1. Select the object (bar, column, pie slice, or other data marker).

2. From the Format menu, choose Patterns. The Area Patterns dialog box appears (see fig. 8.23).

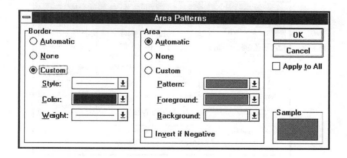

Fig. 8.23

The Area Patterns dialog box.

3. In the Border box, choose a style, color, and weight for the border of the data marker. Your choice appears in the sample in the lower right corner of the dialog box.

4. In the Area box, choose a pattern, foreground color, and background color for the area, or fill, of the data marker. Again, your choice appears in the sample in the lower right corner of the dialog box.

5. Click OK.

Changing the fill of a particular data marker makes that marker stand out on the slide. If you want to emphasize one slice in a pie, for instance, you can fill it with a bright, solid color.

The next section shows you how to change the fonts for text and numbers on the graph.

Choosing Fonts

Using the Chart Fonts dialog box, you can choose the type, style, size, color, and background for the fonts used on your chart. You can change the font for individual elements—the legend, the x-axis labels, the data labels, and the title—without changing the font for the entire graph. Follow these steps:

1. Select the line or object containing the characters you want to change.

2. From the Format menu, choose Font. The Chart Fonts dialog box appears (see fig. 8.24).

The Chart Fonts dialog box.

3. Choose a font type, size, style, and color by clicking the appropriate areas in the box. The Sample box shows how your choices change the text.

4. In the Background area, you see three choices for text background—Automatic, Transparent, and Opaque. Automatic creates a white background to make the text readable; it is the default

choice. If you choose Transparent, the color and pattern of the area behind the text show through. If you choose Opaque, a solid white rectangle encloses the text so that it stands out from the background if the background isn't white.

Adding and Moving the Legend

The *legend* is the box in your graph that identifies each data series. If you choose Series in Columns in the Datasheet window, the column headings appear in the legend box. The legend is positioned in the upper right corner of the graph by default, but it can be moved to another location.

Some graph styles do not create a legend automatically. To add a legend to such a graph, choose the Add Legend command from the Chart menu. A legend appears in the default location.

Using the Legend dialog box, you can move the legend box to the following different positions:

Position	Description
Bottom	PowerPoint centers the legend below the graph.
Corner	PowerPoint places the legend in the upper right corner of the chart window.
Top	PowerPoint centers the legend above the graph.
Right	PowerPoint centers the legend horizontally to the right of the graph.
Left	PowerPoint centers the legend horizontally to the left of the graph.

You can move the legend box to different positions on your graph, or you can delete it entirely. Suppose that you want to move the box from the right side of a pie graph to the top, because you know that explanatory text will fall to the right of the graph when you place it on your slide. Follow these steps to move the legend box:

1. Select the legend box.

2. From the Format menu, choose Legend. The Legend dialog box appears (see fig. 8.25).

3. Choose an option (bottom, top, corner, right, or left), and then click OK. The legend box appears in its new position, and the graph is repositioned.

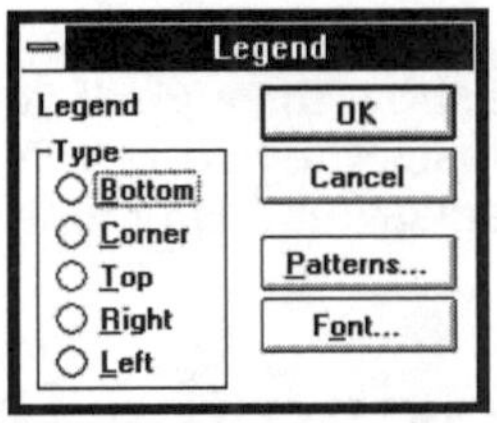

Fig. 8.25

The Legend
dialog box.

Remember that you can move and resize the legend box just as you can any other object. To delete the legend box entirely, choose Delete Legend from the Chart menu. When the legend is deleted, this menu command changes to Add Legend. Use the Add Legend command to restore the legend to the graph.

Inserting the Graph into Your Slide

After you complete a graph, you're ready to insert it into your slide. Follow these steps:

1. From the File menu, choose Exit and Return to Presentation.

2. Choose Yes when asked to update graph in Presentation.

The Graph windows close and you return to the PowerPoint presentation slide you were working on when you entered Graph. Figure 8.26 shows an example of a slide with a graph inserted into it.

The graph is now an object on a slide. You can move it, resize it, fill it, and so on—just like other objects. You can also recolor the graph like a picture to make it blend in with the rest of your color scheme. The graph is saved the next time you save your presentation file.

Editing Your Graph

When you need to edit a graph that you have already placed on a slide, simply point to the graph on your slide and double-click. This step returns you to Graph, where your chart appears on-screen with its associated datasheet.

At this point, you can make changes to the graph or the datasheet using the instructions provided in this chapter. When you're ready to return to your presentation, choose the Exit and Return to Presentation command from the File menu. PowerPoint updates the graph on your slide with the changes you made.

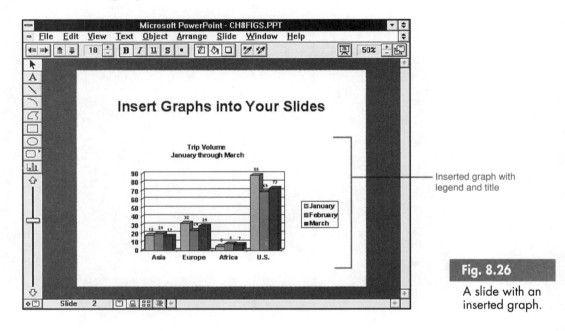

Inserted graph with legend and title

Fig. 8.26

A slide with an inserted graph.

Chapter Summary

This chapter showed you how to move between the Datasheet and Chart windows in the Graph program. It provided instructions for inserting data into the datasheet and manipulating cells by selecting, cutting, and pasting data. It explained the process used to insert and delete rows and columns in the datasheet, and showed you how to use number formats, change text, and vary the width of your columns.

You also learned how to choose the right graph for your data, how to select objects in a graph, and how to change line styles, fills, labels, and fonts. Finally, you saw how to return to PowerPoint and insert your new graph into your presentation. In Chapter 9, you learn to create speaker's notes and handouts to enhance your presentation, and to work with a presentation in outline form.

Creating Notes Pages, Handouts, and Outlines

With PowerPoint, you can create three components of a presentation in addition to slides: speaker's notes, handouts, and an outline. In Chapter 1, you briefly viewed these components; in this chapter, you learn how to create them. You also learn how to work with Microsoft's outlining feature, which is included in many Microsoft products.

Like slides, speaker's notes, handouts, and outlines all have masters. Enter the information into the master that you want to appear on each page. You can display the master for the speaker's notes and the outline by double-clicking the Notes View and Outline View buttons, respectively, or by choosing the commands from the View menu. To display the Handouts Master, double-click the Slide Sorter View button, or choose Handouts Master from the View menu. The view buttons, as well as the View menu, are illustrated in figure 9.1.

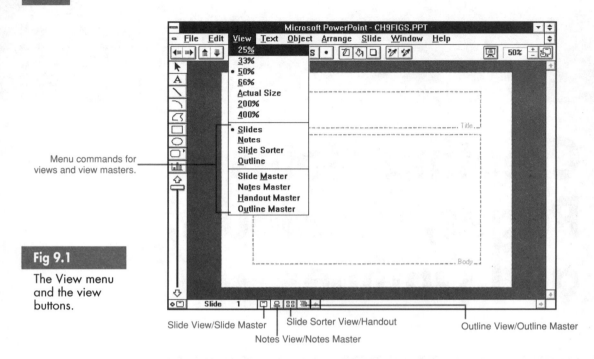

Menu commands for views and view masters.

Fig 9.1

The View menu and the view buttons.

Slide View/Slide Master

Slide Sorter View/Handout

Notes View/Notes Master

Outline View/Outline Master

Creating Notes Pages

The top of the notes page of a presentation contains a reduced view of the slide; the bottom half of the notes page is reserved for you to enter notes about the slide. The Notes Master contains a Master Body Object like the one on the Slide Master. In the Master Body Object, enter any information—such as page numbers—that you want to appear on each notes page. Enter all other text on individual notes pages. You can format the text on a notes page just as you do on a slide. Figure 9.2 shows an example of a notes page. The page number at the bottom of the page was inserted on the Notes Master.

To create notes, follow these steps:

1. Open an existing presentation or create a new one.

2. If you're working with a new presentation, create at least one slide.

3. Display the slide for which you want to create a notes page; then click the Notes View button at the bottom of the screen, or choose Notes from the View menu. A reduced view of the slide appears at the top of the notes page.

4. Double-click the body object in the lower half of the page; then enter the speaker's notes for the current slide.

5. Click anywhere outside the body object to deselect it.

To enter speaker's notes for each slide in the presentation, follow steps 1 through 5 for each slide.

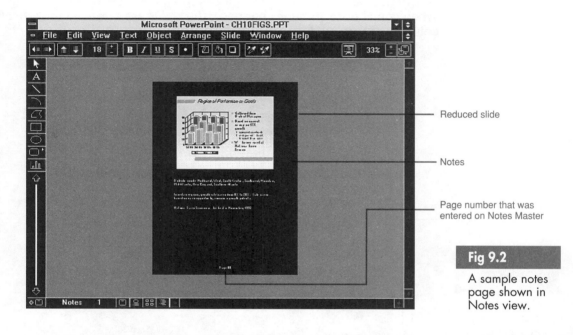

Reduced slide

Notes

Page number that was entered on Notes Master

Fig 9.2

A sample notes page shown in Notes view.

When you work in Notes view, increase the display scale to at least 66%. At scales below 66%, the notes in the lower half of the page are difficult to read.

T I P

Creating Handouts

When you deliver a presentation to an audience, you can help the audience follow the presentation by providing printed copies of the slides. The audience then need not take detailed notes; members can simply annotate the handouts. PowerPoint's Handout Master is designed to create copies of slides. You can format handouts to display two, three, or six slides per page.

The three different format layouts are illustrated on the Handout Master (see fig. 9.3). (Double-click the Slide Sorter button to display the Handout Master on-screen.) The dotted lines show where the slides will appear in each layout arrangement. When you choose two slides per page, one slide appears at the top of the page, and the other appears at the bottom. Three slides per page are arranged vertically on the left side of the page; the right side includes room for notes on the handout. When you choose six slides per page, the slides are arranged in vertical columns of three slides each.

Two-slide layout

Three-slide layout

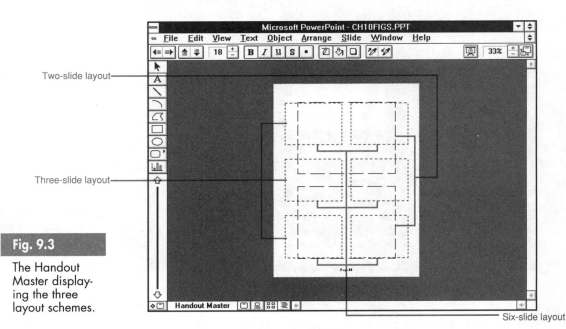

Six-slide layout

Fig. 9.3

The Handout Master displaying the three layout schemes.

The handout is the only part of a presentation that does not have a page that corresponds to its master. For example, the Notes Master has a corresponding notes page, but the Handout Master does not have a corresponding handout page. At this point, you need to work with the Handout Master only if you want to add information that will appear on *each* handout. You might want the title of the presentation to appear at the top of each handout, for example, or your company logo to appear at the bottom of each handout.

You don't have to decide on the layout style at this point; you will determine the layout style when you're ready to print handouts (see Chapter 10, "Creating Output"). Think about which layout style you're likely to use, however. You can then position the repetitive text (or other objects) on the Handout Master without obstructing the slides. If you later choose a different layout style, you can always reposition the objects you added to the Handout Master, if necessary.

As with any other master, you can add text to the Handout Master. This text will then appear on every handout page. To add text to the Handout Master, follow these steps:

> **NOTE** You can add a company logo or other clip art to the Handout Master. For instructions, see Chapter 12, "Inserting Objects."

1. Display the presentation for which you want to create a Handout Master.

2. Double-click the Slide Sorter View button or choose Handout Master from the View menu.

3. To enter text on the master, click the Text tool; then position the mouse pointer where you want to enter text.

4. Click the left mouse button, and then begin typing the text. If you prefer, you can draw a text object by clicking and dragging, and then enter the text into the object.

5. Click anywhere in a blank area of the master to deselect the text object.

Working with Outlines

PowerPoint's outlining feature enables you to enter new text and work with existing text in the form of an outline. The outlining tools let you change the level and position of text in an outline, as you learn later in this chapter. You don't have to work in Outline view to use the outlining tools, however. You can use the outlining tools to create an outline in Slide View as well. Outline view displays your presentation in outline form—without objects, pictures, and clip art.

PowerPoint's defaults are preset to create outlines automatically. When you look at the Slide Master, you see an example of the preset outline format for text (see fig. 9.4).

Figure 9.4 shows a slide in Slide view that uses PowerPoint's default outline format. Text is automatically entered at heading level 1 unless you press Tab. Pressing Tab inserts a bullet and indents the text to the second level in the outline. Pressing Tab again inserts the bullet for the third level and indents the text farther. You can continue to indent text (by pressing Tab) five levels down—to heading level 5.

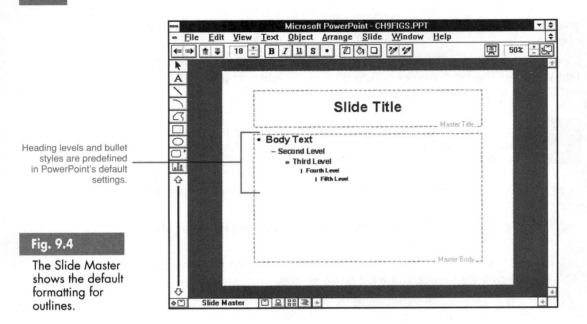

Heading levels and bullet styles are predefined in PowerPoint's default settings.

Fig. 9.4

The Slide Master shows the default formatting for outlines.

Using Outline Tools

To switch to Outline View, click the Outline View button at the bottom of the screen or choose Outline from the View menu. When you work in Outline view, the PowerPoint Toolbar across the top of the screen changes to include special tools used in outlining (see fig. 9.5). The four outlining tools at the far left end of the Toolbar also appear on the Slide View Toolbar. Two other outlining tools—Draft Text and Titles Only—replace the Line, Fill, and Object Shadow tools that appear on the Slide View Toolbar. The Outline view Toolbar contains the following tools:

Tool	Function
Promote	Moves the selected text to the next higher level in an outline.
Demote	Moves the selected text to the next lower level in an outline.
Move Up	Rearranges paragraphs; the selected paragraph is moved above the previous paragraph each time you click this tool. The heading level remains unchanged.
Move Down	Moves the selected paragraph below the next paragraph. The heading level remains unchanged.

Tool	Function
Draft Text/ Formatted Text	Displays the outline with or without any special fonts, formatting, or other styles you might have applied to the text.
Titles Only/ Titles and Bodies	Toggles between displaying slide titles only and displaying the entire content of slides. Displaying only the titles gives you a quick overview of the presentation.

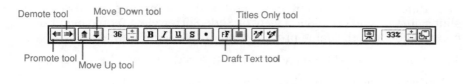

Fig 9.5

The Outline view Toolbar.

Creating Slides in Outline View

You might prefer to enter the text for slides in Outline view. This view enables you to see the content of more than one slide on-screen at once, and because graphical objects do not appear in outline view, you don't have to be bothered with adding or positioning them.

To enter text in Outline view, follow these steps:

1. Create a new presentation or open an existing one.

2. Click the Outline View button at the bottom of the screen, or choose Outline from the View menu.

3. Type the title for the first slide, and then press Ctrl-Enter. PowerPoint moves to the second line, indents it, and adds the bullet for level 1 text.

4. Enter as many level 1 bullets as you like by typing the text and pressing Enter after each one.

5. To enter text at level 2, type the text at level 1, and then click the Demote tool. The text is reformatted to level 2. Press Enter to continue adding more level 2 bullets.

6. Repeat step 5 to enter text at subsequent heading levels.

7. To create the next slide, press Ctrl-Enter.

T   I   P   At any time while you are entering text, click the Promote or Demote tools to change the level of text. When you press Enter, PowerPoint creates text at the last level on which you created text. When you press Ctrl-Enter, PowerPoint creates a new slide.

Cutting, Copying, and Pasting Items

In Outline view, you can cut, copy, and paste paragraphs or entire slides, just as you do in Slide view or Slide Sorter view. You can cut or copy a slide into the same presentation or into a different one.

To cut or copy—and then paste—an entire slide, follow these steps:

1. Display the presentation in Outline view.

2. Click the slide number or the slide icon. To select multiple slides, press and hold the Shift key as you click additional slide icons. The slides you select are highlighted.

3. From the Edit menu, choose the Cut or Copy command.

4. If necessary, open the second presentation into which you want to paste the selected slide. If the presentation is already open, choose the file name from the Window menu.

5. Click to the left of the slide icon where you want the slide inserted. The cursor is blinking between the slide number and the slide icon. (Be sure not to select the slide; just position the cursor.)

6. From the Edit menu, choose the Paste command.

Figure 9.6 illustrates the process of cutting, copying, and pasting. To cut, copy, or paste a text selection within a slide, use the same basic steps you used to cut or copy an entire slide

T   I   P   If you make a mistake while cutting, copying, or pasting, immediately choose Undo from the Edit menu. This command reverses the last action taken.

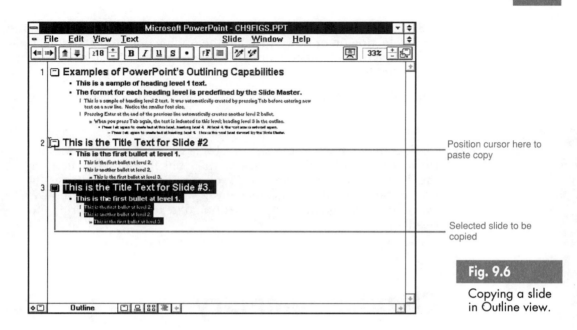

Position cursor here to paste copy

Selected slide to be copied

Fig. 9.6

Copying a slide in Outline view.

Promoting and Demoting Text

To move text to the next higher level in the outline, select the text, and then click the Promote tool. The text is reformatted to the style of the next higher level. If you select text at heading level 3 and then click Promote, for example, PowerPoint reformats the text to level 2 text. When you want to move text to the next lower level in the outline, click the Demote tool. The text is reformatted to the style of the next level.

Rearranging Paragraphs and Slides

The Move Up and Move Down tools make rearranging easy. To rearrange slides or paragraphs within slides, follow these steps:

1. Display the presentation in Outline view.

2. Select the paragraph you want to move. To select an entire slide, click the slide number or the slide icon. The selected paragraph or slide is highlighted.

3. Click the Move Up or the Move Down tool. PowerPoint moves the selection up or down through the outline one step at a time. Continue to click the tool until the selection is positioned where you want it.

4. Click anywhere in a blank area of the screen to deselect the text.

T I P   Don't confuse the Promote/Demote tools with the Move Up/Move Down tools. Look at the pictures on the icons for help remembering the difference between the tools: Promote/Demote tools change the horizontal position—the heading level—of text. The Move Up/Move Down tools change the vertical position of text without altering the heading level.

Chapter Summary

This chapter gave you a sense of the different views available in PowerPoint. You learned how to view a presentation from different perspectives and how to create three new components of a presentation: notes, handouts, and an outline. Notes pages enable you to annotate the comments that you want to make about slides during a presentation. By creating handouts, you can give your audience a copy of the slides in a variety of layout styles. Outlines let you create and manipulate a presentation easily. To add to your slides, you can create as few or as many of these new components as your presentation requires.

Now that you have learned the basics of working with PowerPoint, you're ready to learn what kind of output you can create. The next chapter explains how to print notes, handouts, and outlines, as well as slides and overheads. You will also learn how to create a file from which you can have slides professionally produced by a service bureau.

Creating Output

With PowerPoint, you can create several different types of output, including slides on paper or overhead transparencies, handouts, presentation outlines, and speaker's notes. You can print to a file that a professional service agency can use to create 35mm slides or color transparencies, or you can design your final output to be presented as an online slide show. Regardless of the final output, you'll probably print copies of your slides on paper several times before finalizing a presentation. Printing slides is probably the most common type of printing you'll do.

In this chapter, you learn how to set up your printer for the type of output you're creating. You learn how to change the default format for printing slides, and how to use the computer as a slide projector. You also learn how to print notes pages, handouts, and the outline for your presentation. Finally, you learn how to send your PowerPoint slides to Genigraphics by modem to have your photographic slides created for you.

Setting Up Your Slides

To begin creating a presentation, you must set up the slide format. This first step is important because the layout of the slides is affected by the slide setup—if you change the setup after the slides are created, you might have to reformat your slides.

In most cases, you can use the default settings, which print slides in landscape mode at 10 inches wide by 7.5 inches tall. This size fits well on 8.5-by-11-inch paper. If your final output will be an on-screen slide show, 35mm photographic slides, or paper of an unusual size, you'll need to change the slide setup.

To change the slide setup, follow these steps:

1. Open the presentation you want to change, or open a new presentation.

2. Choose Slide Setup from the File menu. The Slide Setup dialog box appears (see fig. 10.1).

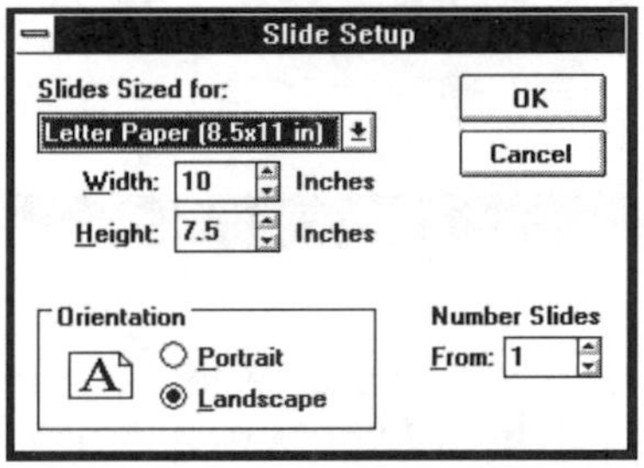

Fig. 10.1

The Slide Setup dialog box.

3. Choose an option in the Slides Sized For drop-down box. (See table 10.1 for an explanation of each option.)

4. To change the print orientation from Landscape (the slide content appears horizontally on the page), click Portrait (the slide content appears vertically on the page).

5. To begin numbering slides from a number other than 1, type a number in the Number Slides From box.

6. When all settings are correct, click OK.

If you changed an existing presentation, be sure to check each slide's layout in case you need to make adjustments. If you changed the settings for a new presentation, you might notice a slight change in the size of the background area shown on the slide.

Table 10.1 Slide Setup Dialog Box

Option	Description
On-Slide Show	Sets the dimensions to 10 inches by 7.5 inches and the orientation to landscape so that the slides fill the screen.
Letter Paper	The default setting. Sets the dimensions to 10 inches by 7.5 inches and the orientation to landscape.

Option	Description
A4Paper (210x297 mm)	Sets the width to 26 cm (10.83 inches) and the height to 18 cm (7.5 inches). The orientation is landscape.
35mm Photographic slides	Sets the width to 11.25 inches and the height to 7.5 inches in landscape orientation so that the content fills the slide area.
Custom	Enables you to specify the dimensions you want. Use this option when the paper you are using is a nonstandard size paper (not 8.5 by 11 inches). Click the up and down arrows in the Width and Height boxes.

Setting Up Your Printer

You've probably already installed and set up your printer for other Windows applications. In most cases, you will not need to change the printer setup. If you do, you'll see the Windows Setup dialog box, the same dialog box you see when using the Windows Control Panel for setting up printers.

You might want to print slides on one printer and print handouts, notes pages, and outlines on a different printer. In this situation, you can specify different default printers for different printing tasks.

To check the current printer setup or to specify two different default printers, follow these steps:

1. Open an existing presentation or create a new one.

2. From the File menu, choose Print. PowerPoint displays the Print dialog box (see fig. 10.2). In this figure, the HP LaserJet III printer is chosen to print slides (as shown in the Print box).

3. Click the Print Setup button. PowerPoint displays the Print Setup dialog box (see fig. 10.3). The box contains two areas. The upper portion sets the printer for slides, and the lower portion sets the printer for notes, handouts, and an outline. The default printer for slides appears in the upper portion of the dialog box, the default printer for notes, handouts, and an outline appears in the lower portion.

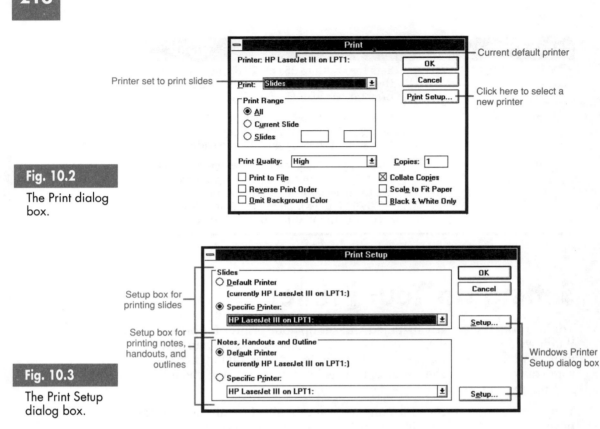

Fig. 10.2

The Print dialog box.

Fig. 10.3

The Print Setup dialog box.

4. To change the default printer for slides, click the Specific Printer option in the upper half of the dialog box; then choose a printer from the drop-down list.

5. To change the default printer for Notes, Handouts, and Outline, click the Specific Printer option in the lower half of the dialog box; then choose a printer from the drop-down list.

6. To change the actual printer setup for the new printer you chose in steps 4 or 5, click the Setup button to the right of the printer name. PowerPoint displays the standard Windows Setup dialog box. To change these printer settings, refer to your Windows documentation and your printer manual for instructions.

7. When all settings are correct, click OK to return to the Print Setup dialog box shown in figure 10.3.

8. Click OK to close the Print Setup dialog box and return to the Print dialog box of the active presentation.

9. Click OK to close the Print dialog box and return to the Print dialog box shown in figure 10.2.

Until you change these settings, they remain in effect for all presentations. You should not need to change these settings unless you install a new printer or change the default printers.

Printing

With PowerPoint, you can print any part of a presentation: slides, notes pages, handouts, or an outline. The basic procedures for printing each element are the same. These steps are outlined in the following section.

Printing Slides

You will probably print slides more frequently than other parts of the presentation. You can print slides in final form, or, if your printer supports a lower print resolution, you can eliminate the background shading and print in only black and white to speed up the printing of preliminary copies. These options and others are described in table 10.2.

To print slides, follow these steps:

1. Open the presentation you want to print.

2. Choose Print from the File menu. The Print dialog box appears (see fig. 10.4).

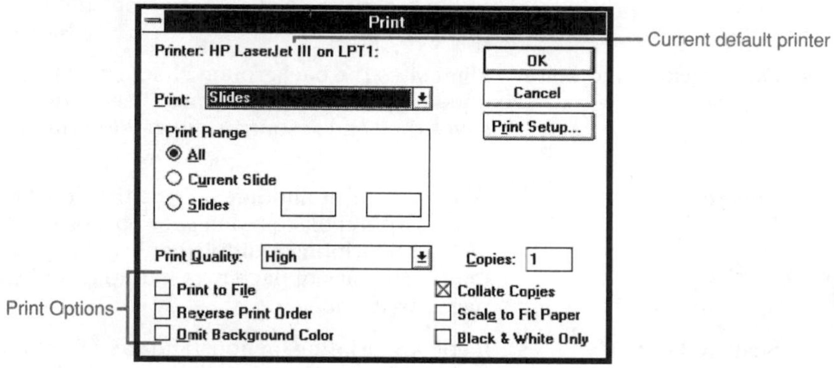

Fig. 10.4

The Print dialog box.

3. In the Print drop-down box, choose whether to print Slides, Notes Pages, Handouts, or Outline view.

4. In the Print Range box, choose All to print all pages, Current Slide to print only the active slide, or Slides to print a selected range. With the Slides option, type the beginning page number in the From box and the ending page number in the To box. To print only one page, such as page 5, type the same page number in both the From and To boxes.

5. In the Print Quality box, choose a print resolution. For some printers, this option might not be available. Check your printer manual for information on print resolution options.

6. To print more than one copy, type the number of copies in the Copies box.

7. Choose any check box print option by clicking the box to display the X. See table 10.3 for a description of each print option.

8. To change any default settings for the specified printer, click the Print Setup button. PowerPoint displays the Print Setup dialog box. From this box, you can click the Setup button to display the Windows Setup dialog box, if necessary. When all settings are correct, click OK until the Print dialog box returns.

9. In the Print dialog box, click OK. PowerPoint begins printing.

Table 10.2 Print Options in the Print Dialog Box

Option	Description
Print to File	Prints the slides to a file that can later be used to produce 35mm photographic slides or slides from a desktop film recorder.
Reverse Print Order	Begins printing from the last page and prints to the first page. (Not an option on some printers.)
Omit Background Color	Eliminates the background shading from slides, notes, handouts, and outlines. This option saves time and resources when you print a draft.
Collate Copies	When you print multiple copies, the Collate Copies option places each set of pages in order instead of printing multiple copies of page one, multiple copies of page two, multiple copies of page three, and so on.
Scale to Fit Paper	If you are printing on nonstandard paper; that is, not 8 1/2 by 11 inches, scales each slide to fit the paper.

Option	Description
Black and White Only	Converts all color and fill to white and all text and lines to black. This option is useful for printing drafts, or for printing crisp, clear notes and handouts pages.

Printing Notes Pages

In Chapters 3 and 9, you learned how to view and enter text into the notes pages of a presentation. To print notes pages, follow the same basic steps you learned for printing slides. Because notes pages are printed one to a page, specify the print range for the slides you want to print. For example, if you want to print notes pages only for slides 1 through 4, specify From 1, To 4 in the Print Range box.

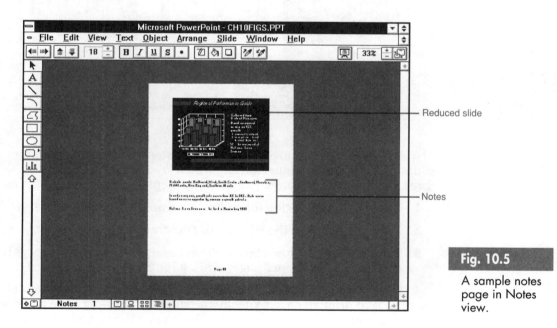

— Reduced slide

— Notes

Fig. 10.5

A sample notes page in Notes view.

Printing Handouts

One useful feature of PowerPoint is the flexibility it offers when printing handouts. Often, printing two, three, or even six slides per handout page is more efficient than printing one slide per page. PowerPoint offers each of these layout options.

To see how a handout page will look with each of these layout options, double-click the slide Sorter View button, or choose the Handout Master command from the View menu. You see the slide shown in figure 10.6. The dotted lines show how the handouts will look with two, three, or six slides per page.

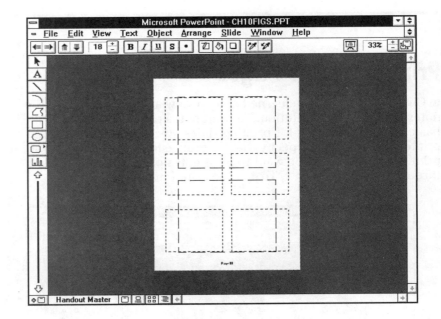

Fig. 10.6

Layout options for handouts.

To print handouts, you use the same basic steps you used for printing slides. In addition, you must specify which layout option to use: two, three, or six slides per page. Follow these steps to print handouts:

1. Open the presentation for which you want to print handouts.

2. Choose Print from the File menu. The Print dialog box appears.

3. In the Print drop-down box, choose Handouts (2 slides per page), Handouts (3 slides per page), or Handouts (6 slides per page).

4. In the Print Range box, choose All to print all pages. If you don't want to print all pages, specify the *slide numbers*—not the pages—that you want to print. You then don't need to calculate which page a certain slide appears on.

   For example, if you have specified 3 slides per page and you want to print slides 4, 5, and 6, enter From 4, To 6 in the Print Range box. Because 3 slides appear on each page, PowerPoint prints all of page 2, which contains slides 4, 5, and 6.

5. Click OK to begin printing.

Printing an Outline

An outline prints just as it was last displayed in Outline view. If, for example, you clicked the Titles Only tool to hide the body text, PowerPoint prints only the titles of the slides. If you increased the scale to 66 percent, the outline will print at 66 percent. If you clicked the Draft Text tool to display the outline in draft text, PowerPoint will print the outline in draft text.

To print an outline, follow the steps for printing slides outlined in the section titled "Printing Slides," but choose the Outline View option in the Print box. In the Page Range box, enter the slide numbers you want to include on the outline page. For example, if you enter From 3, To 7, PowerPoint includes only those slides on the outline page that is printed.

Creating a Slide Show

Until recently, PowerPoint's only output options were slides printed on paper, overhead transparencies, or a special file from which 35mm photographic slides could be produced. Now, however, you can use your computer screen as the output medium to run a slide show. With the right kind of projection device, you can project the slide show on your computer to a screen large enough to be viewed by an audience. If your computers are networked appropriately, you can display the slide show on several personal computers at the same time.

You can run a PowerPoint slide show manually by using the mouse or keyboard to move to the next slide when you're ready. You can also set up your slide show to run automatically, setting the amount of time each slide should remain on-screen and specifying a transition style between slides. The *transition style* determines how one slide is removed from the screen and the next one is presented. Dissolving from one slide to the next, and covering one slide with another from the left down are two examples of transition styles.

Setting Transition Styles and Timing

To set timing between slides and to specify transition styles, follow these steps:

1. Display your presentation in Slide Sorter View.

2. Select the slide for which you want to set timing and transition. If you want to use the same settings for multiple slides, select those slides as a group.

3. Click the Transition tool at the far left end of the Toolbar (see fig. 10.8), or choose the Transition command on the Slide menu. PowerPoint displays the Transition dialog box shown in figure 10.7.

The Transition dialog box.

4. Choose a transition style from the Effect dialog box. Below the box, click Slow, Medium, or Fast for the transition speed.

5. In the Advance box, choose a timing option. If you want the selected slide to remain on-screen until you click the mouse, choose Only on Mouse Click. Choose Automatically after N Seconds to set a specific time for the slide to appear on-screen. Type the number of seconds in the box. You can specify more than 60 seconds if you want the slide to remain on-screen longer than one minute.

6. Click OK. PowerPoint displays the time for the slide below the bottom left corner. If you set a transition for the slide, a symbol similar to the Transition tool icon also appears at the bottom left corner of the slide, directly to the left on the transition time.

Running a Slide Show

When you're ready to run a slide show, you have several options for advancing the slides manually, using set timings, or rehearsing new timings. Follow these steps:

1. Open the presentation.

2. Choose Slide Show from the File menu. The Slide Show dialog box appears (see fig. 10.9).

3. In the Slides box, choose All, or specify the slide numbers in the From and To boxes.

4. In the Advance box, choose Manual Advance if you want to control the slide show manually with the mouse. If you have set slide timings, you can choose the Use Slide Timings option; otherwise this option is not available. If you want to set new timings for the slide show, click the Rehearse New Timings option.

5. To have the slide show run continuously, and then repeat, choose the Loop Continuously Until 'Esc' option.

6. Click OK to begin running the slide show. Press Esc at any time to end the slide show.

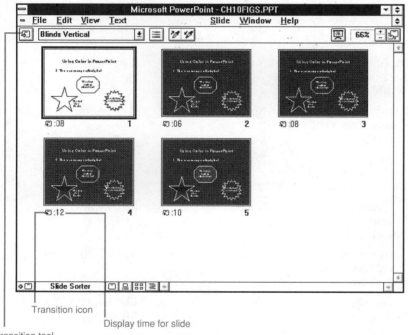

Fig. 10.8

Transition symbols and timing (in seconds) appear at the lower left corner of slides.

Fig. 10.9

The Slide Show dialog box.

Table 10.3 explains the different ways that you can use the mouse and the keyboard to control the slide show.

Table 10.3 Navigating in the Slide Show		
Activity	**Using the Mouse**	**Using the Keyboard**
To show next slide	Click left button	Space bar, N, right arrow, down arrow, PgDn
To show preceding slide	Click right button	Left arrow, up arrow, PgUp
To show a particular slide	None	Type the number and press Enter
To show or hide the mouse pointer (toggle)	None	A or equal sign (=)
To toggle between a black screen and the current slide	None	B or period (.)
To toggle between a white screen and the current slide	None	W or comma (,)
To return to the presentation in PowerPoint	None	Esc, hyphen (-), or Ctrl-Break
To pause and resume an automatic slide show	None	S or + (plus sign)
To end slide show and return to the presentation in PowerPoint	None	Esc, hyphen (-), or Ctrl-Break

Linking with Genigraphics

As you see in Chapter 12, "Inserting Objects and Creating Special Effects," you can use Genigraphics Corporation's professionally drawn clip art in your own slides. Genigraphics is a leading maker of slides for businesses. PowerPoint gives you the benefit of outstanding software and outstanding artistic design capabilities at the same time.

You can use the expertise of Genigraphics and Microsoft to *create* your slides and benefit from the expertise of both companies when you output your slides. PowerPoint and the Genigraphics software combine to produce your file. You can use Genigraphics as your "output device" and have slides sent back to you by overnight express.

You need a Hayes-compatible modem to use the direct connection to Genigraphics. (If you prefer, you can take a diskette to a Genigraphics office. See your PowerPoint documentation for a list of Genigraphics offices around the country.) When you install printer drivers during setup, install Genigraphics Driver on GENI. Refer to the Windows documentation for information on installing printer drivers.

To link with Genigraphics, Choose Printer Setup from the File menu, and then choose 'Genigraphics Driver on GENI' as your target printer. When you create your slides, the fonts, slide dimensions, and orientation will be appropriate for processing by Genigraphics. Figure 10.10 shows the Genigraphics Setup dialog box, which you use to set up to print with Genigraphics.

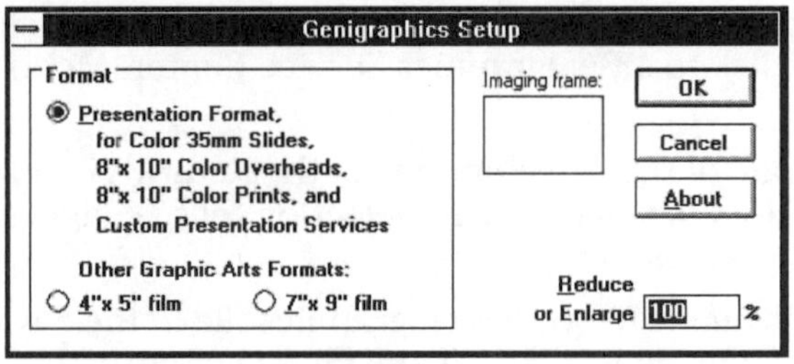

Fig. 10.10

The Genigraphics Setup dialog box.

Creating a Genigraphics File

Follow these steps to "print" your presentation with Genigraphics:

1. With Genigraphics as your target printer, choose Print from the File menu. The Print dialog box appears.

2. From the Print dialog box, choose OK. The Genigraphics Job Instructions dialog box appears (see fig. 10.11). In figure 10.11, the Custom button was chosen. The Custom button expands the Genigraphics Job Instructions dialog box to display the box in which you type specific instructions.

   You choose to have one or more copies made of one or more of the following types of output: 35mm photographic slides on plastic mounts, 35mm photographic slides on glass mounts, 8-by-10-inch overheads, and 8-by-10-inch prints.

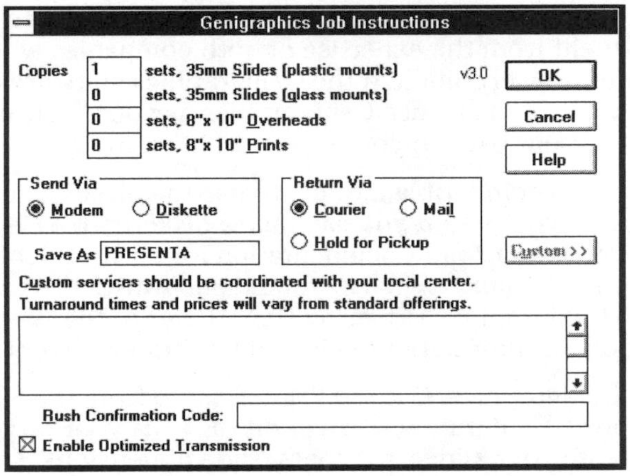

Fig. 10.11

The Genigraphics
Job Instructions
dialog box.

3. Type the number of copies you want of each type of output.

4. In the Send Via box, choose Modem if you intend to transmit the file electronically; choose Diskette if you intend to send or deliver a floppy disk to a Genigraphics Service Center. Modem is the default.

5. Choose one of the three options in the Return Via box: Courier, Mail, or Hold for Pickup. This selection tells Genigraphics how to return the slides to you.

6. Type a file name for your Genigraphics file in the Save As box (the default extension is .GNA). If you click the button on the bottom right, labeled Custom, you can type specific instructions regarding your print job.

7. Choose the Custom button to expand the dialog box (refer again to fig. 10.11).

   A wide range of custom services and formats is available. Call your Genigraphics Service Center before you specify any custom service or format. After you speak with a Genigraphics representative, type the necessary information about customization in the box.

   If you need a rush order, get a rush confirmation code from the service center when you call, and type that number in the Rush Confirmation Code box.

   The check box in the lower left labeled Enable Optimized Transmission is set to on automatically. Do not turn off this option unless the Genigraphics Service Center tells you to do so.

8. When all settings are correct, choose OK. The Genigraphics driver begins to save your slides.

   If you choose the Modem option in step 4, the Genigraphics driver saves the file to the Genigraphics directory. If you choose the Diskette option, the standard PowerPoint Save As dialog box appears. In the dialog box, you can indicate the directory to which you want to save your file.

   The Genigraphics Billing Information dialog box now appears (see fig. 10.12).

9. Fill in the fields in the dialog box as necessary. The information includes the shipping—and, if different, billing—address and name. It also includes the form of payment: by credit card, Genigraphics account, or cash on delivery (COD). You also can enter your tax-exempt ID number, if relevant.

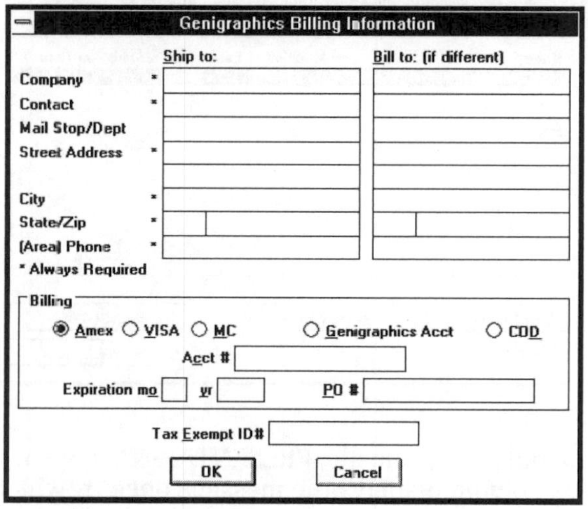

Fig. 10.12

The Genigraphics Billing Information box.

10. Choose OK.

If you choose the Modem option for transmission in the Genigraphics Job Instructions box, you receive a message to run GraphicsLink in order to transmit the file. The next section discusses how to use GraphicsLink.

Using GraphicsLink To Transmit Files

The preceding section tells you how to create and save a file in the proper Genigraphics format. Use the following steps to transmit the file by modem to a Genigraphics Service Center:

 NOTE To make certain that you have made all the proper arrangements, call Genigraphics before you send a file for the first time. The phone number at Genigraphics Corporate Headquarters in Shelton, Connecticut, is 1-901-795-9088.

1. Start the GraphicsLink program in the Applications window in Program Manager by double-clicking the GraphicsLink icon. You see the GraphicsLink dialog box (see fig. 10.13).

GraphicsLink - c:\windows\system\geni

<u>F</u>ile <u>E</u>dit <u>H</u>elp

File Name	Status	Last Modified	Estimated Transmission Time
PRESENTA.GNA	Unsent	07/15/92	2 minutes

[<u>J</u>ob Instructions...] [<u>B</u>illing Information...] [<u>T</u>ransmitted Info...]

[Send]

Fig. 10.13

The GraphicsLink dialog box.

In this example, only one file, PRESENTA.GNA, appears on the list. The Status column displays the message Unsent, which changes to Sent after you transmit the file; the date the file was last modified; and the approximate transmission time.

The dialog box contains three buttons: Job Instructions, Billing Information, and Transmitted Info. The latter is unavailable in this example because no file has been transmitted. When available, the Transmitted Info button gives information about transmitted files. If you choose the Job Instructions or Billing Information buttons, the Genigraphics Job Instruction or Genigraphics Billing Information dialog box appears (refer again to figs. 10.11 and 10.12). You can change information in these two boxes as necessary.

Before sending your file, you must choose Communications Setup from the File menu. The Communications Setup option enables you to change the default numbers for setup as necessary. The options include Modem Speed; Dialog Type; Port; Parameters; and special choices such as Initialization Command, Dialog Prefix, Disconnect Sequence, and Hardware Flow Control. Consult your modem manual for details on the options you need to use. In addition, you must specify the destination, which you choose from the list of Genigraphics Service Centers that appear on-screen.

2. When you are satisfied with all the options, click OK to return to the main GraphicsLink menu.

3. To choose a file or files to send, click the file name or click and drag the files.

   You also can use the Edit menu options—Select All, Select Unsent, and Select Sent—to select files. Select All selects all files; Select Unsent selects only those files you haven't sent.

4. Click the Send button in the bottom right corner of the dialog box.

Transmission begins and a special box provides a report of the progress made. At the end of the transmission, another message tells you whether the transmission was successful. You can try again, if necessary. If the transmission was unsuccessful, the message tells you when the transmission failed. If successful, a report replaces the file on disk. This report appears on the GraphicsLink screen under the same name as the file, and the message sent appears in the Status column.

Chapter Summary

In this chapter, you completed the final step in creating presentations: outputting your presentation to a variety of devices. You began by learning how to set up the slide format and how to set up your printer. Then you learned how to print slides, notes pages, handouts, and an outline. You learned how to create a slide show and set timing and transitions between slides. And finally, you learned how to use the Genigraphics slide service.

You have now learned all the steps you need to know to create a presentation. You learn how to use PowerPoint's advanced capabilities for text, graphs, and color in Part II of this book.

PowerPoint Advanced Features

Quick Start: Working with Pictures

I n previous quick starts, you learned to create a presentation, add text and objects, and choose a color scheme. In this quick start, you use advanced PowerPoint capabilities to work with pictures. You turn several PowerPoint objects into a single picture, copy and paste the picture, and then crop and recolor it.

In this chapter, you also work with PowerPoint's clip art, an invaluable feature. The PowerPoint clip art library is a large collection of professionally drawn and colored pictures. As you learn in this chapter, selecting and copying clip art onto your slides doesn't require much skill or experience. Clip art gives you a "quick start" to creating polished and professional-looking slides for your PowerPoint presentations.

Converting Objects to a Picture

Converting objects and text boxes into pictures makes them easier to manipulate. For example, you can convert many objects into one picture that you can move, recolor, resize, and crop. This section shows you how to create a logo for a firm by converting several objects into one picture. You then learn to recolor the logo, cut or copy it, and paste it onto a slide as a picture. You can crop this new picture and resize it as needed.

Suppose that you want to create a picture like the one in figure 11.1 as a company logo.

Fig. 11.1

A logo created with PowerPoint drawing tools.

This logo's elements—the text and the drawn objects—are parts of one picture, but each element was typed or drawn separately.

T I P   To avoid covering other objects, draw new objects in a blank area of the screen. You can then move the new objects where you want them to go.

To create the upper portion of the umbrella, follow these steps:

1. Use the Ellipse tool to draw a large circle for the top of the umbrella. Fill the circle with gray or another color.

2. Use the Rectangle tool to draw a rectangle that covers the lower half of the circle. While the rectangle is still selected, click the Line tool to remove the lined border of the rectangle. Because the border of the rectangle is invisible, the circle you drew looks like a half circle.

3. Group the two objects by selecting both objects (see fig. 11.2), and then choosing Group from the Arrange menu. Grouping the two objects enables you to select and move them as a single object.

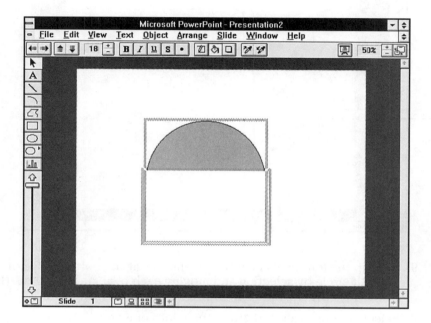

4. Use the Ellipse tool to draw an oval approximately one-quarter the width of the lower edge of the half circle. The oval will be used as one-quarter of the lower edge of the umbrella.

5. Use the Rectangle tool to draw a rectangle that covers the lower half of the oval. While the rectangle is still selected, click the Line tool to remove the lined border of the rectangle. Because the rectangle's border is invisible, the oval you drew appears to be a half oval.

6. Select both the oval and the rectangle (see fig. 11.3), and then choose Group from the Arrange menu. Grouping the two objects enables you to select and move them as a single object.

7. To copy the object, select the oval, and then choose Copy from the Edit menu or press Ctrl-C.

8. Make three additional copies of the oval by choosing Paste from the Edit menu three times or by pressing Ctrl-V three times.

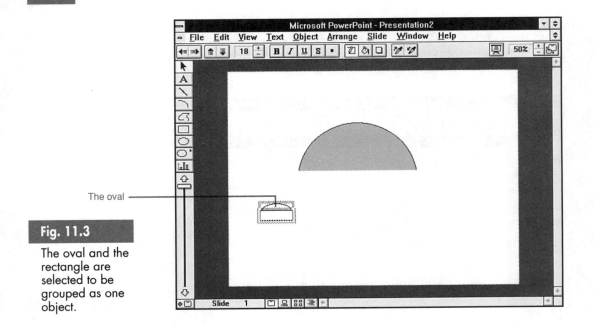

Fig. 11.3

The oval and the rectangle are selected to be grouped as one object.

9. Line up the four ovals next to one another at the bottom edge of the half circle by selecting and moving each oval, one at a time. (If necessary, use the Line tool to draw a horizontal guide line.)

10. Select all four ovals and group them into one object. Delete the horizontal guide line, if you drew one.

11. If necessary, reposition the ovals (now one object) under the circle, and resize the circle to make it fit the ovals.

12. Select the ovals and the circle (see fig. 11.4). Then group the ovals together to make the top and bottom of the umbrella one object.

To create the umbrella handle, the raindrops, and the company name to complete the logo, follow these steps:

1. To draw the curved handle of the umbrella, use the Ellipse tool to draw a small circle.

2. Use the Rectangle tool to draw a rectangle that covers the upper half of the small circle. Click the Line tool to remove the border from the rectangle.

3. Select both objects (see fig. 11.5). Then choose Group from the Arrange menu to group the multiple objects as one object.

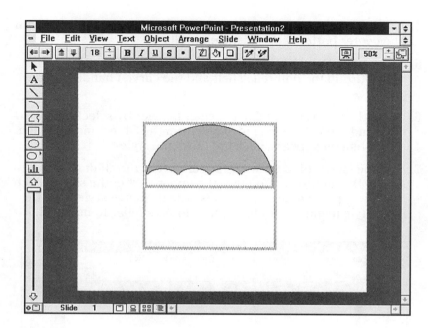

All objects are
selected to be
grouped as one
object to form
the top of the
umbrella.

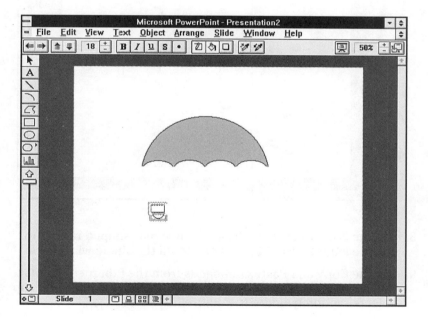

The circle and
rectangle that
form the umbrella
handle are
selected to be
grouped as one
object.

4. Using the Line tool, draw the umbrella shaft straight down from the center bottom edge of the umbrella.

5. Move the curved handle into position at the lower edge of the shaft. Group the umbrella shaft and the curved handle as one object.

6. Make the umbrella handle and shaft heavier by selecting the object, and then choosing Line Style from the Object menu. When the submenu appears, click the third line style.

7. Use the Line tool to draw the upper part of the shaft (centered above the umbrella). To make the upper part of the shaft match the lower part of the shaft, choose the third line style from the Line Style menu. Your picture now looks similar to figure 11.6.

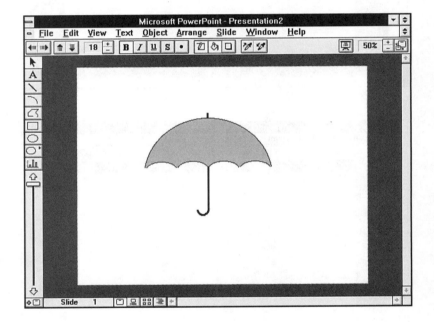

8. Use the Freeform tool to draw a simple tear-shaped rain drop. Choose Fill from the Object menu to fill the shape with black.

9. Use the Copy and Paste commands from the Edit menu to make several copies of the rain drop object. Reposition the rain drop objects randomly under the umbrella.

10. Click the Text tool, and then type the name *Weather Beaters* near the lower right corner of the umbrella.

11. While the name is still selected, choose Font from the Text menu, and then click the Lucida Blackletter font. Click the Font Size tool to change the size of the name to 24 points. Your slide now looks like figure 11.1, which appears at the beginning of this chapter.

Pasting Objects as a Picture

In the preceding section, you learned how to combine several drawn objects to create a picture—in this case, a picture for a logo. Throughout the steps, you grouped some of the related objects so that those objects could be moved together. At this point, however, most of the objects are still separate. That is, the objects are not grouped together as one picture. To group the objects as a picture, follow these steps:

1. Choose Select All from the Edit menu. The outline of each object appears (see fig. 11.7).

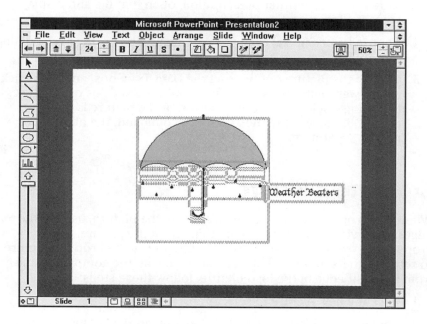

Fig 11.7

All objects are selected.

2. Choose Group from the Arrange menu. The individual selection outlines are replaced by a single selection outline that encloses all the objects.

The single selection outline indicates that the object is a single picture. To copy or move a picture to another slide, choose the Copy or Cut commands from the Edit menu, and then use the Paste command from the Edit menu. You can then reposition the picture as necessary.

You might want PowerPoint to treat several separate objects as a single picture. Suppose, for example, that you're not ready to group all the objects that comprise the umbrella logo, but you want to paste them onto another slide as a single picture. The Paste Special command enables you to paste separate objects as a single object. Follow these steps:

1. Select each object you want to include. To select all objects, choose Select All from the Edit menu.

2. Choose Cut or Copy from the Edit menu. If you choose Cut, the objects are removed and placed on the Clipboard. If you choose Copy, the objects remain on the current slide and a copy is placed on the Clipboard.

3. Display the slide in which you want to paste the picture. If the slide is part of another presentation, open that file and display the correct slide.

4. Choose Paste Special from the Edit menu. The Paste Special dialog box appears.

5. Choose the Picture option from the Data Type box, and then click OK. PowerPoint pastes the objects onto the slide as one picture. (The single selection box indicates that the picture is now one object.) If you choose the Edit Paste command, the objects are pasted separately.

Cropping a Picture

When you crop a picture, you block some of the picture, usually the edges, from view. You don't cut anything from the picture; think of cropping as "reframing" the picture. Later, you can uncrop the picture to return it to its original shape and size. To trim the company name from the right edge of the logo picture, follow these steps:

1. Click the new picture to select it.

2. Choose Crop Picture from the Object menu. The mouse pointer changes to the Cropping tool (see fig. 11.8).

3. Position the center of the Cropping tool over the lower left resize handle on the selection box.

4. Click and drag the tool to the left until the company name falls outside the selection box; then release the mouse button.

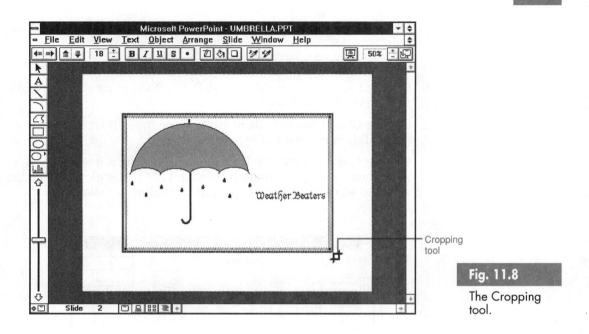

Fig. 11.8

The Cropping tool.

To reframe a picture after it has been cropped, select the picture, and then choose Crop Picture from the Object menu. Use the Cropping tool to drag one of the sizing handles until the picture is reframed the way you want it. Click anywhere away from the picture to deselect it.

Using Clip Art

PowerPoint comes with a collection of professionally drawn pictures, or clip art, stored in PowerPoint's clip art directory. Transferring clip art to a slide in your presentation is easy. In this section, you transfer a picture of a hot air balloon to a slide to illustrate a presentation about a new company called Up, Up, and Away Balloon Rides. To transfer a clip art picture, follow these steps:

1 1. Choose Open Clip Art from the File menu. The Open Clip Art dialog box appears (see fig. 11.9). The clip art directory is the current directory. The files in this directory appear beneath the File Name box.

2. Click the Open Untitled Copy check box to protect the original file from being altered.

3. Double-click the transprt.ppt file. After a few seconds, the slides in the transportation file are listed in Outline view on-screen.

4. Double-click slide number 12, Hot Air Balloon. The clip art picture appears on-screen.

5. Click the balloon to select it.

6. Choose Copy from the Edit menu. PowerPoint places a copy of the picture on the Clipboard.

7. Choose Close from the File menu to close the clip art file. Your presentation returns to the screen.

8. Choose Paste from the Edit menu. A copy of the hot air balloon is pasted into your presentation (see fig. 11.10). The picture remains selected so that you can crop, resize, recolor, or make other changes.

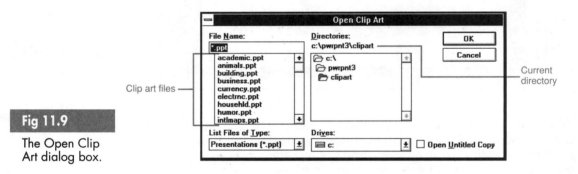

Clip art files ──

Current directory

Fig 11.9

The Open Clip Art dialog box.

 NOTE   PowerPoint always pastes clip art into the center of a slide. After it is pasted, you can move the picture to the correct position on the slide.

You can move, resize, and crop the clip art pictures just like the picture you created earlier in this chapter. In the next section, you learn to recolor the clip art picture.

Recoloring a Picture

When you copy a picture or clip art from another file into your active presentation, you might find that the colors don't blend well. To recolor the hot air balloon you just copied, follow these steps:

1. Select the picture that you want to recolor; in this case, the hot air balloon.

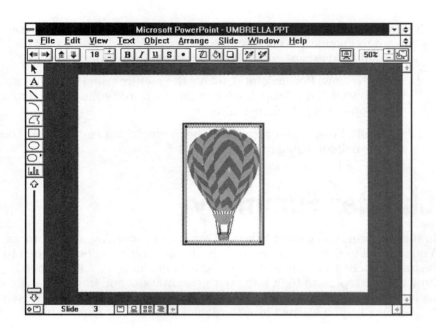

Fig. 11.10

A clip art picture pasted into the active presentation.

2. Choose Recolor Picture from the Object menu. The Recolor Picture dialog box appears (see fig. 11.11). A copy of the picture appears on the left of the dialog box. Notice that the Colors option at the bottom of the dialog box is checked. The Colors option displays the solid colors used in the picture. The Fills option displays the colors used for patterned fills.

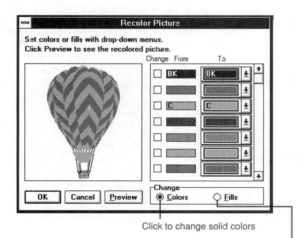

Fig. 11.11

The Recolor Picture dialog box.

Click to change solid colors

Click to change patterned fill colors

3. To choose new colors, click the drop-down box for the color you want to change. In this example, click the drop-down box for the second (teal green) color. From the drop-down list, choose RD8.

4. Click Preview. PowerPoint displays the picture using the new colors. Now click the drop-down box for the third (aqua) color. From the drop-down list, choose BU5.

5. Click OK. PowerPoint returns to the presentation and recolors the hot air balloon using RD8 and BU5.

Chapter Summary

In this chapter, you gained hands-on experience working with pictures. You learned to draw, combine, group, and arrange objects, and then to paste the pictures to a new location as a single picture. You learned how to crop a picture to fit into your presentation, and how to transfer a clip art object from a PowerPoint clip art file to a slide in your presentation. Finally, you learned how to recolor a picture or clip art file.

The next few chapters go into greater detail about the features presented in this lesson.

Inserting Objects and Creating Special Effects

I n Chapter 3, "Creating a Presentation," you learned to work with an entire multiple-slide presentation. Often, however, you will want to include in your presentation information from another PowerPoint presentation or information from an outside application. In this chapter, you learn how to copy or cut text and objects from one presentation and paste them into another, and how to insert clip art from PowerPoint's clip art library into your presentation.

In this chapter you also learn how to import objects from applications outside PowerPoint into your presentation. You learn the easiest cut/copy and paste procedure, and the steps for creating linked and embedded objects. Finally, you learn how to create special effects to enhance your slides.

Copying Objects and Clip Art

Copying and moving objects from one presentation to another presentation is similar to moving objects within the same file; it requires only the added step of opening the second PowerPoint presentation. In addition to copying and moving objects, you can copy pictures from PowerPoint's clip art library into your presentation.

In this section, you learn how to copy and move objects from one presentation to another and how to insert clip art.

Copying Objects from Another Presentation

Any object in a PowerPoint presentation can be moved or copied to another presentation. Remember that when you copy the entire object, text is also considered an object. To cut or copy a portion of a text object, follow these steps:

1. Open the presentation and display the slide into which you want to copy or move an object.

2. Open the presentation that contains the object you want to copy or move.

3. Select the object (or objects) you want to copy or move.

4. Choose Cut or Copy from the Edit menu. Your selection is moved or copied to the Clipboard. Figure 12.1 illustrates a selected object.

5. To switch to the presentation into which you want to copy the object, choose the name of the presentation from the Windows menu or, if a portion of the Presentation window is visible, click it.

6. Choose Paste from the Edit menu. The contents of the Clipboard are pasted into the presentation (see fig. 12.2).

 NOTE If you cut or copied formatted text, the text loses its formatting when you use the Paste command. To retain the formatting, use the Paste Special command, which is described later in this chapter.

Copying Clip Art

PowerPoint comes with a large collection of clip art—professionally drawn pictures that you can add to your presentations. Clip art is convenient and easy to use. If you are unsure of your artistic abilities, using clip art can save you the time and trouble of creating pictures yourself.

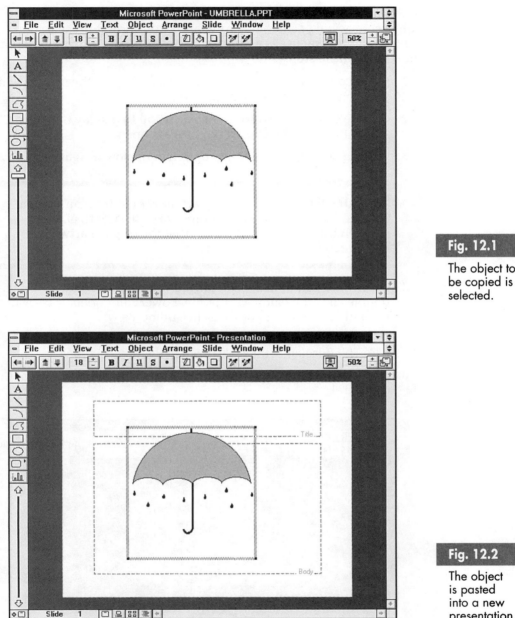

Fig. 12.1

The object to
be copied is
selected.

Fig. 12.2

The object
is pasted
into a new
presentation.

PowerPoint's clip art library contains 19 categories of related images—
from business items to sports symbols to international maps and flags.
For a complete list of file names, see Appendix C.

In this section, you learn how to copy a picture from the clip art subdirectory and paste the picture into a PowerPoint presentation. The sample picture you use is a Russian cathedral from the landmark.ppt file. Follow these steps:

1. Open your PowerPoint presentation and display the slide in which you want to paste a clip art picture.

2. Choose Open Clip Art from the File menu to display the Open Clip Art dialog box. The clip art directory is open.

3. Click the Open Untitled Copy option in the lower right corner.

> **CAUTION:** When using clip art, never cut from an original presentation in the clip art directory. Be sure to click the Open Untitled Copy option so that the original artwork is protected.

4. In the Files list, double-click the file you want to open. In this case, double-click the landmark.ppt file. PowerPoint opens a copy of the file and displays a list of slides in Outline View.

5. Double-click a slide to display it. In this case, double-click Slide #14. The Russian cathedral shown in figure 12.3 appears.

6. Select the item to copy it. In this example, click the picture of the cathedral.

Fig. 12.3

A selected clip art picture.

7. From the Edit menu, choose Copy.

8. From the File menu, choose Close. This step closes the clip art file from which you copied (unless you will use it again) and returns you to the PowerPoint presentation.

9. From the Edit menu, choose Paste. Your slide now looks like figure 12.4.

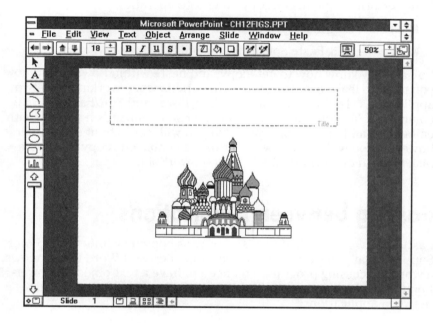

Fig. 12.4

The picture pasted into a slide.

The pasted object is selected in the slide so that you can make changes. You can move, copy, resize, crop, and recolor the object—just like any other graphics object.

Inserting Objects from Other Applications

Thanks to the power of Microsoft Windows, you can bring information from other Windows applications into a PowerPoint presentation. Sharing information between Windows applications saves you the trouble of re-creating work. For example, suppose that you used a drawing program to create a picture that you now want to include in your slide presentation. Instead of redrawing the picture in PowerPoint, you can paste a copy of the picture into your presentation. Or suppose that you typed an explanation of a business graph into a Windows word processing program. Instead of retyping the explanation in PowerPoint, you can copy it from your word processing file into your presentation.

When you want to bring objects into PowerPoint from other applications, you have three choices:

■ Perform a simple cut/copy and paste operation

■ Use the Edit/Insert command

■ Use the Edit/Paste Special command

You already know how to cut, copy, and paste within PowerPoint; now you need to learn how to use these functions when working with two applications. To do so, you use the Edit/Insert and Edit/Paste Special commands. The difference between the two commands has to do with embedded and linked objects, which you will learn about shortly. First, however, you will learn how to perform a simple cut/copy and paste task from an outside application into PowerPoint.

Pasting between Applications

Pasting between applications is as easy as copying within PowerPoint. Suppose that you want to copy text from Microsoft Word for Windows, a word processing program. You need to have a text object in PowerPoint into which you can paste the text. Follow these steps to paste between applications:

 If you are pasting a picture or other object, see the section "Using Embedded and Linked Objects," later in this chapter.

1. Create a text object in PowerPoint to receive the imported text. If a text object already exists, you can use that object, or use the body object.

2. Using standard Windows procedures, open the application from which you want to copy; then open the correct document or file from which you want to copy.

3. Select the items or text that you want to copy. Your screen now looks similar to figure 12.5.

4. Use the appropriate command (in this case, Cut or Copy from the Edit menu in Word for Windows) to place the selected text onto the Clipboard.

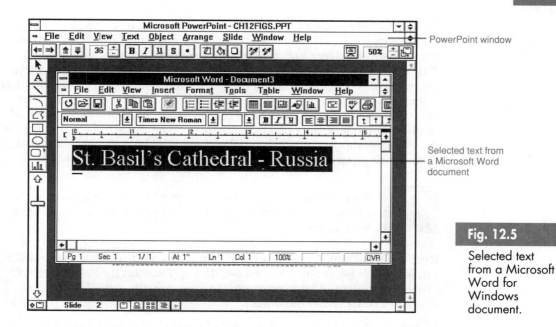

PowerPoint window

Selected text from
a Microsoft Word
document

Fig. 12.5

Selected text
from a Microsoft
Word for
Windows
document.

5. Return to the PowerPoint window by clicking any visible portion of the Window or by pressing Alt-Tab until PowerPoint is displayed.

6. Double-click in a text box to display the text cursor.

7. From the Edit menu, choose Paste.

Using Embedded and Linked Objects

Because of the way PowerPoint is designed, you have access from within PowerPoint to other Microsoft applications that exist on your system. For example, if you have Microsoft Excel installed on your system, you can access Excel from within PowerPoint. When an application is accessed from within PowerPoint, it is called an *embedded application*. The information you create using an embedded application is referred to as an *embedded object* because you create the object within PowerPoint.

Suppose, for example, that you access Microsoft Excel from within PowerPoint to create a simple spreadsheet. The spreadsheet you create becomes part of your PowerPoint presentation, even though you used Excel to create it. The spreadsheet does not exist as a file in Excel.

The advantage to using an embedded application to create an embedded object is that all the instructions your computer needs to display the embedded object are stored with the PowerPoint presentation. This means that your PowerPoint presentation file is always complete; you can run your presentation on another computer and the embedded objects will display correctly. The embedded application (such as Excel) does not have to be installed on the other computer. If you intend to give someone a copy of a presentation on a floppy disk to display on his or her computer, embed the objects you include so that the instructions for displaying the objects are included in the PowerPoint file.

NOTE   You can only access the embedded application used to create an embedded object if the application is installed on your computer.

By double-clicking an embedded object, you can directly access—without leaving PowerPoint—the embedded application that was used to create the object. When you return to PowerPoint, any changes you made are reflected in the object.

Although linked and embedded objects appear the same on-screen, the two items are quite different. A *linked object* is an object for which the instructions for displaying the object are stored *outside* PowerPoint—that is, in another application.

Suppose, again, that your presentation contains an Excel worksheet, but the worksheet is a linked object rather than an embedded object. The worksheet you see on the slide is located in Excel, as if you are looking through a hole in your presentation slide into Excel to view the worksheet you created. The worksheet itself is not part of your PowerPoint presentation file. The instructions for displaying the worksheet in PowerPoint are stored with Excel rather than with PowerPoint. If you want to give someone a copy of your file on disk, the worksheet object is not displayed because the PowerPoint file contains no instructions for displaying it. It doesn't matter whether or not the person who receives the file has Excel on his or her computer. Your computer contains the instructions needed to display the file.

A linked object maintains an active connection with its source document. If you update your Excel worksheet, therefore, the object in PowerPoint is updated as well.

Some guidelines for choosing between embedded and linked objects follow.

Use embedded objects:

- ■ If you want the objects to be visible on someone else's computer when you give the person a copy of your file

- ■ If you want to edit the object without leaving PowerPoint

- ■ If it doesn't matter whether or not the file for the object is attached to PowerPoint (that is, that the file doesn't exist on its own and cannot be edited elsewhere)

- ■ If the size of your PowerPoint file is not a concern (files with embedded objects can become quite large)

Use linked objects:

- ■ If you want the object to be updated in PowerPoint when you update the source document

- ■ If the file for the object you are embedding already exists, or if you want the file to exist independently of PowerPoint so that you can edit it independently

- ■ If the size of your PowerPoint file is a concern (linked objects don't significantly increase the size of your PowerPoint files)

Creating Embedded Objects

In the following example, you learn how to create a simple worksheet in Microsoft Excel and embed it in a PowerPoint presentation. Use the same basic steps to embed objects from other applications. (A complete list of supported file types and applications is shown when you display the Insert Object dialog box.) Follow these steps:

1. Display the presentation and the slide in which you want to place an embedded object.

2. Choose Insert from the Edit menu; then choose Object from the submenu that appears. The Insert Object dialog box appears (see fig. 12.6).

3. In the Object Type list, choose Microsoft Excel Worksheet; then click OK. Microsoft Excel opens and appears in the active window. Notice that the document is named Worksheet in *Filename*, where *filename* is the same name as your presentation.

4. Create the embedded object. For this example, create a simple worksheet in Excel several columns wide and several rows long.

5. From the Excel File menu, choose Update. The object in Power-Point is updated with the worksheet you created.

The object is selected so that you can move, resize, or make other modifications.

Fig. 12.6

The Insert Object
dialog box.

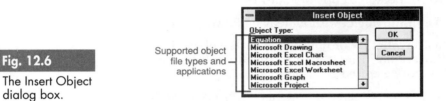

In this example, the worksheet is small when embedded in PowerPoint. In figure 12.7, the worksheet has been resized and moved to a new location.

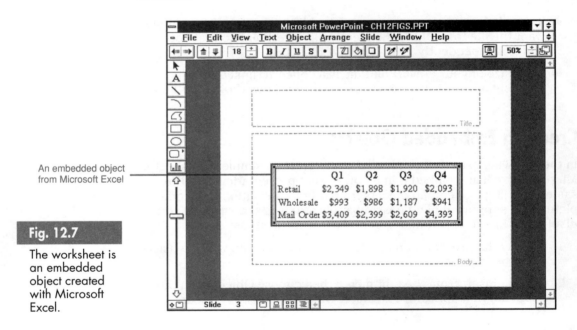

An embedded object
from Microsoft Excel

Fig. 12.7

The worksheet is
an embedded
object created
with Microsoft
Excel.

When you want to update the worksheet, double-click the worksheet object. Microsoft Excel opens and displays this file. Edit the worksheet, and then repeat steps 5 and 6 to update the object and return to PowerPoint.

NOTE The steps outlined may seem familiar from Chapter 8, in which you learned to create basic graphs. In fact, you were creating an embedded object when you created a graph. Instead of selecting the Insert command from the Edit menu, you clicked the Graph tool to open the Graph application. You created the graph, exited and returned to PowerPoint (the same step as updating in Excel), and the graph became an embedded object.

Creating Linked Objects

In this section, you again use an Excel worksheet as the example, but you create it as a linked object rather than an embedded object. You can use the same procedure to link objects from other applications. Follow these steps:

1. Open the presentation and display the slide where you want to place the linked object.

2. Open Microsoft Excel, and then open the file you want to link. (You can create a new file or use an existing one. If you create a new one, save and name it before you continue.)

3. Select the cells in the worksheet that you want to include in the linked object.

4. Choose Copy from the Edit menu to place a copy of the worksheet on the Clipboard.

5. Switch back to PowerPoint. (The fastest way is to press Alt-Tab until PowerPoint is displayed.)

6. Choose Paste Special from the Edit menu. The Paste Special dialog box appears (see fig. 12.8).

7. The Microsoft Excel Worksheet Object option should be selected in the Data Type box. If not, select it.

8. Click the Paste Link button. PowerPoint pastes the worksheet onto the slide and links it to the source document in Excel. The object is selected so that you can make changes. Click anywhere outside the object to deselect the object.

The worksheet is resized, cropped, and repositioned, (see fig. 12.9).

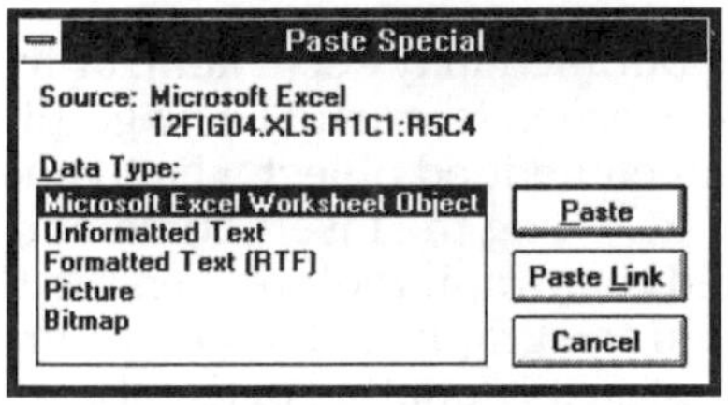

Paste Special

Source: Microsoft Excel
12FIG04.XLS R1C1:R5C4

Data Type:
Microsoft Excel Worksheet Object
Unformatted Text
Formatted Text (RTF)
Picture
Bitmap

Paste
Paste Link
Cancel

Fig. 12.8

The Paste Special
dialog box.

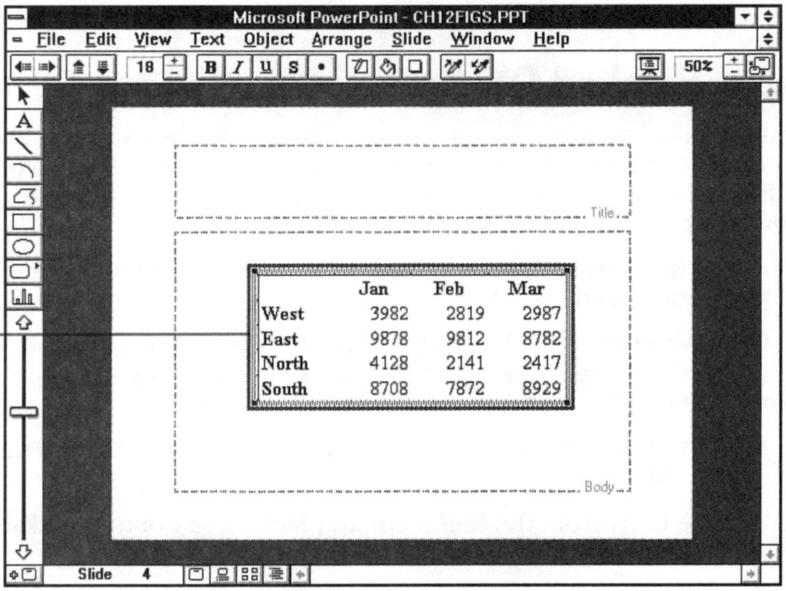

Microsoft PowerPoint - CH12FIGS.PPT

File   Edit   View   Text   Object   Arrange   Slide   Window   Help

18   B I U S   •   50%

Title

	Jan	Feb	Mar
West	3982	2819	2987
East	9878	9812	8782
North	4128	2141	2417
South	8708	7872	8929

Body

A linked object from
Microsoft Excel

Slide   4

Fig. 12.9

The worksheet is
a linked object.

When you want to update the worksheet, start Excel and open the
worksheet file, make the appropriate changes, and then return to
PowerPoint. The worksheet is automatically updated in PowerPoint.

Inserting a Text Outline

PowerPoint's Text Outline feature can save you a great deal of time
creating slides. If you have outlined text in a word processing document, you can bring the file into PowerPoint to create new slides in a
presentation.

Some word processing programs, such as Lotus Manuscript and
Microsoft Word, come with an outliner that you use to create an outline. You can then transfer the text of the outline to PowerPoint. If your

word processing program does not have an Outliner tool, you can create an outline yourself, using a tab for each heading level in the outline. PowerPoint will still accept the text and incorporate it into slides. Provided that the file type for the document is .doc, .txt, or .rtf, PowerPoint can create slides from the file.

Suppose that you have a document that contains outlined text, such as the one in figure 12.10. This particular example shows a simple outline created in Microsoft Word with the Microsoft Word outliner, but you can use any outline or series of headings created using tabs.

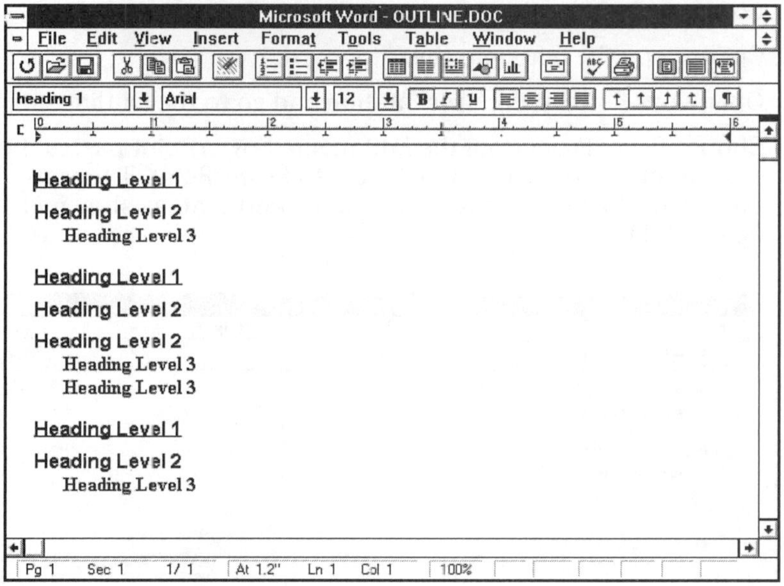

Fig. 12.10

A sample of outlined text in a Microsoft Word document.

You can create a set of PowerPoint slides from this file in one of three ways:

- Cut or copy the text from the word processing document, and then paste it into PowerPoint

- Use the File Open command in PowerPoint to open the .doc, .txt, or .rtf file

- Choose the Edit Insert command, and then choose Outline to insert the .doc, .txt, or .rtf file

This chapter covers all three methods. In each case, PowerPoint creates a new slide at every level 1 heading and uses the text of the level 1 heading as the slide title. Subheadings are included on the same slide as body text. When the document is short, any of the three methods work well. When the document is long, the last two methods are more efficient and easier to perform.

Cutting or Copying an Outline

To cut or copy an outline from a .doc, .txt, or .rtf file and paste it into PowerPoint, follow these steps:

1. Open the word processing document that contains the outline text. Save the file with a file extension of .doc, .txt, or .rtf.

2. Cut or copy the text onto the Clipboard.

3. Open your PowerPoint presentation and go to the Outline view.

4. Choose Paste From from the Edit menu. PowerPoint pastes the content of the .doc, .txt, or .rtf file into PowerPoint. The word processor document is recreated in PowerPoint, as shown in figure 12.11.

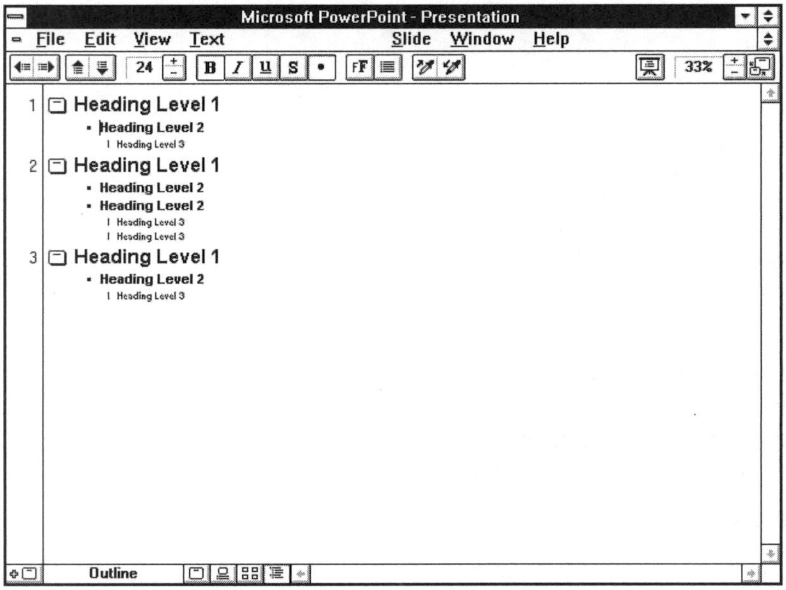

Fig. 12.11

The document shown in Outline View was pasted from Microsoft Word.

Opening an Outline File

To open a .doc, .txt, or .rtf file directly from PowerPoint and create new slides, follow these steps:

1. Make sure that the word processing document that contains the outline text is saved with a file extension of .doc, .txt, or .rtf.

2. Open the PowerPoint presentation where you want to insert the outline, and choose Slide View or Outline view.

3. From the File menu, choose Open. The Open dialog box appears (see fig. 12.12).

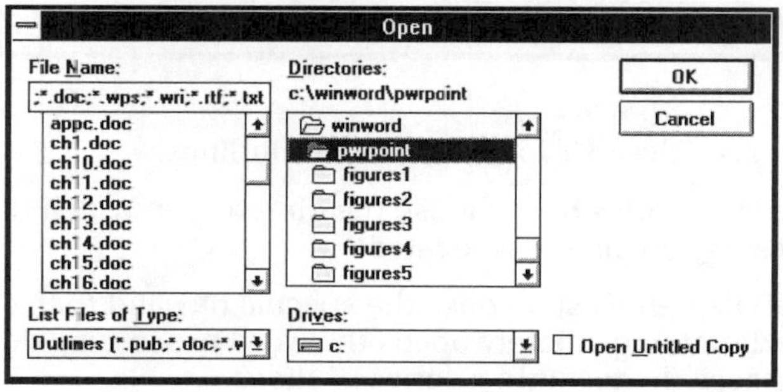

Fig. 12.12

The Open dialog box.

4. In the List Files of Type box, choose Outlines.

5. In the Directories list, choose the directory in which the word processing document is located.

6. In the File Name list, choose the specific file, and then click OK. PowerPoint immediately opens the word processing document and places the text into a series of slides. The screen looks similar to figure 12.11.

Inserting an Outline File

To use the Edit Insert Outline command to insert a .doc, .txt, or .rtf file in PowerPoint, follow these steps:

1. Make sure that the word processing document that contains the outline text is saved with a file extension of .doc, .txt, or .rtf; otherwise PowerPoint cannot read the file.

2. Open the PowerPoint presentation where you want to insert the outline, and choose Slide view or Outline view.

3. From the Edit menu, choose Insert. From the submenu, choose Outline. PowerPoint displays the Insert Outline dialog box (see fig. 12.13).

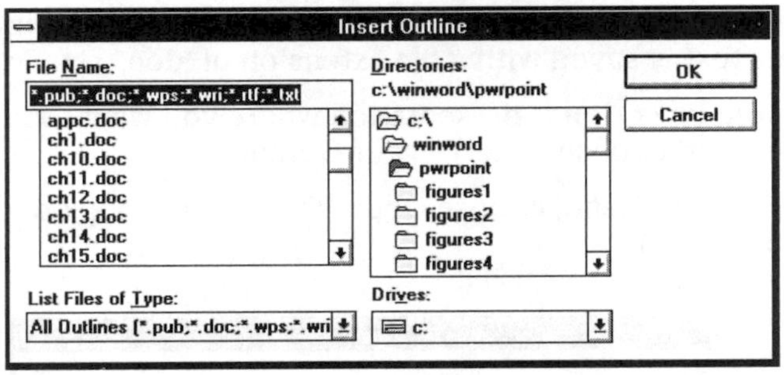

Fig. 12.13

The Insert Outline dialog box.

4. In the List Files of Type box, choose Outlines.

5. In the Directories box, choose the directory in which the word processing document is located.

6. In the File Name list, choose the specific file, and then click OK. PowerPoint immediately opens the word processing document and places the text into a series of slides.

Use any of these three methods to import a word processing document or outline into PowerPoint. After the file is in PowerPoint, you can move, copy, rearrange, reformat, or add to or delete the content, as you can in any other PowerPoint file.

Inserting a Picture

When you want to insert a picture that exists in an application outside of PowerPoint, use the Edit Insert Picture command. You can insert pictures from applications that support any of the following file extensions: *.wmf, *.dxf, *.eps, *.pcx, *.cgm, *.pic, *.dib, *.drw, *.hgl, *.tif, *.plt, *.wpg, *.pct, *.bmp. Follow these steps:

1. Display the presentation and the slide where you want to insert a picture.

2. From the Edit menu, choose Insert. From the submenu, choose Picture. PowerPoint displays the Insert Picture dialog box (see fig. 12.14).

4. In the List Files of Type box, choose a category or specific file type for the picture file you're inserting.

5. In the Directories box, choose the directory in which the picture is located.

6. In the File Name list, choose the specific file to insert, and then click OK. PowerPoint pastes the picture into the current slide.

Figure 12.15 shows a toucan, a clip art picture copied from Windows Draw!, a Micrographx program.

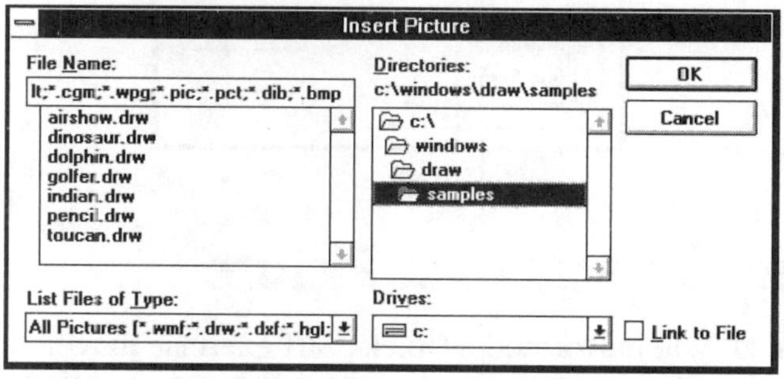

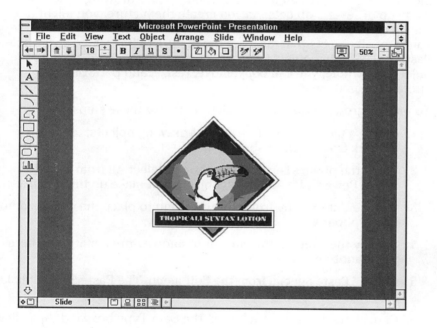

Fig. 12.14

The Insert Picture dialog box.

Fig. 12.15

A clip art picture copied from Windows Draw!

Note that for certain file types, a filter dialog box, similar to the one shown in figure 12.16, might be displayed. The filter dialog box enables PowerPoint to convert the file type so that it can be used in PowerPoint. Choose the options you want to use, and then click OK.

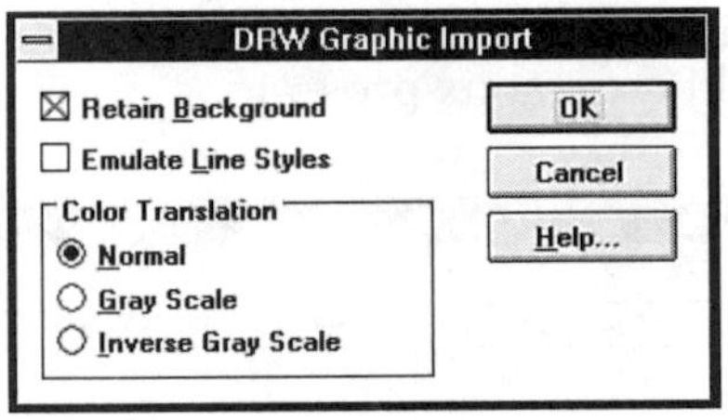

Fig. 12.16

A filter dialog
box.

Pasting Objects as a Picture

In Chapter 11, you performed a Quick Start exercise in which you selected a group of objects and pasted them to a new location as one
picture. This feature can be useful when you are drawing a picture
made up of several objects. As you create the picture, you might not
want to group the objects together, but when the picture is complete,
you want all objects that make up the picture to be treated as a whole.
Pasting all selected objects as a whole enables you to manipulate the
object as a whole; you can copy, move, resize, and perform other
operations on the entire picture.

To paste a group of objects as a picture, follow these steps:

1. Create a picture using PowerPoint drawing objects, text, or
   artwork from another source.

2. When the picture is complete, choose Select All from the Edit
   menu. PowerPoint selects all objects that make up the picture.

3. Choose Cut or Copy from the Edit menu to place the objects onto
   the Clipboard.

4. Display the slide (in the current or another presentation) where
   you want to paste the picture.

5. Choose Paste Special from the Edit menu. The Paste Special dialog
   box appears.

6. Choose the Picture option from the Data Type box, and then click
   Paste. PowerPoint pastes the objects onto the slide as one picture. The single selection box around the picture indicates it is
   now one object.

Cropping an Object

Often you may create or import into a presentation a picture that needs
to be cropped. *Cropping* means blocking the edges of the picture from

view. You might crop a picture that includes too much information or that is surrounded by unnecessary white or blank space. When you crop a picture, you don't lose any part of it; you simply "cover" unwanted areas of the picture.

To crop a picture, follow these steps:

1. Display the slide that contains the picture you want to crop; then select the picture by clicking it.

2. From the Object menu, choose Crop Picture. The mouse pointer changes to the Cropping tool.

3. Position the center of the Cropping tool over one of the resize handles on the selection box.

4. Click and drag the tool to block out the extraneous parts of the picture; then release the mouse button.

To return a cropped picture to its original form, select the picture, and then choose Crop Picture from the Object menu. Place the Crop tool over the lower left resize handle and drag the handle out until the frame freezes. When the frame cannot be enlarged further, the picture is restored to its original form. Release the mouse button.

Creating Special Effects

You can create a variety of special effects with PowerPoint. PowerPoint provides templates with special effects, and you can also customize your own effects.

The process of creating special effects usually involves drawing, coloring, copying, pasting, grouping, and then repeating these steps as many times as necessary. In this section, you learn how to create the repeating pattern for a slide background shown in figure 12.17. The slide background was created with a patterned fill. The diagonal lines were drawn with the Line tool, colored, copied, then positioned on the slide.

Usually, you want the colors in the pattern and the background to be similar. Otherwise, any text or objects you draw on the slide become less visible. Follow these steps to create the pattern shown in figure 12.17. Before you begin, delete the title and body objects from the slide. To use the pattern on all slides, create it on the Slide Master.

1. Using the Line tool, draw a diagonal line in the upper left part of your slide. (Hold down the Shift key as you draw to make a perfect diagonal line.) Choose a thin line style from the Line Style submenu on the Object menu.

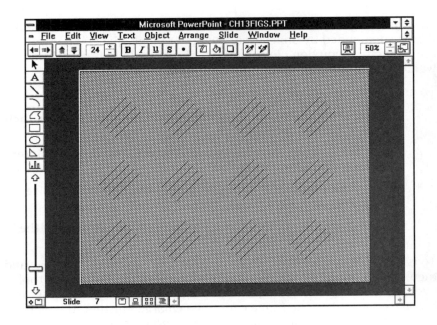

Fig. 12.17

A repeating pattern created with the Line drawing tool.

2. To color the line, choose Line from the Object menu. Choose a color from the list shown, or click Other Color to choose a color outside the current scheme.

3. Copy and paste the line three times. The Paste command in PowerPoint places the pasted lines down and to the right. You can move the pasted lines if you want.

4. Select all four lines, and then choose Group from the Arrange menu. The four lines are now grouped as one object.

5. Draw a horizontal guide line about 2 inches from the top of the slide. You will use this line to position the lines.

6. Copy and paste the object three times. Position each object along the line to form the top row of lines as shown in figure 12.17.

7. Select all four objects, and then choose Group from the Arrange menu. The top row of lines are now grouped as one object.

8. Copy and paste the object two times. Place the two copies into position to form the second and third rows of lines on the slide.

9. Create a shaded background for the lines. Use the Rectangle tool to draw an object the same size and dimensions as the slide background.

10. While the rectangle is still selected, choose Send to Back from the Arrange menu to move the background behind the line objects you just drew.

11. From the Object menu, choose Fill. When the submenu appears, choose the Patterned option.

12. In the Patterned Fill box, choose a pattern, a foreground, and a background color. In figure 12.17, the left-diagonal line pattern (third pattern in the second row) was used to fill the rectangle.

13. Click OK to close the Patterned Fill dialog box.

At this point, your screen should look like the one shown in figure 12.17. You can now add title and body objects to the slide. (Use the Add Title and Add Body commands on the Slide menu.) Figure 12.18 shows how the slide looks with a title and body text. The background shows through the Title and body objects because their fill default is None. If you add other text objects to the slide, be sure to specify None for the fill to have background show through behind the text.

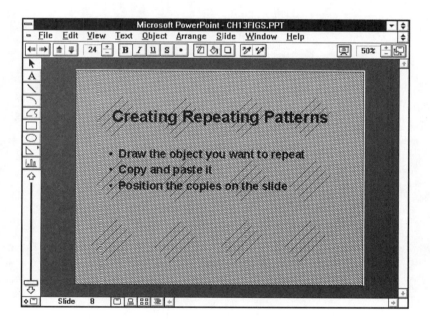

Fig. 12.18

A title and body text was added to the custom background.

Chapter Summary

In this chapter, you learned how to copy and move objects from one PowerPoint presentation into another. You also learned the steps for copying objects from other applications into PowerPoint. In this context, you discovered the difference between embedded and linked objects and reviewed the guidelines for determining when to use each type of object. You also learned how to copy an outline and a picture or clip art from another application into PowerPoint. These skills help you learn to use PowerPoint and other applications efficiently.

In the next chapter, you learn about advanced features of PowerPoint text.

Using Advanced Text Features

PowerPoint offers more word processing flexibility than many word processors. In fact, PowerPoint provides so many formatting combinations and possibilities that ordinary functions such as indenting and spacing can become quite complicated. But you do not need to know everything about these capabilities to use them effectively. After you feel comfortable with the basics, you might want to learn and use some of PowerPoint's advanced text features. This chapter will get you started.

This chapter shows you how to display the ruler, how to set indents and tabs using the ruler, and how to apply those indents and tabs to text. It discusses the options that PowerPoint provides for line and paragraph spacing, and provides directions for changing default settings (either for the current presentation or for all future presentations). Finally, it shows you how to work with the custom dictionary in your spelling checker—how to add and delete special words, names, and acronyms.

Understanding PowerPoint's Ruler

Every text object in PowerPoint has an associated *ruler* that is used to set the indents, wraps, and tabs for that text object. To display the ruler for a text object, first select the text object; then choose the Show Ruler command from the Text menu or press Ctrl-R. Figure 13.1 shows the ruler for the body object on the Slide Master.

As shown in previous chapters, the body object can accommodate up to five indented heading levels; each time you press the Tab key, PowerPoint automatically indents your text to the next heading level. The Slide Master shown in figure 13.1 provides a good visual example because it includes a sample of text entered at each heading level. This chapter shows you how PowerPoint creates these levels.

The ruler displays *indents*, which set the left margin for complete paragraphs, and *tabs*, which enable you to insert text at a specified column location on the current line. Indents set both the starting point of the current line and the *wrap*, or the starting point of succeeding lines. Tabs set text positions for only the current line. If the text wraps to additional lines after a tab has been set, the text returns to the initial left margin.

The markings on the ruler denote inches on a printed slide, not on-screen. If you have set your operating environment for the metric system, the marks on the ruler represent centimeters.

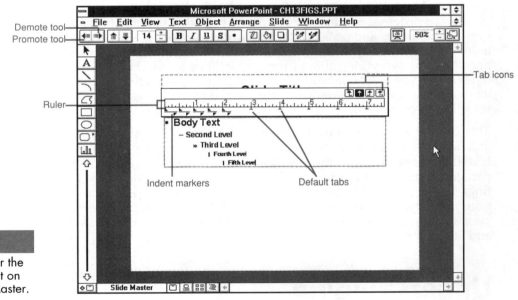

Fig. 13.1

The ruler for the body object on the Slide Master.

Indenting Text

Each indent that has been set on the ruler can be identified by two markers: an upper triangle that shows the indent position for the first line, and a lower triangle that shows the indent position for the remaining lines in the paragraph (the wrap). The first pair of indent markers (an upper and lower triangle joined by a dotted line) indicate the positioning of text at heading level 1. Each additional pair of indent markers indicates the positioning of text at each of the other four heading levels.

To enter text at heading level one, begin typing and continue typing (don't press Enter) until you're ready to type a new entry. When an entry is longer than one line, the characters *wrap* (move down) to the next line and are aligned at the position of the lower triangle— the wrap for remaining lines in the paragraph. When you press Enter, PowerPoint begins a new heading level 1 entry; that is, the insertion point returns to the upper triangle position.

To indent your text to a new heading level, press the Tab key, or click the Demote tool (again see fig. 13.1), and then start typing. Each time you press Tab or click Demote, the text you entered after the Tab appears at the next heading level.

Indenting text at different heading levels is also know as *outlining*. For more information on outlining and changing text from one heading level to another, see Chapter 9, "Creating Notes Pages, Handouts, and Outlines."

T I P

Changing Indentation

If you do not set indents the way you want them *before* entering your text, you can also change the indentation of existing text. If you insert a ruler after you begin typing, the settings apply to text that you type afterward. Suppose that you want to change the indentation of the text shown in figure 13.2. This figure shows several paragraphs that are aligned at each of the five indentation levels; the text at levels 2 through 5 includes bullets to help illustrate the points at which text entries wrap.

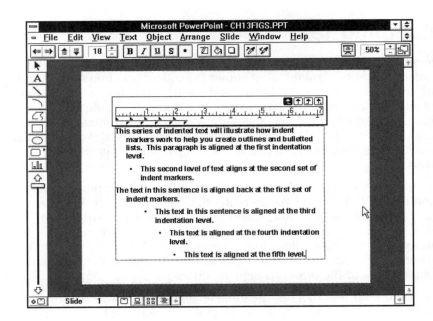

Fig. 13.2

Text indented at different levels.

Suppose that you want to align all the text under the first heading at the left margin, eliminating the indented wrap. Follow these steps:

1. Select the text object that contains the text you want to indent.

2. Choose Show Text Ruler from the Text menu. On the ruler, you see the five pairs of triangles that mark the heading levels.

3. To move an indent marker, click the triangle and drag it to the new position. In this case, drag the first lower marker to the left until it lines up with the first upper marker.

4. To switch off the ruler, click outside the text object.

The text in the first paragraph now lines up according to the new position of the first indent markers (see fig. 13.3).

In some cases, you might want to move a set of markers together without altering their relative position, instead of moving them independently. If you want to move the second indent level in the sample text slightly to the left, for example, follow these steps:

1. Select the text object that contains the text you want to indent.

2. Choose Show Text Ruler from the Text menu. On the ruler, you see the five pairs of triangles that mark the heading levels.

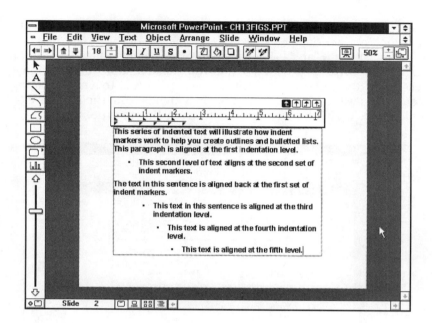

Fig. 13.3

First paragraph
text realigned
with the new
indent markers.

3. Click the dotted line between the markers and drag it to the new position on the ruler. In this case, drag the second pair of markers a space or two to the left. Figure 13.4 shows how your text might look after taking this step.

NOTE If you move the second set of indent markers to the right (instead of to the left), you cannot move them past the third set of indent markers. If you attempt to do so, you simply push the level 3 markers farther to the right.

4. To switch off the ruler, click outside the text object.

If you want to move text from one existing indentation level to another, you do not need to alter the indent markers. Simply click the Demote or Promote tool on the Toolbar. Refer to Chapter 9 for complete instructions on changing text levels.

Setting Tabs

Unlike indents, tabs determine how text is positioned *within* the current line. A tab enables you to enter text at a specified column location (or locations) within the current line. PowerPoint places a default tab at every inch marker on each ruler. A later section of this chapter— "Resetting Default Tabs"—shows you how to change these default tab positions. In order to position text at the next available tab position, press Ctrl-Tab. (Pressing Tab alone moves your text to a new heading level.) If you want a line of text to begin 3 inches from the left, for example, press Ctrl-Tab three times before starting to type.

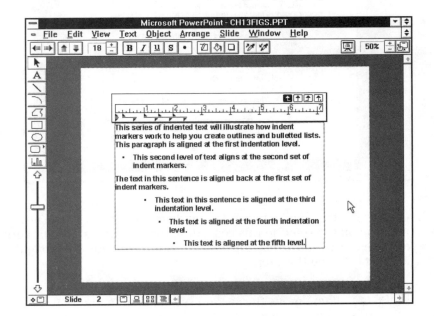

Fig. 13.4

Text with the second indentation level moved slightly to the left.

The default tabs on the ruler are *left-aligned tabs*. They can be changed as needed. You can also add new tabs that are *right-aligned*, *center-aligned*, or *decimal-aligned*.

Figure 13.5 shows four text entries produced using left-, center-, right-, and decimal-aligned tabs. Text typed at a left-aligned tab appears to the right of the tab. At a right-aligned tab, the text entered appears to the left of the tab. When you enter text at a center-aligned tab, PowerPoint spaces it equally to the right and left of the tab.

Decimal-aligned tabs are used to enter columns of numbers rather than text; they serve a different function than the other three types of tabs. When you enter text at a decimal-aligned tab, PowerPoint vertically aligns the decimal points in your entries.

To set and use tabs, follow these steps:

1. Use the Text tool to create a text block; choose the Show Ruler command from the Text menu to display the text ruler.

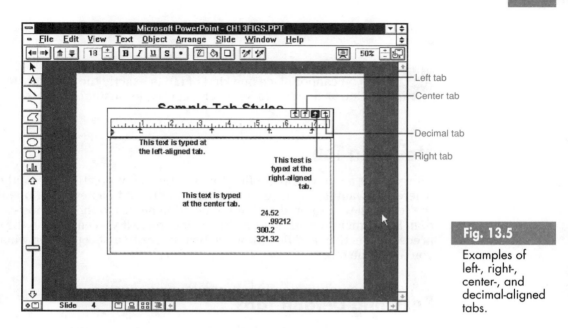

Fig. 13.5

Examples of left-, right-, center-, and decimal-aligned tabs.

2. Choose one of the tab tools (left, center, right, or decimal) from the right side of the ruler. The default tab type is left-aligned. For this example, choose the Center tab tool.

3. Position the mouse pointer at the point underneath the rule line in the text ruler box where you want the tab stop to appear. Click once. For this example, click under the 3-inch mark. The tab marker appears below the ruler.

4. Click the beginning of a line in the text object.

5. Press Ctrl-Tab until the cursor is positioned under the tab.

 NOTE The number of times you press Ctrl-Tab depends on how many indent markers and tabs appear before the tab you want to use. The cursor stops at the next indent marker or tab each time you press Ctrl-Tab.

6. Type the text you want to align at the tab. For this example, type *This text is typed at a center-aligned tab.* You are typing at a center tab, so the text moves alternately to the right and left of the center point as you type.

7. Click anywhere outside of the text object to hide the ruler and deselect the object.

You can use these steps to set and use left, right, and decimal tabs, as well.

 You cannot place one kind of tab in exactly the same position as another (a left over a center, for instance).

Moving a Tab

After setting a tab, you might find that the tab is not positioned exactly where you want it. To move a tab, click and drag it to a new position on the ruler. All text entered at that tab position moves to the new position. Experiment with this procedure using the text you entered in the preceding section, and note how the text moves to a new position when you move the tab.

Resetting Default Tabs

You can respace PowerPoint's default tabs by clicking one tab and dragging it to a new position. (Note that you cannot *delete* PowerPoint's default tabs.) Suppose that you want to place default tabs every one-half inch rather than every inch. Click any default tab and hold down the mouse button. All default tabs are removed from the ruler except the one immediately to the right or left of the selected tab. Drag the tab you clicked until it is positioned one-half inch from the other tab. When you release the mouse button, the default tabs reappear on the ruler at one-half-inch intervals.

Deleting Tabs

To delete a tab, simply click the appropriate tab marker and drag it off the ruler above or below the ruler line. The selected tab disappears from the ruler. Remember that you cannot delete default tabs.

Setting Line and Paragraph Spacing

Line spacing determines the amount of space that appears between lines of type; *paragraph spacing* determines the amount of space that appears between paragraphs. Setting line and paragraph spacing might seem a simple matter of specifying the number of blank lines to be placed between lines of type or paragraphs, but it is not that simple. When you set line spacing to 1, for example, you create what is commonly known as *single-spaced* text. But a look at the resulting document makes it clear that the lines of text are not separated by single blank lines, even though the line spacing is set to 1. This perceived discrepancy results because one *spacing line* is defined as 120 percent of the largest point size used in the line. If you are using a 10 point font and you set line spacing to 1, one line of spacing is equal to 12 points. So *line spacing* doesn't refer to the space *between* lines, but to the total height of the line of text and the blank space between it and the line preceding it.

NOTE Unless you need precise measurements on a slide, do not get too analytical about line and paragraph spacing. It's often just as easy to set line spacing based on subjective qualities, the most important of which is *readability*. Always make sure the text is readable for the type of presentation you're delivering.

PowerPoint enables you to change line and paragraph spacing using units of lines or points. If you're not accustomed to working with points, one point is equal to 1/72 inch. When you work with an 18-point font, for example, the height of the text is actually 18/72 inch, or one-quarter inch. PowerPoint does enable you to change the spacing units from lines to points.

Paragraph spacing can become confusing because it involves two different settings: the space *before* a paragraph and the space *after* a paragraph. Many new users make the mistake of specifying an amount for *both*; they don't realize that the two amounts are combined when PowerPoint spaces between paragraphs. If you set the space after a paragraph to 1.5 and the space before a paragraph to 1.5, for example, the total space between paragraphs is 3. For this reason, change one setting—usually the space before a paragraph—and leave the other setting at 0.

You can select as much or as little text as you want when you are making spacing changes. To change the spacing for all text in a text object, select the text object. To change line spacing for a single paragraph, select a part of the paragraph or position the cursor anywhere within the paragraph. To change spacing for multiple paragraphs, select some text from each of the paragraphs.

To adjust line and paragraph spacing, follow these steps:

1. Select the text you want to adjust.

2. Choose Line Spacing from the Text menu. The Line Spacing dialog box appears (see fig. 13.6). Notice that line spacing in the figure is set to .90, or 90 percent, rather than 120 percent—slightly less than one spacing line.

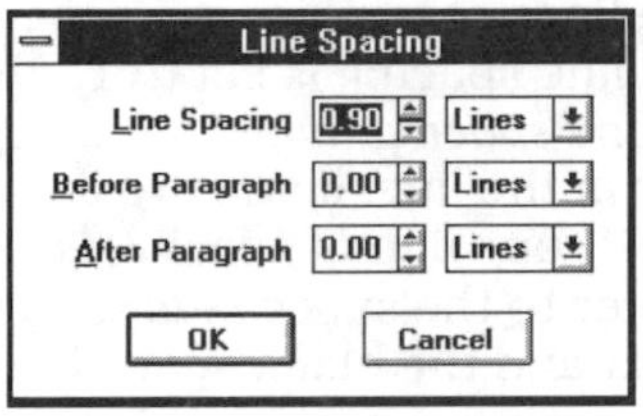

Fig. 13.6

The Line Spacing dialog box.

3. Set the line spacing by clicking the up or down arrows (or typing a number) in the Line Spacing box.

T I P   As you adjust the number in the box, PowerPoint reformats the selected text to the new setting. Move the dialog box out of the way, if necessary, so that you can see the changes to the text as you work.

4. Set the space before a paragraph by clicking the up or down arrows (or typing a number) in the Before Paragraph box.

5. Set the space after a paragraph by clicking the up or down arrows (or typing a number) in the After Paragraph box.

6. When the settings are correct, click OK.

Figure 13.7 shows several on-screen examples of various line and paragraph spacing.

T I P   If you prefer to work with points rather than lines as a unit of measure, click the drop-down box for each option and select Points. When you switch to points, PowerPoint automatically converts the current setting into its equivalent in points. If the selected text is 24 points and line spacing is set to 1, for example, the number shown changes to 29 (120 percent of 24) when you change the unit to points.

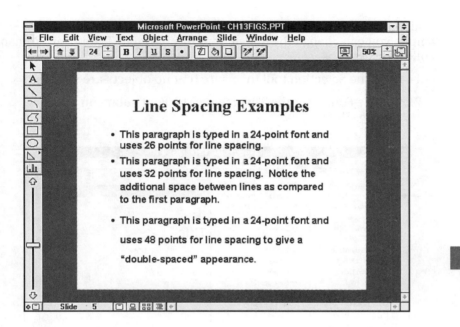

Fig. 13.7

Examples of line
and paragraph
spacing.

NOTE You should always have a good reason for changing the spacing of a document, such as to distinguish one section of text from another or a heading level from its text. Line spacing on slides should be slightly wider than what you would normally use for a printed document; more space between lines makes text more readable on-screen.

Creating New Default Settings

When you are working on a new presentation and choose the Use Default Format option in the New dialog box, PowerPoint applies the default settings to the file. *Defaults* are the initial settings that PowerPoint uses for text color, font size, outline, fill, and shadow color. PowerPoint uses many default settings, some of which you may never be aware of or use. PowerPoint's default options are indicated by a diamond shape on the submenus where those settings appear. See Appendix B for listings of the various PowerPoint default settings.

You can change the default settings for the presentation you are working on at any time, but it's best to change them before you begin. The new default settings then apply to every element on each slide. If you change default settings after you begin a presentation, the objects that have been entered already do not change to the new default settings.

You follow a basic set of steps to change default settings. As an example, you can change the default font from Arial to Times New Roman. Follow these steps:

1. Click the Selection tool to ensure that no objects are selected.

2. Choose Font from the Text menu. The Font submenu appears (see fig. 13.8).

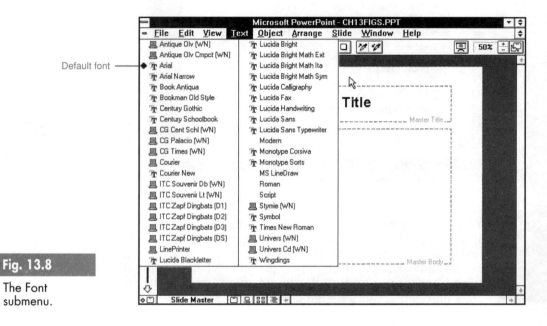

Default font

Fig. 13.8

The Font submenu.

3. Choose the Times New Roman font, and then release the mouse button. The default font becomes Times New Roman; the diamond shape now appears in the new location (see fig. 13.9).

PowerPoint also enables you to change the default settings used for all new presentations. These settings are determined by the masters in a file called default.ppt. You can reset PowerPoint's defaults manually, or you can replace them with the defaults from an existing presentation. Follow these steps:

1. Open the presentation that contains the settings you want to use as new defaults, or create a new presentation and change the defaults.

2. Choose Save As from the File menu. The Save As dialog box appears (see fig. 13.10).

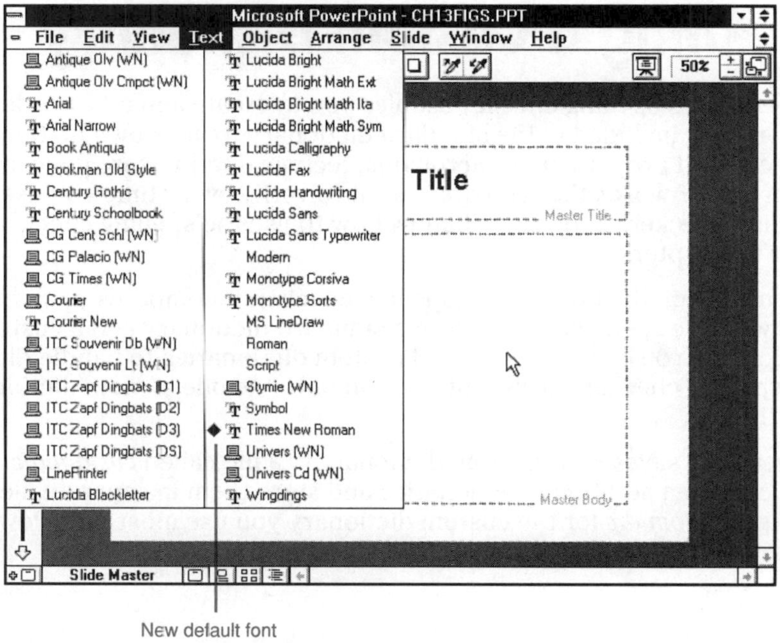

Fig. 13.9

The new default
font.

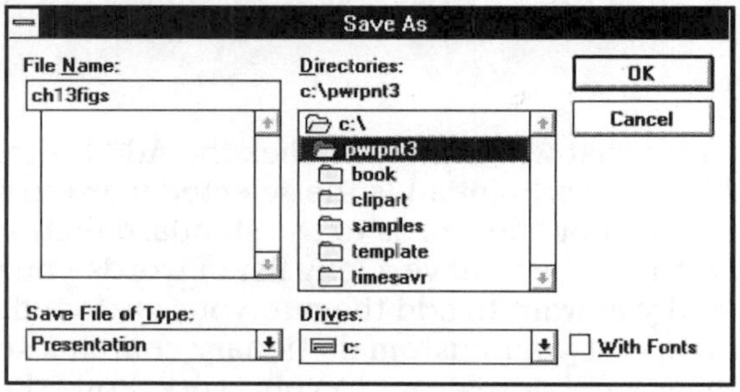

New default font

Fig. 13.10

The Save As
dialog box.

3. Select the PowerPoint directory, usually named *pwrpoint*. In figure 13.10, this directory is named *pwrpnt3*.

4. In the File Name box, type *default.ppt*, and then click OK.

Think twice before resetting PowerPoint's defaults. These default settings have been developed with care to work well with a variety of presentation styles. Your own variations might work well for some presentations, but they might not work as well as the original defaults for others. Remember that when you change the original defaults, you permanently change the *default.ppt* file. The only ways to restore the original defaults at that point are to reset them all manually or to recover the old *default.ppt* file from a backup.

Creating a Custom Dictionary

PowerPoint's spelling checker enables you to create and add words that are not included in the standard dictionary to your own dictionary. You can add proper names, acronyms, technical terms, foreign words, or any other words that you don't want to verify every time you use the spelling checker. If you do not know how to use the spelling checker, refer to Chapter 4.

When you run the PowerPoint spelling checker, it compares your spellings with the spellings of words in a standard dictionary and a custom dictionary. You can create several custom dictionaries to handle different spelling checking tasks, but you can only use one custom dictionary at a time.

PowerPoint saves your custom dictionary in a file called *custom.dic*. You can open additional dictionaries and store them in separate files, but use *custom.dic* for the custom dictionary you use most. The Power-Point spelling checker automatically starts with this file.

T I P If you create extra dictionary files, store them in the same directory as PowerPoint. Then when you do a spelling check, you can instruct PowerPoint to check those dictionaries one at a time.

Chapter 4 explains that whenever you click the Add button while checking spelling, PowerPoint adds the selected word to the custom dictionary. (You cannot add words to the standard dictionary file.) Suppose, however, that you have a long list of words you use routinely in your work and you want to add them to your custom dictionary all at once. Or suppose that your custom dictionary contains some words that are no longer valid or relevant to your work. PowerPoint lets you add or remove these words quickly in order to keep your custom dictionary up to date. Follow these steps to open the custom dictionary and make changes:

1. Open any presentation, or create a new presentation.

2. Choose Spelling from the Text menu. The Spelling dialog box appears (see fig. 13.11).

3. Click the Dictionary button. The Custom Dictionary box appears (see fig. 13.12).

   The dictionary displayed in the Custom Dictionary box is *custom.dic*—PowerPoint's default custom dictionary.

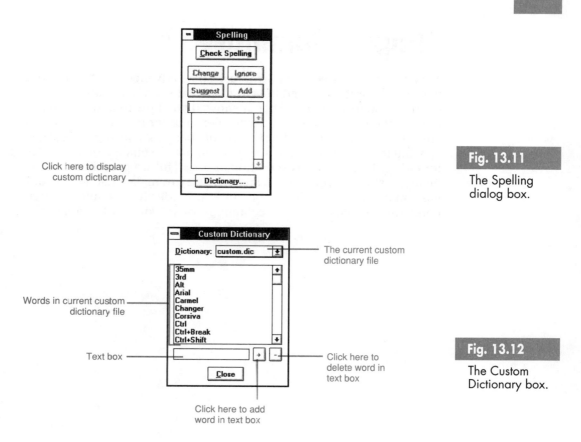

Click here to display
custom dictionary

Fig. 13.11

The Spelling
dialog box.

The current custom
dictionary file

Words in current custom
dictionary file

Text box

Click here to
delete word in
text box

Fig. 13.12

The Custom
Dictionary box.

Click here to add
word in text box

4. If you have created other custom dictionaries and want to make changes in one of them, select it from the drop-down list.

5. To add a new word to the dictionary, type the new word in the text box to the left of the +/– buttons, and then click the plus (+) button. PowerPoint adds the word to the existing list and displays it with the other words in alphabetic order.

6. To remove a word from the dictionary, select it from the list. The word appears in the word box. Click the minus (–) button and PowerPoint removes the word from the list.

The changes you make in a custom dictionary take effect the next time you use the spelling checker. The words you added are not questioned again.

Chapter Summary

This chapter showed you how to use some advanced text formatting features. First it explained how to display the text ruler and how to change indents and tabs. Then it showed you how to add left, right, center, and decimal tabs on a text ruler in order to enter text in some special ways. It covered the process of changing line and paragraph spacing in text objects, and showed you how to change default settings for either the current presentation or for all future presentations. And finally, it showed you a quick and easy way to make changes to your custom dictionaries. The next chapter provides helpful information concerning some advanced techniques for working with graphs.

Using Advanced Graph Features

Chapter 8, "Creating Basic Graphs," showed you how to express your data using the graph types available in PowerPoint. It explained PowerPoint's many options for displaying data in the Datasheet window and creating graphs in the Chart window. This chapter expands on the material covered in Chapter 8 and provides information concerning the more advanced features of the datasheet and the available graph forms.

This chapter covers the processes of creating custom number formats, excluding and including rows and columns, and formatting data for a scatter graph. It also shows you how to hide or display axes, how to change the scales used on axes, and how to change tick marks and their labels. It explains gridlines, shows you how to display data labels on a graph, and gives you instructions for copying a graph to another application, such as Microsoft Word.

This chapter also outlines procedures for replacing the default datasheet and graph that appear when you first enter Graph, and importing data from other applications, such as spreadsheets. In addition, the chapter includes instructions for importing charts directly from Microsoft Excel.

Customizing the Datasheet

You can use a number of advanced features when you work in the datasheet. You can design a custom format, include or exclude rows from chart calculations, and format the axes for a scatter graph. This section discusses these options.

Designing a Custom Format

As you learned in Chapter 8, PowerPoint Graph comes with an impressive array of number formats. You might find, however, that the available formats do not always meet your needs. If you need to use a format that PowerPoint does not provide, you can create your own.

Table 8.2 in Chapter 8 lists some of the symbols that can be used to modify Graph number formats. Table 14.1 in this chapter displays some of the additional symbols you can use to customize Graph's number formats. For a complete list, see on-line Help or the Microsoft PowerPoint Handbook.

Table 14.1 Symbols for Numeric Formats

Symbol	Description	Example
"text"	Displays the text enclosed in quotation marks.	If the format is "No." 0000, the entry 1395 is displayed as No. 1395.
[color]	Displays the contents of the cell in the specified color. Colors include Black, White, Red, Green, Blue, Cyan, Yellow, and Magenta.	If the format is is [red]#,###, the number is displayed in red.
$ - + ( ) space	Of these characters, displays the character you specify.	If the format is 00-00-0000, the number 21334987 is displayed as 21-33-4987.
,	Displays the comma as a thousands separator.	If the format is #,###, the number 2109 is displayed as 2,109.
*	Repeats the next character specified in the format enough times to fill the column width.	If the format is *&, the entry 29.11 is displayed as &&&&&&.

Creating a Custom Format

The following steps show you how to create a custom format in which you change the display color of a cell entry. You can use the principles outlined in these steps, along with the information in tables 8.2 and 14.1 (refer to Chapter 8 for table 8.2), to create other types of custom formats.

1. Select the cell or cells that you want to format.

2. Choose Number from the Format menu. The Number dialog box appears (see fig. 14.1).

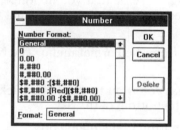

Fig. 14.1

The Number dialog box.

3. Choose the format that looks most similar to the one you want to create. This step is not essential, but it can save you time. For this example, choose #,##0.

   The chosen format appears in the Format box, located at the bottom of the dialog box. If you do not select a format, the default format—General—appears in this box.

4. Click the format displayed in the Format box at the bottom of the dialog box; the mouse pointer changes to a line cursor. Now you can change the format as needed.

5. Use the arrow keys, Del key, and character keys to create the format you want. For this example, change #,##0 to [green]#,##0.

6. Click OK.

The new format now applies to numbers entered in the selected cells. In this example, the numbers in the selected cells now appear in green.

PowerPoint adds the format you created to the list of available formats in the Number dialog box; it can be chosen from the list (rather than re-created) the next time you open the Number dialog box. You can create up to 43 custom formats for your datasheet.

As shown in the Number dialog box format list, some formats contain more than one section of information. You can create custom formats that contain up to three sections. The first section formats negative numbers, the second section formats positive numbers, and the third section formats the cell if it contains a numeric value of zero. Each section must be separated from the next section by a semicolon. If you create a format with only one section, that format applies to all numbers entered. If you create a format with only two sections, the first section applies to positive numbers and to zeros; the second section applies to negative numbers.

Deleting a Custom Format

At some point, you might decide that you no longer need a custom format that you created earlier. To delete a format that you created, follow these steps:

1. Choose Number from the Format menu. The Number dialog box appears.

2. Choose the format you want to delete by clicking it. Custom formats appear at the bottom of the list.

3. Click the Delete button in the dialog box.

4. To delete additional custom formats, repeat steps 2 and 3.

5. Click OK to close the dialog box.

You can only delete custom formats; the Delete button cannot be used when you select a built-in PowerPoint format.

Including and Excluding Rows and Columns

When you *include* or *exclude* rows or columns, you do not delete them. Rows and columns can be excluded temporarily so that the data in those rows or columns does not appear on the chart for your datasheet. This function can be useful when some of the data in your datasheet is irrelevant, incomplete, or superfluous for a particular graph you are creating. Because the data is not actually deleted, you can always include it on a graph produced later. When you exclude data instead of deleting it, you save the trouble of retyping the data when you're ready to include it in your chart. Follow these steps to exclude a row or column:

1. Select the row(s) or column(s) to exclude. For this example, select the column labeled *4th Qtr* in the default Graph datasheet.

2. Choose Exclude Row/Column from the DataSeries menu. The selected row or column on the datasheet turns gray. The data in the excluded row or column does not appear in the graph. Figure 14.2 shows how the default graph looks after excluding the 4th Qtr column.

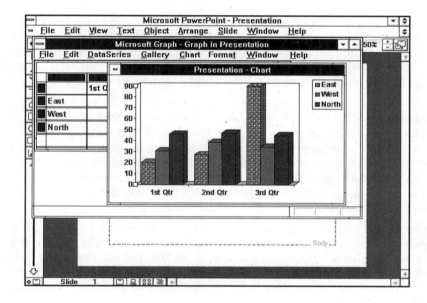

Fig. 14.2

The default graph with the 4th Qtr column excluded.

If you select only a single cell rather than a row or column, PowerPoint displays the dialog box shown in figure 14.3.

Click either the Exclude Row or Exclude Column option; then click OK.

When you're ready to include the excluded data for display in a new graph, follow these steps:

1. Select the row(s) or column(s) you want to include.

2. Choose Include Row/Column from the DataSeries menu. The previously excluded columns or rows appear normal again in the datasheet and are automatically included in the chart.

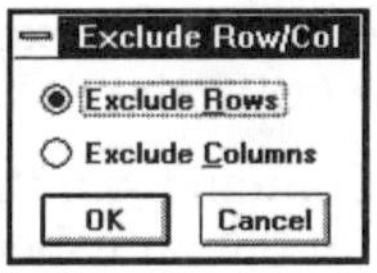

Fig. 14.3

The Exclude
Row/Col dialog
box.

Formatting Scatter Graphs

Most of the PowerPoint graph types plot labels on one axis and numeric values on the other. Scatter graphs are different, because their
scattered data points are determined by *two* numbers: an *x*-value and a
y-value. In order to provide two values for each data point on a scatter
graph, your datasheet must contain more than one data series.

By default, PowerPoint uses the data entries on the first row of the
datasheet as x-values. These values determine the position of data
points along the horizontal (x) axis. The entries in one of the other
rows can then be used as y-values that determine the position of data
points along the vertical (y) axis. With this default arrangement, the
graph is displayed correctly only if you have arranged it in rows rather
than in columns. If you arrange your data in columns, you need to
specify a new set of data to plot on the x-axis.

Figure 14.4 shows a datasheet that contains values to be plotted on a
scatter (XY) graph. The Time/Temperature row is represented on the
x-axis by default, as indicated by the white X in the selection box to the
left of the row. Because this first row contains no meaningful numeric
data, the portion of the chart that is visible shows nonsense values on
the x- and y-axes.

The problem here is quite simple. Because the data series in this
datasheet are arranged in columns, the first *column* (rather than the
first row) should be represented on the x-axis. To correct the problem,
choose the Plot on X Axis command from the DataSeries menu. With
this option, you can change the series that Graph represents on the
horizontal axis. To select the data in the first column for representation
on the x-axis, follow these steps:

1. Open the DataSeries menu.

2. Choose Series in Columns. The white X appears above the first
    column, indicating the new X data series, and PowerPoint modi-
    fies the graph accordingly (see fig. 14.5).

To specify a column other than column 1 as the data series to be used
in plotting x-values, click the selection box above the column before
choosing the Plot on X Axis command from the DataSeries menu; then
follow the preceding steps.

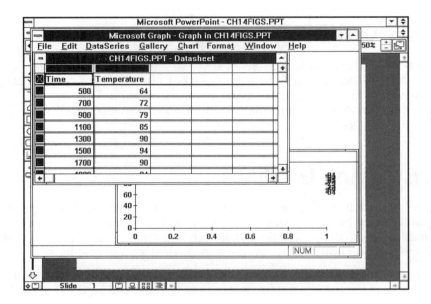

Fig. 14.4

Data to be plotted on a scatter graph.

Data in column 1 is used to plot X values

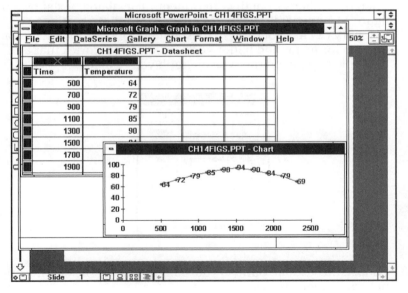

Fig. 14.5

The graph is reformatted using the first column data as the X values.

Customizing Graphs

Each PowerPoint chart consists of several elements, including the graph type, the axes, and the legend. All of these elements can be customized to suit the needs of a particular presentation. This section provides some helpful information about options available with PowerPoint graphs.

Displaying Gridlines

Gridlines are lines that cross the graph at each tick mark; they improve graph clarity by pinpointing the location of data points. PowerPoint enables you to create gridlines that highlight major and/or minor units of measure on both the horizontal and vertical axes of graphs.

Suppose that you want to draw as many lines as possible across your graph to make the exact data points easy to read. Follow these steps to add horizontal gridlines:

1. Select the Chart window to make it active.

2. Choose Gridlines from the Chart menu. The dialog box shown in figure 14.6 appears. The box is divided into three sections—Category (X) Axis, Series (Y) Axis, Value (Z) Axis—which contain options for major and minor gridlines. The categories that are available depend on the type of graph you're using.

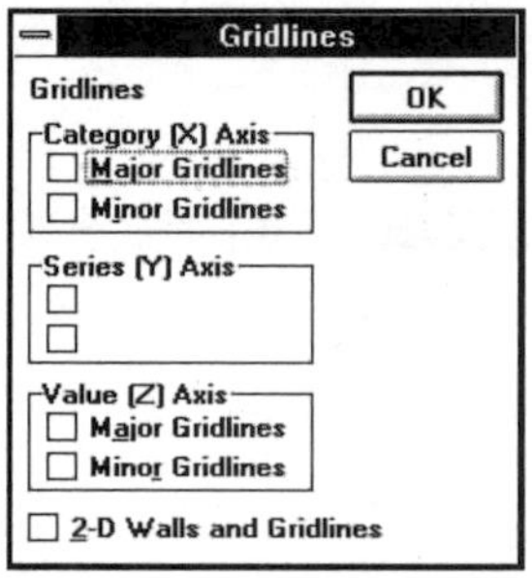

Fig. 14.6

The Gridlines dialog box.

3. Choose the gridline options you want to add by clicking the appropriate check boxes.

4. To show the gridlines in 2-D rather than 3-D, click the 2-D Walls and Gridlines check box.

5. Click OK to return to the graph and display the gridlines. Figure 14.7 shows the default graph with major unit 3-D gridlines on both horizontal and vertical axes.

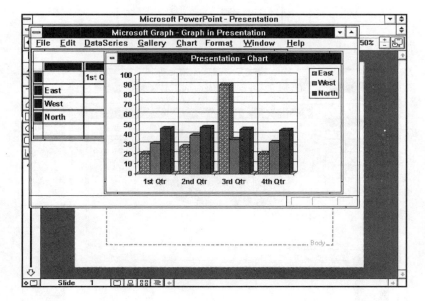

Fig. 14.7

The graph contains horizontal and vertical major gridlines in 3-D.

Displaying Data Labels

To make the graph more readable, you can add data labels to each data marker on the graph. Data labels can show numeric values, percentages (pie graphs only), text, or a combination of text and percentages. The options that are available depend on the type of graph you're using. Suppose that you display the default graph in pie format and want to label each individual slice with the percentage of the whole that it represents. Follow these steps to add percentage labels:

1. Choose Data Labels from the Chart menu. The dialog box shown in figure 14.8 appears.

2. Choose any of the options. You can choose only one option at a time. For the current example, choose Show Percent.

3. Click OK to display the graph with the selected data labels. Figure 14.9 shows the default graph with percentage labels added.

Fig. 14.8

The Data Labels
dialog box.

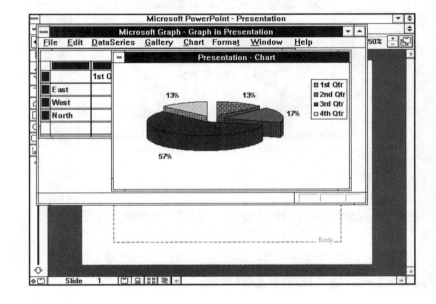

Fig. 14.9

A pie graph with
percent labels.

Adding an Arrow

PowerPoint enables you to call attention to a specific area on a graph
by adding an arrow. After an arrow is on-screen, you can move it to
different positions, vary its length, and rotate it 360 degrees. To add an
arrow to a graph, follow these steps:

1. Choose Add Arrow from the Chart menu. An arrow appears on the
   chart. The arrow is selected; resize handles appear at each end.

2. To move the arrow, click anywhere on the line and drag it to a
   new position.

3. To adjust the length of the arrow, click either resize handle and
   drag the handle in or out.

4. To rotate the arrow, click the handle you want to rotate (the other
   end remains anchored) and turn the arrow to a new position.

5. When the arrow is positioned where you want it, press Esc to deselect the arrow.

Figure 14.10 shows an arrow added to the default pie graph. When you place the chart on your presentation slide, you can add a text box to explain the significance of the data highlighted by the arrow.

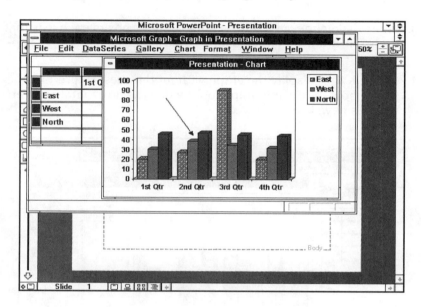

Fig. 14.10

An arrow was added, resized, and rotated to the proper position.

Changing the Axes

You can change the axes of a graph in a number of ways. You can choose whether or not to display the x- and y-axes; you can specify the scale of measurement; you can alter the position and appearance of tick marks (unit markers). The following sections show you how to make these changes in the axes on a graph.

Hiding the Axes

Graph automatically displays horizontal and vertical axes on its default chart. If you prefer to display only one axis, or neither axis, you can *hide* one or both of them. Follow these steps:

1. Select the Chart window to make it active.

2. Choose Axes from the Chart menu. The 3D Axes dialog box appears (see fig. 14.11).

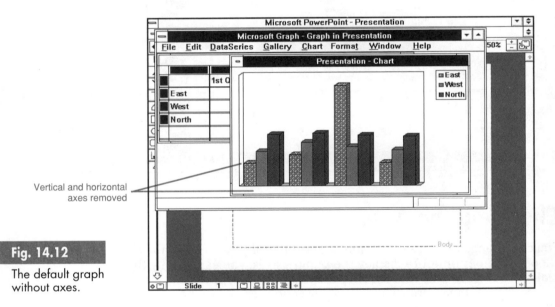

Fig. 14.11

The 3D Axes
dialog box.

3. In the dialog box, an X appears in the check box of each axis that is currently shown on the chart. To turn off an axis, click the appropriate check box to remove the X.

4. Click OK to redisplay the graph without the axes. Figure 14.12 shows how the default graph looks when the horizontal and vertical axes have been removed.

Vertical and horizontal
axes removed

Fig. 14.12

The default graph
without axes.

Scaling the Axes

If you don't turn the axes off, you might want to change the scaling (or ruling) on one or both of them. PowerPoint enables you to change the scaling on a small section of the graph or to adjust the units of measurement that the tick marks represent. You can change the scale to pinpoint exactly the data points displayed on the graph.

The dialog boxes displayed for formatting the horizontal and vertical axes are different. Follow these steps to format the *horizontal* axis:

1. Select the Chart window to make it active.

2. Click the horizontal axis to select it; then choose the Scale command from the Format menu. The Format Axis Scale dialog box shown in figure 14.13 appears.

```
┌─────────────────────────────────────────┐
│ ▄  Format Axis Scale                      │
├─────────────────────────────────────────┤
│ Category [X] Axis Scale        ┌────────┐ │
│                                │   OK   │ │
│ Number of Categories           └────────┘ │
│ Between Tick Labels: [1]       ┌────────┐ │
│                                │ Cancel │ │
│ Number of Categories           └────────┘ │
│ Between Tick Marks: [1]        ┌────────┐ │
│                                │Patterns│ │
│ ☐ Categories in Reverse Order  ├────────┤ │
│ ☒                              │ Font...│ │
│                                ├────────┤ │
│                                │ Text...│ │
│                                └────────┘ │
└─────────────────────────────────────────┘
```

Fig. 14.13

The Format Axis Scale dialog box for the horizontal axis.

To change the arrangement of tick marks and labels, use these boxes:

Number of Categories between Tick Labels: When this option is set to 1, each category is labeled. Change the number to change the frequency of categories labeled. If you change this number to 2, for example, every other category (first, third, fifth, and so on) on the horizontal axis gets a label.

Number of Categories between Tick Marks: When this option is set to 1, each category is indicated on the x-axis by a tick mark. Change the number to change the frequency of tick marks. If you change this option to 2, for example, every other category (first, third, fifth, and so on) is marked by a tick mark on the horizontal axis (see fig. 14.14).

3. You can also reverse the order in which categories are displayed on the chart by clicking the Categories in Reverse Order check box. An example is shown in figure 14.15.

4. Click OK to return to the graph and view the changes to the horizontal axis.

In order to change the scale of the *vertical* axis, follow these steps:

1. Select the Chart window to make it active.

2. Click the vertical axis, and then choose Scale from the Format menu. The Format Axis Scale dialog box shown in figure 14.16 appears.

3. Type the highest number you want to display on the vertical axis in the Maximum box. The default graph shows a maximum value of 90.

4. Type the lowest number you want to display on the vertical axis in the Minimum box. The default graph shows a minimum value of 0.

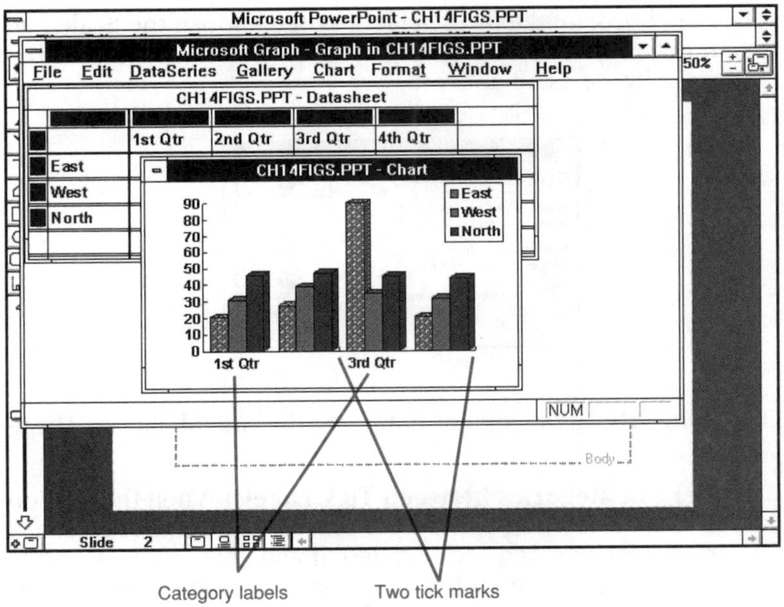

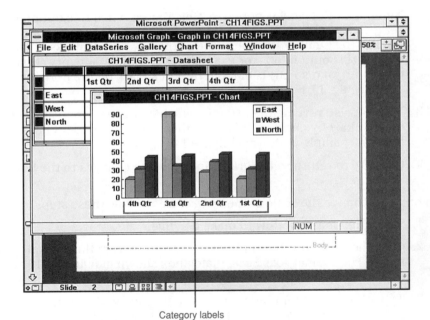

Fig. 14.14

Every other category is labeled and has a tick mark.

Fig. 14.15

Categories in reverse order.

```
┌─────────────────────────────────────┐
│ ▬           Format Axis Scale         │
│ Value [Z] Axis Scale      ┌─────────┐ │
│ Auto                      │   OK    │ │
│  ☒ Minimum:    [C    ]    └─────────┘ │
│                           ┌─────────┐ │
│  ☐ Maximum:    [100 ]     │ Cancel  │ │
│                           └─────────┘ │
│  ☐ Major Unit: [10  ]     ┌─────────┐ │
│                           │Patterns.│ │
│  ☐ Minor Unit: [5   ]     └─────────┘ │
│                           ┌─────────┐ │
│  ☒ Floor [XY Plane]       │  Font.. │ │
│                           └─────────┘ │
│    Crosses At: [0   ]     ┌─────────┐ │
│                           │  Text.. │ │
│  ☐ Logarithmic Scale      └─────────┘ │
│  ☐ Values in Reverse Order            │
│  ☐ Floor [XY Plane] Crosses at Minimum Value │
└─────────────────────────────────────┘
```

Fig. 14.16

The Format Axis Scale dialog box for the vertical axis.

5. In the Major Unit box, type a number to specify the increment between major tick marks on the axis. To mark 10, 20, 30, 40, and so on as major units, enter *10* in this box (this is the case with the default graph).

6. In the Minor Unit box, type a number to specify the increment between major and minor tick marks. The default graph does not show minor tick marks.

7. Click OK to return to the graph and view the changes to the vertical axis.

The default graph in figure 14.17 has been changed to show a scale from 0 to 100 that is broken down into major increments of 10 units (labeled) and minor increments of 5 units.

Changing the Tick Marks

Tick marks are the lines that mark the scale on the vertical axis and the categories on the horizontal axis. You can place the tick marks inside, outside, or across the axis lines; you can choose whether or not to display the major and minor units of measure. The Axis Patterns dialog box shown in figure 14.18 enables you to make these changes. The following steps, for example, can be used to place major unit tick marks outside and minor unit tick marks inside the vertical axis:

1. Select the Chart window to make it active.

2. Click the vertical axis to select it.

3. Choose Patterns from the Format menu. The Axis Patterns dialog box shown in figure 14.17 appears.

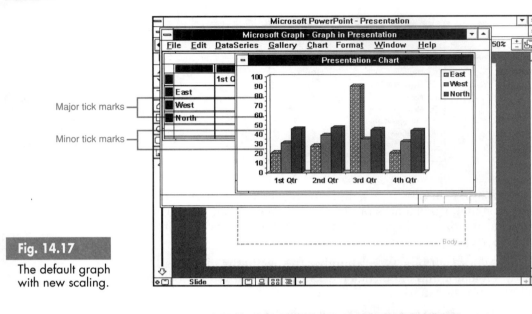

Fig. 14.17

The default graph with new scaling.

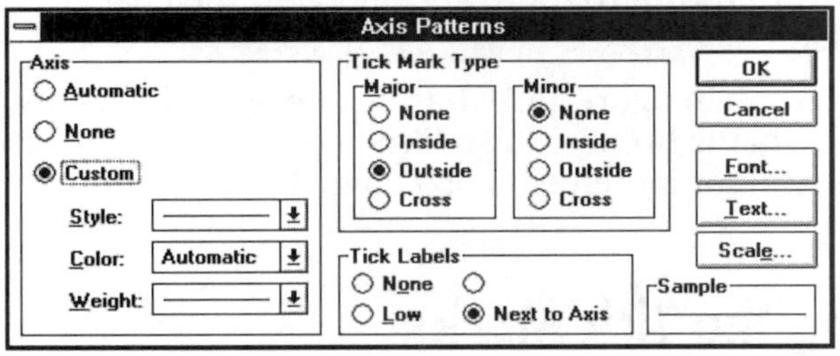

Major tick marks

Minor tick marks

Fig. 14.18

The Axis Patterns dialog box.

The Tick Mark Type box contains four setting—None, Inside, Outside, and Cross—for major and minor tick marks. If you choose None, the tick marks are hidden from view. If you choose Inside, tick marks appear on the right side of the vertical axis. The Outside option displays tick marks on the left side of the axis; the Cross option displays them centered on the axis (combining inside and outside marks).

For this example, click the Outside option for the Major Tick Marks and choose the Inside option for the Minor Tick Marks.

4. Click OK to return to the graph and view the new tick mark format. Figure 14.19 shows the results for the sample case.

Minor tick
marks
inside
axis

Major tick
marks
outside
axis

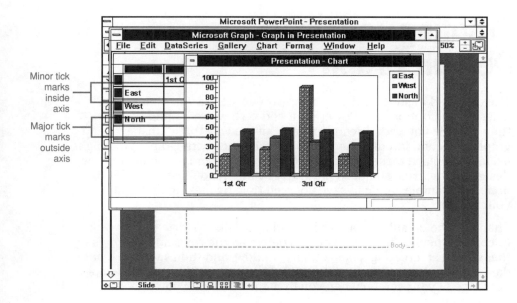

Fig. 14.19

A graph with
major unit tick
marks outside
and minor unit
tick marks inside
the axes.

Notice that the earlier figures showing the default graph (previous to fig. 4.16) did not show the minor units of measure on the y-axis, because the None option was selected for Minor Tick Marks.

The same basic steps that were used previously in this chapter can also be used to format the tick marks on the horizontal axis. The same dialog box appears—the Axis Pattern dialog box—and the same options are available.

This dialog box also enables you to specify the way that labels for tick marks are displayed. Using the Tick Labels box, you can choose one of four positions for the labels: None, Low, High, or Next to Axis. Try the different options to see how they affect your chart.

So far, this chapter has shown you how to customize the datasheet and the graph separately. You can also use advanced capabilities that apply to the graph and datasheet together. The following sections show you how to replace the default graph with a default of your own and how to import data into Graph from other files.

Creating Your Own Default Graph

The default datasheet and graph appear every time you choose the Insert Graph option on a PowerPoint slide. They are helpful because they provide you with a ready example of the way that datasheets and graphs look and interact. As you gain experience with Graph, you might prefer to replace these defaults with a datasheet and graph of your own design. If you use a standard pie graph routinely to illustrate sales figures, for example, you can save yourself time by making that graph your default.

Changing the default can also be useful if you like to format your cells to certain specifications. Or you can delete all the rows and columns in the datasheet, creating a blank Chart window, and then save the blank datasheet and graph as your new defaults. Figure 14.20 shows the appearance of your screen when you first enter Graph if you choose this final option.

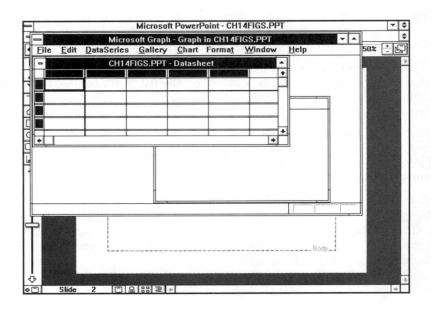

Fig. 14.20

A blank datasheet and graph.

To save a default datasheet and graph for future use, follow these steps:

1. Prepare the graph you want to save, or simply delete all the data in the datasheet to create a blank graph.

2. With the Chart window active, open the File menu.

3. Choose Set as Default Chart.

You now have a new default datasheet and graph, which PowerPoint stores in a file called *default.gra*. If you want to remove your default and return to the original PowerPoint default, delete the default.gra file in the main Windows directory using DOS or the Windows File Manager.

Exporting a Graph to Other Applications

Chapter 8, "Creating Basic Graphs," showed you how to place a finished graph on a presentation slide. This section explains how to copy a graph onto the Clipboard and transfer it to other applications, such as word processors. In each case, only the graph is transferred; you cannot transfer a datasheet.

Suppose that you want to transfer a particular graph to Microsoft Word for Windows in order to illustrate an article. Follow these steps to make the transfer:

1. After activating the Chart window, open the Edit menu. Copy Chart is the only choice available in the drop-down menu.

2. Choose Copy Chart. PowerPoint copies the contents of the Chart window onto the Clipboard.

3. Exit Graph and enter the application in which you want to use the chart; use that application's paste function to insert the graph from the Clipboard.

This technique enables you to incorporate a graph into your word processor (or other application) with only a few keystrokes. You don't need to worry about file compatibility between your graphics program and your word processor. Windows, which loads multiple applications into memory at once, enables you to copy the graph to another application as easily as to a PowerPoint presentation. Note, however, that this copy function only works when copying from one Windows application to another.

Importing Data and Charts

You might regularly use other applications to create items such as charts and spreadsheets. PowerPoint lets you *import* these items into a presentation. Importing data saves you the trouble of recreating work in PowerPoint that you created in another package. The following sections explain how to import spreadheets from a variety of applications and how to import charts from Microsoft Excel.

Importing Data

You can produce a graph in PowerPoint by using data from a spreadsheet such as Lotus 1-2-3, Lotus Symphony, or Microsoft Excel. Table 14.2 lists the file types you can import into PowerPoint.

Table 14.2 Data Files You Can Import

File	Extension
ASCII text-only files that use commas or tabs to separate fields	.TXT
Lotus 1-2-3 (Version 1A) and Microsoft Works files	.WKS
Lotus 1-2-3 files (Version 2.0)	.WK1
Lotus Symphony files	.WR1
Microsoft Excel spreadsheets	.XLS
Multiplan, Excel, and other symbolic link (SYLK) files for exchanging data between spreadsheets and applications	.SLK

Most cell formats are imported automatically with these files. Formulas, however, are not imported; only the numbers in formula cells are transferred into the resulting PowerPoint datasheet.

T I P   You can import files up to 4,000 rows by 256 columns in size.

Suppose that you want to use data from a Symphony file called MOVILLE.WR1 in PowerPoint. The following steps show how to import that file into Graph:

1. Activate the Datasheet window and select the beginning cell for the data. For the example, select the blank first cell at the top left, just under the row of black cells.

2. Choose Import Data from the Graph File menu. The Import Data dialog box appears (see fig. 14.21).

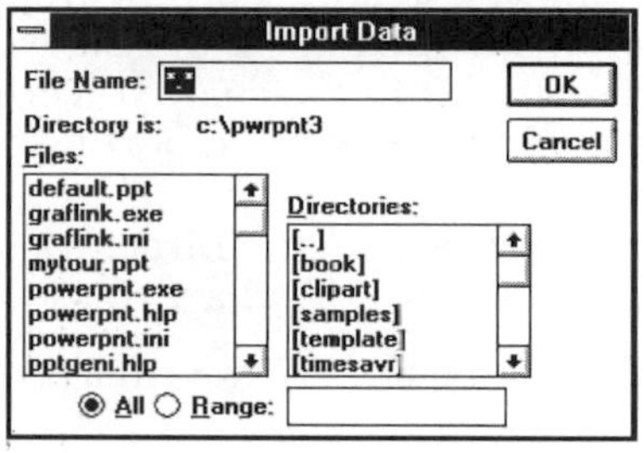

Fig. 14.21

The Import Data dialog box.

3. Follow the standard Windows procedure to select the file you want to import; go to the correct directory, and then choose the file.

   You don't have to import all the data in the file. The All and Range buttons at the bottom of the dialog box give you a choice of importing a complete data file or a selected range of data. The All option is the default. If you choose to select a range of data, follow steps 4 through 6.

4. Click the Range option button, and then click in the box next to Range. The mouse pointer changes to a line cursor.

5. Type the cell range, separated by two periods (*C1..G200*, for example). You can also use a range name, if appropriate. (For Excel, type *C1:G200*.)

6. Click OK. PowerPoint copies the selected data into the datasheet.

Sometimes labels are not imported with the data. When this happens, you can copy the labels from the file of origin, enter Graph, and paste the labels into the datasheet.

Importing Excel Charts

If you have Microsoft Excel for Windows on your hard disk, you can import a chart rather than just data. PowerPoint automatically converts the Excel chart so that you can edit it as a PowerPoint graph and place it on a presentation slide. To import an Excel graph, follow these steps:

1. After activating the Chart window, open the File menu.

2. Choose the Open Microsoft Excel Chart command. The Open Microsoft Excel Chart dialog box appears.

 NOTE At this point, Graph displays a warning message reminding you that the current graph shown in the Chart window and the data in the Datasheet window will be overwritten with the chart you are importing. To return to Graph without importing the file, click Cancel.

3. Select the correct directory in the Directories box; using the Files box, select the file name for the chart you want to import.

4. Click OK. The data and chart are now in a form that you can edit and place on your slides.

Chapter Summary

This chapter showed you how to use advanced Graph features. The section on customizing datasheets showed you how to create custom number formats for your cells, how to exclude rows and columns temporarily from graphs, and how to format scatter graphs. The section on customizing graphs showed you how to hide or display horizontal and vertical axes, how to change the scales used on both axes, and how to change the types of tick marks and labels used. This chapter also showed you how to use gridlines, how to display data labels on graphs, and how to copy whole graphs to other applications in Windows. And finally, it gave you instructions for replacing the PowerPoint default graph with one that better suits your needs and for importing data and charts from other applications such as Excel. The next chapter provides some helpful information concerning the advanced uses of color.

Using Advanced Color Features

Visual artists know that color can offer countless ways to enhance your presentation. In PowerPoint, you can create and use any color you want. In Chapter 7, "Working With Color," you learned some basic ways to use color in PowerPoint, such as copying the color scheme from a template, creating a unique color scheme to suit your needs, and coloring individual objects. But PowerPoint offers more possibilities. As you learned in Chapter 7, the eight colors used most often make up the color scheme. These eight colors are directly available through the color menu options.

In this chapter, you learn how to use more than the eight basic colors in the color scheme, whether you use the default color scheme or choose another color scheme. You learn how to use additional colors available in PowerPoint and how to create new colors. You learn how to choose a color for a particular object and how to add colors to the menu so that you can use them as you use other colors.

As you become proficient with the basic tools, you can use color in more sophisticated ways. For example, after you create colors to use in your own color scheme, you can use that color scheme in other presentations, as you learn in this chapter. Finally, you learn to recolor pictures imported from other Windows applications.

Using Other Colors

As you saw in Chapter 7, the color scheme provides eight basic colors. Suppose, however, that you want to use colors other than those in the color scheme. Through features available on the Slide menu, Power-Point enables you to choose or create the exact colors you need.

Many colors are already available in PowerPoint through the Other Color option, and through the Extra Colors option, which adds colors to the color scheme. You can create custom colors with the More Colors option available in certain dialog boxes, as explained in the section "Creating a Color."

Viewing Existing Colors

Few users remember all the colors in the current color scheme. To quickly view all the colors at once, choose the Fill, Line, or Shadow command from the Object menu. These commands display submenus that show the colors in the current color scheme. To view all the colors and identify how PowerPoint uses each one, display the Color Scheme dialog box. Follow these steps:

1. Choose Color Scheme from the Slide menu to display the Color Scheme dialog box (see fig. 15.1). The Scheme column displays each color, and the Recommended Use column identifies the objects to which PowerPoint applies the colors.

2. Click Cancel to exit the Color Scheme dialog box and return to the slide.

Using the Other Color Option

When you choose the Fill, Line, or Shadow commands from the Object menu or the Color command from the Text menu, the Other Color option appears at the bottom of the submenu. You use this command to select a color that you will use infrequently—perhaps when you want to use a new color for one or two objects but you don't want to add the new color to the color scheme. (For information regarding using additional colors frequently, see the section "Adding Colors to the Scheme" later in this chapter.)

The slide in figure 15.2 displays a box with a black frame. Suppose that you want to draw attention to the box by using a brighter color for the frame. To change the color of the rectangle's frame, follow these steps:

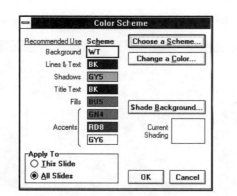

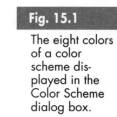

Fig. 15.1

The eight colors of a color scheme displayed in the Color Scheme dialog box.

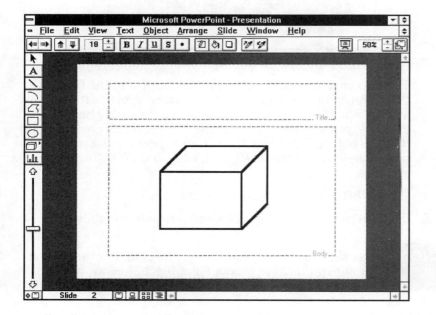

Fig. 15.2

An object with a black frame.

1. Select the object for which you want to change the color; in this example, choose the rectangle.

2. Choose Line from the Object menu.

3. Choose Other Color from the Line submenu. The Other Color dialog box appears (see fig. 15.3).

The Line option is selected

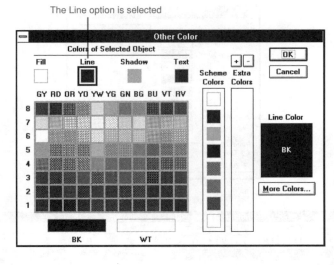

Fig. 15.3

The Other Color
dialog box.

This screen may look familiar, as it is identical to the Change a
Color screen discussed in Chapter 7, which explains the options
available on this screen. Along the top of the dialog box in this
example, you see a black frame, the current frame color, around
the Line object. This black frame also appears in the preview box
on the right side of the dialog box, labeled BK (for "black") in this
example.

4. Choose BG7 for the frame of the rectangle.

5. Click OK to close the dialog box and return to the slide.

NOTE Use these same steps to change the color of other objects
by substituting the Object/Fill, Object/Shadow, or Text
Color commands for the Object/Line command in step 2.

On the slide, the frame now appears in the new color, as shown in
figure 15.4.

Sometimes you want to color more than one object with a new color.
You might want an additional color available for use throughout your
presentation. The next section explains how to add a new color to the
current color scheme.

Adding Colors to the Scheme

Any extra colors appear on the submenu when you choose the Fill,
Line, or Shadow commands from the Object menu, or when you choose

the Color command from the Text menu. You can access the extra colors from these menus.

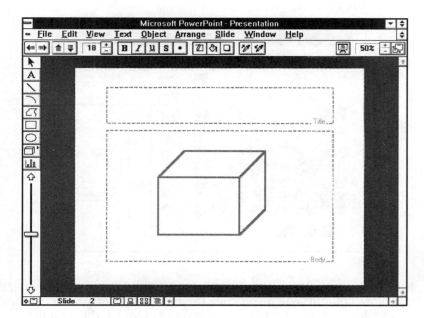

Fig. 15.4

The object with a new frame color.

Adding an extra color is similar to changing a color or using a color through the Other Color option. Suppose that you want the text in an object to appear in a special new color, which you intend to use for other text in this slide. Unlike the Other Color option, which applies only to what you have chosen on your screen, the extra colors you add to the menu are available whenever you want to use them in the presentation. To add a color to the menu, follow these steps:

1. Choose Color Scheme from the Slide menu; then click the Change a Color button.

   You see the Change a Color dialog box shown in figure 15.5. This dialog box is the same as the one in figure 15.3, but with a different name. Notice that the first color, the background color, is selected in the Scheme Colors column. This will become very important in step 4.

2. Choose any color from the color table. The color is displayed in the preview box on the right side of the dialog box.

3. Click the plus (+) sign above the Extra Colors column. The color appears in the Extra Colors column. Repeat steps 2 and 3 to add as many colors as you want—up to eight.

To delete a color you have added, click the color in the Extra Colors column; then click the minus (–) button. The color disappears from the column.

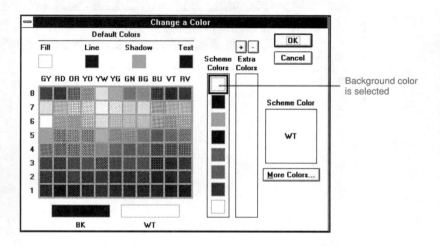

Fig. 15.5

The Change a Color dialog box.

4. Click again on the first color, the background color, in the Scheme Colors column. When you click the color, it becomes selected and should display the original background color (in the default scheme, white). If you forget this step, the background color is changed to the first color you added in the Extra Colors column. Click OK to return to the Color Scheme dialog box.

5. Check to see that all colors shown are correct. Click OK to return to the slide.

All the colors you added now appear on the submenus when you choose the Fill, Line, or Shadow commands from the Object menu, or when you choose the Color option from the Text menu. Choose any one of these commands; a submenu appears that is similar to the one shown in figure 15.6.

To change the text to the new color, select the text and choose Color from the Text menu; then choose the new color at the bottom of the color submenu.

You now have seen how to add an extra color to your menu of permanent color choices. You also can create a new color, as you learn in the next section.

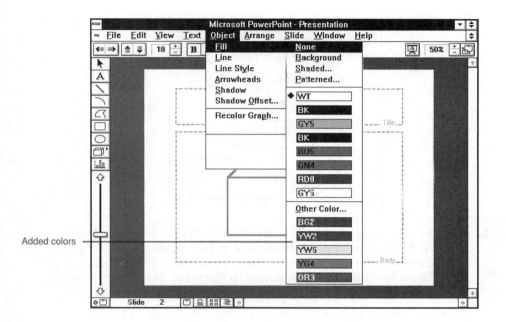

Added colors

Fig. 15.6

Colors added to
the color scheme
appear on any
submenus that
display colors.

Creating a Custom Color

You can create custom colors using the More Colors dialog box. You
access the More Colors dialog box through the Color Scheme dialog
box, and then through the Change a Color dialog box.

In Chapter 7, you learned how to use the Change a Color dialog box to
change a color in your color scheme. Here, you use the Change a Color
dialog box to create a custom color and *add* it to your color scheme.
Follow these steps:

1. Choose Color Scheme from the Slide menu. The Color Scheme
   dialog box appears.

2. Click the Change a Color button. The Change a Color dialog box
   appears.

3. In the color table, choose a color that is close to the color you
   want to create.

4. Click the More Colors button in the lower right corner of the dialog box. The More Colors dialog box appears (see fig. 15.7). Two
   boxes appear at the top of the dialog box: Original Color and New
   Color. At this point, both colors are the same.

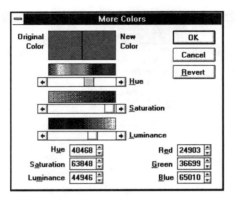

Fig. 15.7

The More Colors
dialog box.

5. Drag the scroll bars for the Hue, Saturation, and Luminance. The
   Hue scroll bar reflects the color shown in the Original Color box.
   Saturation refers to the color intensity. Luminance shows how
   much black or white has been added to the color. Watch the New
   Color box as you alter the Hue, Saturation, and Luminance.

   As you change the color, the New Color box changes, but the
   Original Color box does not. You therefore have a good comparison of old and new at all times. Continue to drag the scroll bars
   until you're satisfied with the color you have created.

T I P   If you want to retrieve an original color when you work in the More
Colors dialog box, click the Revert button or click the Original Color
box. The original color is restored and the scroll bar positions revert
to their previous settings.

6. Click OK to close the More Colors dialog box and return to the
   Change a Color dialog box.

7. Click the Plus (+) button above the Extra Colors column to add
   this custom color to the color scheme.

8. Click the first color (the background color) in the Scheme Colors
   column. This step selects and displays the background color in
   the Scheme Color box on the right side of the dialog box.

 NOTE   Step 8 is very important; if you forget it, the background color is changed to the first color in the Extra
Colors column.

9. Click OK to close the Change A Color dialog box and return to the Color Scheme dialog box. Check the colors in this box to verify that they are correct.

10. Click OK to return to the slide.

To verify that your custom color was added to the color scheme, choose the Fill, Line, or Shadow command from the Object menu. The new color appears below the Other Color option.

In this section, you have seen how to create a color in PowerPoint. The next section explains how to create matching slides.

Recoloring Pictures

In PowerPoint, *pictures* include logos, maps, photographs, and colored artwork. As you saw in Chapter 12, you can import pictures from other presentations and applications. PowerPoint always retains the original colors in imported pictures, even if the colors do not exist in Power-Point. A special menu option on the Object menu enables you to re-color pictures, one color at a time. You can also change black and white to other colors. But you cannot increase the number of colors already in the picture—you must use the same number of colors that were used to create the picture.

Suppose that you want to include a humorous illustration in your pre-sentation. The humor.ppt file in the clip art subdirectory includes a picture of a money-hungry man (see fig. 15.8). (For instructions on in-serting clip art into a presentation, see Chapters 11 and 12.)

Follow the steps below to recolor the picture. Be sure that you copied the clip art to your presentation as a Picture using the Paste Special command from the Edit menu. If the picture is not really a Picture, the following steps will not work.

> **NOTE** The Recolor Picture option is not available with objects you draw yourself unless you group the objects, copy them, and then choose Paste Special from the Edit menu to paste the grouped objects as a picture.

In the picture, the man's tie is pink. To change his tie to red, follow these steps:

1. Select the picture that you want to recolor. In this case, select the picture of the money-hungry man.

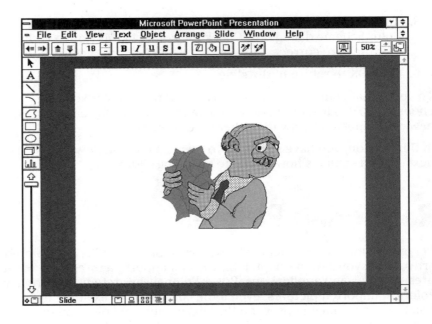

Fig. 15.8

A clip art picture of a money-hungry man.

2. Choose Recolor Picture from the Object menu. The Recolor Picture dialog box appears (see fig. 15.9). A copy of the picture is displayed on the left slide of the dialog box.

   Notice that the Colors option at the bottom of the dialog box is checked. The Colors option displays the solid colors used in the picture. The Fills option displays the colors used for patterned fills.

3. On the right side of the dialog box, you see the To column. In the drop-down boxes of the To column, choose new colors to replace the colors you want to change.

   The current color appears in the From column. Use this column to find the color you want to change. When you change a color, an X appears in the Change column in the check box next to the color.

   For this example, scroll down the list to display the pink color used in the tie. Choose a shade of red (RD8 in this case) in the drop-down box. As soon as you choose a color, an X appears in the check box. The X means that PowerPoint will change this color as indicated.

4. Click Preview to see how the new color affects the picture. In this example, the tie changes to red when you click the Preview button.

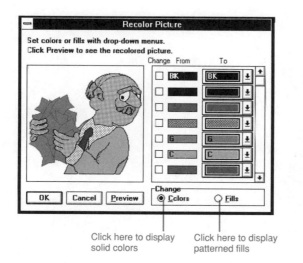

Click here to display
solid colors

Click here to display
patterned fills

Fig. 15.9

The Recolor
Picture dialog
box.

5. To experiment with other colors, repeat steps 3 and 4. To change patterned fills, click the Fills button to display the patterned fills used in the picture. (In this example, the man's shirt and face are two examples of filled patterns.)

   After experimenting, you might decide to use some colors and not others. To revert to the original color in any color choice, click the Change box beside any color. The X disappears. The color shown in the To column stays as it was, showing the new color you chose. But without the X in the check box, PowerPoint will not apply the new color to the picture.

6. When you are satisfied with the new colors, click OK. PowerPoint returns to the presentation and recolors the picture. To return to the presentation without changing any colors, click Cancel.

Chapter Summary

In previous chapters, you learned to use PowerPoint's powerful coloring capabilities to choose from a multitude of existing color schemes and to change the colors in those color schemes. In this chapter, however, you learned how to create colors not listed in the color scheme and how to add a color to your permanent list of available colors. Finally, you learned how to use the Recolor Picture option to change the color of pictures you import into PowerPoint.

In the next chapter, you learn about PowerPoint's timesaver presentations.

Using PowerPoint's Timesaver Presentations

A t this point, you should feel comfortable with PowerPoint. You have learned all the basics and many advanced features, which will help you create slides, notes pages, outlines, and handouts. You have learned how to use PowerPoint's built-in templates and color schemes, and how to create your own. You have used a wide variety of custom features to incorporate objects, graphs, and pictures into your slides, and you know how to share data with other Windows applications. You now have the tools and the skills to create many kinds of slides for any presentation.

Still, you want to get your job done as quickly and efficiently as possible. When you're in a hurry and you need to create a slide using common business forms, charts, or tables, why reinvent the wheel? PowerPoint's timesaver presentations can come in handy.

To make your jobs easier, PowerPoint includes a directory of timesaver presentations. The presentations include the building blocks for various types of forms, charts, tables, and so on. The timesvr directory includes the presentation files for

- Organization charts
- Flow charts
- Calendars
- Timelines
- Tables
- Graphs

If you want to create a flow chart, for example, you could copy slides from the flowchart.ppt presentation, where most of the work has been finished for you already. Just choose the slide that matches most closely the chart you're trying to create, and then add your own text. If no slide closely represents what you're trying to create, use selected objects from a slide and copy them into your chart (see "Using Elements from a Timesaver Presentation," later in this chapter).

Each timesaver presentation contains a wide selection of slides. The calendar.ppt file, for example, contains 31 calendars that begin with July of 1992 and end with December 1994; the flowchrt.ppt file has 11 slides that contain various flow chart elements and flow chart styles. The first slide in every presentation gives you instructions and suggestions for ways to use the slides in the presentation.

Browsing the Directory

Before you use any of the timesaver presentations, browse through the directory. You will get a sense of each presentation's organization and learn what kinds of elements are included on the slides. To browse the directory, follow these steps:

1. Choose Open from the File menu. The Open dialog box appears (see fig. 16.1).

2. Click the Open Untitled Copy check box in the lower right corner of the dialog box. This step is important because it protects the original files.

3. In the Directories box, click the timesavr directory under the main PowerPoint directory.

4. In the File Name box, click the file you want to open; then click OK. PowerPoint opens the presentation in Outline view, and lists each slide title. An example is shown in figure 16.2.

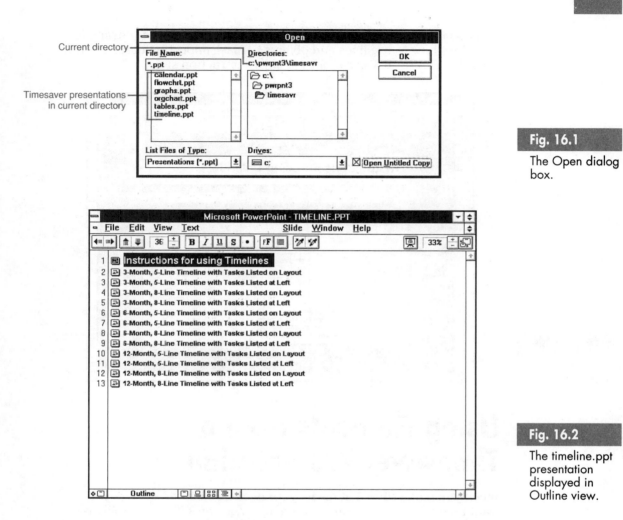

Current directory

Timesaver presentations in current directory

5. When you finish browsing through the slides, close the file. To view another presentation, repeat these steps.

Viewing the Instruction Slides

Each timesaver file contains an instruction/suggestion slide at the beginning of the presentation. These slides can help you, especially when you are still new to PowerPoint and don't remember all the commands and procedures for accomplishing tasks. The suggestions on this slide often give you new ideas for using the elements of the slides in creative ways. The instruction slide for the calendar presentation, for example, describes how to use lines and objects to mark important dates on the calendar. Figure 16.3 shows the calendar instruction slide.

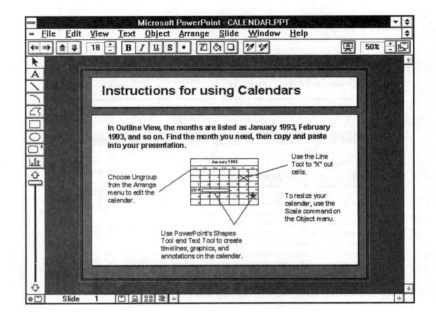

Fig. 16.3

The calendar instruction slide.

Using Elements from a Timesaver Presentation

When you find a slide that meets your needs, select the objects you want to use and copy them to your slide. You can select multiple objects at the same time and copy them together. If you want to copy the entire slide, switch to Slide Sorter view and select the slide (or multiple slides); then copy and paste it into your presentation.

Often several objects are grouped as one object. You can separate the objects by choosing the Ungroup command from the Arrange menu. Don't assume that you should separate all objects, however. Sometimes objects are grouped to help you maintain horizontal and vertical alignment between objects that go together, such as the elements that comprise an organization chart.

Reviewing Sample Presentation Slides

This section shows a sample of one slide from each presentation file. Browse through each presentation to see the wide selection of slides.

Figure 16.4 shows a sample organization chart, slide #4 in the orgchart.ppt file.

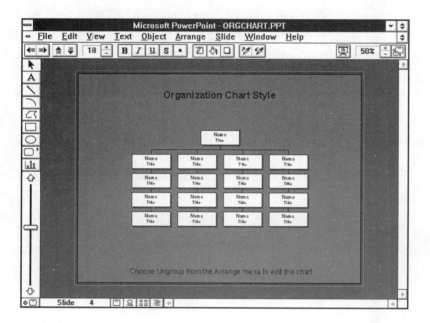

Fig. 16.4

A sample organization chart from the orgchart.ppt file.

Figure 16.5 shows a sample flow chart, slide #7 in the flowchrt.ppt file.

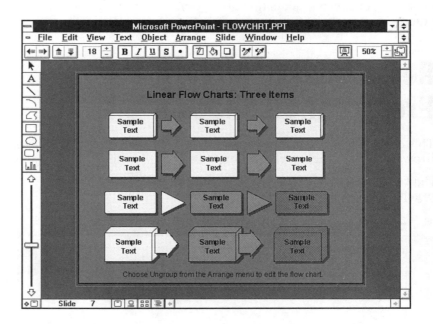

Fig. 16.5

A sample flow chart from the flowchrt.ppt file.

Figure 16.6 shows a sample calendar, slide #7 in the calendar.ppt file.

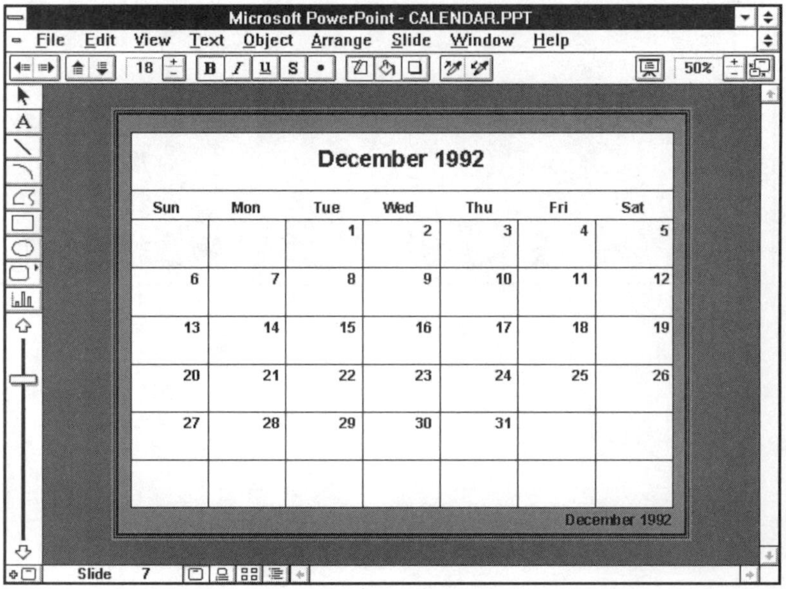

Fig. 16.6

A sample calendar from the calendar.ppt file.

Figure 16.7 shows a sample timeline, slide #4 in the timeline.ppt file.

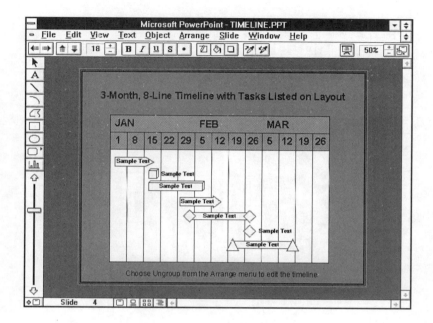

Fig. 16.7

A sample
timeline from the
timeline.ppt file.

Figure 16.8 shows a sample table, slide #12 in the tables.ppt file.

Fig. 16.8

A sample
table from the
tables.ppt file.

Figure 16.9 shows a sample graph, slide #9 in the graphs.ppt file.

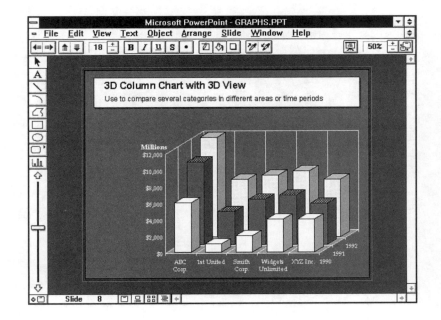

Fig. 16.9

A sample graph from the graphs.ppt file.

Chapter Summary

This chapter introduced a PowerPoint feature designed to make your job easier—timesaver presentations. These presentations (located in PowerPoint's timesavr directory) contain sample organization charts, flow charts, calendars, schedules, tables, and graphs. When you need to create a presentation containing one or more of these elements, you can save time by copying all slides, selected slides, or selected elements from a slide to your own presentation. The first slide of each timesavr presentation contains instructions or suggestions for using the slides.

Installing PowerPoint

Because PowerPoint runs only under Windows 3.1, you must have Windows installed on your hard drive before you can install PowerPoint. If you haven't installed Windows, do so before you continue with this section. Refer to your Windows documentation for Windows installation instructions.

Copying Your Source Disks

To keep your original disks safe, copy the PowerPoint disks to another set of disks before you install the program. Keep the original disks in a safe place and use only the copies. If you then damage any disks during installation, you will still have the originals.

You can copy your disks using the Windows File Manager. You must have enough formatted blank disks to copy each PowerPoint disk (approximately six). If the disks are not yet formatted, use the Format Disk command on the Disk menu. When the disks are formatted, use the Copy Disk command on the Disk menu to copy each PowerPoint disk. Follow the instructions on-screen. For detailed instructions, refer to your Windows documentation.

You can also copy the PowerPoint disks using DOS commands. Follow these steps:

1. Label the target disks (the disks onto which you copy the files) something such as *PowerPoint Working Copies*. Number the disks 1, 2, 3, 4, and 5 (or 1-4 if you're using 3 1/2-inch disks).

2. At the DOS prompt, type *diskcopy*, followed by the floppy disk drive letter typed twice; for example, type the following:

   diskcopy a: a:

   DOS displays this message:

   ```
   Insert source diskette in drive A:
   Press any key when ready...
   ```

3. Insert the original PowerPoint Disk 1 into the floppy disk drive and press any key.

   After a short time another message appears:

   ```
   Insert target diskette in drive A:
   Press any key when ready...
   ```

4. Insert the target disk (use disk number 1 the first time) into the floppy disk drive and press any key.

   DOS copies files onto this disk. DOS might prompt you to change source and target disks several times because of the large number of files involved. When you have copied all the files to the target disk, you see the following message:

   ```
   Copy another diskette (Y/N)?
   ```

5. Press Y to indicate yes, and repeat these steps to copy the remaining PowerPoint disks. Don't forget to use disks with matching numbers (disk 2 with disk 2, and so on).

6. When you see the prompt Copy another diskette (Y/N)? after all files on all disks have been copied, press N.

Now use the working copies to install PowerPoint, as explained in the next section.

Installing PowerPoint

To install PowerPoint, you must have Windows 3.1 installed on your computer. Make sure that your computer is turned on and in the ready state before beginning installation. Follow these steps:

1. Start Windows (type *win* from the DOS prompt). The Windows Program Manager window appears on-screen. If the Program Manager isn't open, double-click the Program Manager icon.

2. Insert the PowerPoint Working Copy Disk 1 into your floppy disk drive.

3. Choose Run from the Program Manager File menu.

4. Type *a:setup* in the command line box, and then press Enter or click OK.

5. The Welcome box appears. Click Continue, type your name and company, and then click Continue again. A message appears that prompts `Please wait while Setup copies its working files to your hard disk`. This copying might take up to a minute. You then see the first screen in the Setup installation program.

6. In the PowerPoint Installation Options dialog box, choose either the Complete Installation or Custom Installation. Microsoft recommends the complete installation so that you can take full advantage of PowerPoint's features. Choose the Custom Installation only if you need to conserve disk space.

   When you choose the Custom Installation, you select only those options you want to install, and you follow the on-screen instructions. If necessary, you can run the Setup program again later to install the options you bypassed.

7. Follow the on-screen instructions; the PowerPoint installation is fully automated. When the installation is complete, the PowerPoint icons are added to the Microsoft PowerPoint group in the Windows Program Manager.

PowerPoint Defaults

Defaults are settings that PowerPoint uses unless you specify otherwise. Defaults can help keep you oriented as you work in PowerPoint. You can change the defaults easily, as you see in Chapter 3 and elsewhere in this book. Defaults are a safety feature; they conform to rules of good usage. From time to time, you might want to restore some or all of the defaults.

When you enter PowerPoint, the presentation you see has default settings in most of the menus. This appendix lists defaults by category. For explanations of the meanings of any of the terms used, refer to the appropriate chapters in the book.

Printer Defaults

The printers for slides, notes pages, and handouts are the current printers for your operating system. The printers use the orientation, paper size, and other options set in your operating system.

View Defaults

The slide scale is initially 50 percent. The Slide Master has a centered title at the top, set in boldface in Arial 36 point (if available). The Notes Master centers a reduced 50 percent scale slide at the top of the notes page. The default handout page contains no text or objects.

Text Default

The default text style in Text objects is Arial 18-point bold. Text is left-justified. Text boxes receive the Adjust Object Size to Fit Text feature.

Object Default

In Draw, the default settings for a drawn object are transparent (not opaque), framed in black, filled with white, and unshadowed. The default line style is the thinnest line in the menu, without arrowheads.

In addition, with the Snap to Grid option on the Arrange menu, the guides do not appear on-screen, and the edges of drawn objects do not appear unless you specify this option.

Color Defaults

The eight colors available in the default color scheme are WT (background), BK (lines and text), GY5 (shadows), BK (title text), BU5 (fill), GN4 (accents), RD8 (accents), and GY6 (accents).

Clip Art

The following is a complete list of the individual slides in the CLIPART subdirectory in PowerPoint. You will find a specific piece of art more quickly by glancing through this appendix than by going straight into the presentations in the CLIPART subdirectory. The CLIPART subdirectory contains 19 presentations in all. Those presentations are listed as follows:

- ACADEMIC AND MEDICAL
- ANIMALS
- BUILDINGS
- BUSINESS
- CURRENCY
- ELECTRONIC
- HOUSEHOLD
- HUMOR
- INTERNATIONAL MAPS
- INTERNATIONAL MAPS AND FLAGS
- LANDMARKS
- PEOPLE
- PRESENTATION HELPERS
- SCENIC BACKGROUNDS
- SHAPES

- SIGNS
- SPORTS
- TRANSPORTATION
- U.S. MAPS

This appendix lists the slides in each presentation.

ACADEMIC AND MEDICAL (academic.ppt)

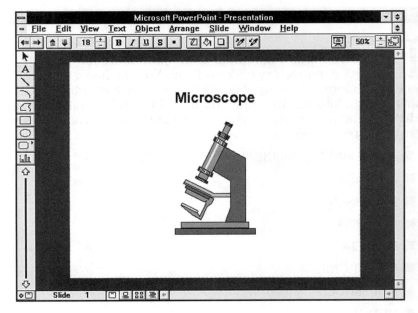

1   Graduation cap

2   Diploma

3   School fish

4   Books

5   Textbook

6   Dictionary

7   Notebook binder

8   School supplies

9   Pencil

10   Hand writing

11   Paper cutouts

12   Lecture

13   Seminar

14   Professor

15   Girl student

16   Boy student

17   Test tubes

18   Microscope

19   Reflective telescope

20   Telescope

21   Magnifying glass

22   Anatomy

23   Anatomy of the ear

24   Syringe

25   Caduceus

ANIMALS (Animal.ppt)

1   Bull

2   Cow

3   Horse

4   Donkey

5   Elephant

6   Piggy bank

7   Rabbit

8   Cat

9   Turtle

10   Shark

11   Tropical fish

12   Eagle

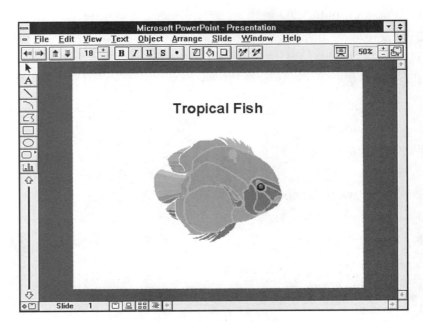

BUILDINGS (building.ppt)

1   City block

2   3-D skyline

3   Factory

4   Courthouse

5   Victorian house

6   Contemporary house

7   Residential house

8   High-rise building

9   Office building

10   Hotel

11   Two office buildings

12   Nuclear power plant

13   Farm

14   Church

15   Oil rig

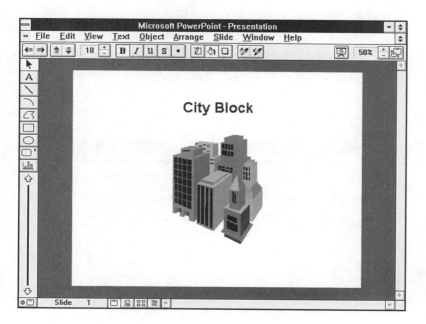

Fig. C.3

City block, slide 1 in this file.

BUSINESS (business.ppt)

1   Personal computer

2   Personal computer with mouse

3   Laptop computer

4   Laptop computer with handle

5   Monitor

6   Hard disk

7   Computer chip

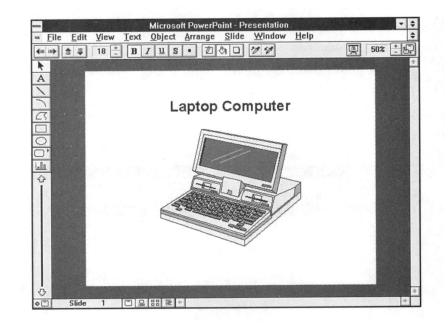

8   Diskette 3.5

9   Diskette 5.25

10   Printer

11   Computer paper

12   Stacked computer paper

13   Computer paper (vertical)

14   Copy machine

15   Typewriter

16   Calculator

17   File cabinets

18   Business postcards

19   Clipboard

20   Rolodex

21   Check

22   Appointment book

23   Calendar

24   Business envelope (front/back)

25   Digitized alphabet (see-through/borders)

26   Digitized alphabet (solid/borders)

27   Digitized numbers (solid/bordered and see-through/unbordered)

28   Digitized numbers

29   Satellite

30   Satellite with panels

31   Satellite dish

CURRENCY (currency.ppt)

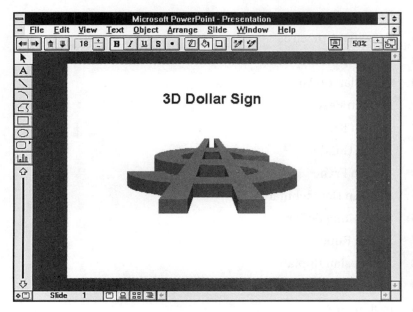

Fig. C.5
A 3-D dollar sign, slide 8 in this file.

1   Dollar bill

2   Stack of dollar bills

3   Stack of coins

4   Penny

5   Nickel

6	Dime
7	Quarter
8	3-D dollar sign
9	Stack of money
10	Foreign currency
11	International money
12	Bag of money
13	Hand holding bag of money
14	Argentine Peso
15	Australian dollar
16	Austrian Schilling
17	Belgium Franc
18	Brazilian Cruzeiros
19	British pound sterling
20	Canadian dollar
21	Chilean Peso
22	Danish Krone
23	Dutch Guilder
24	French Franc
25	German Deutschmark
26	Hong Kong dollar
27	Indian Rupee
28	Indonesian Rupiah
29	Irish pound
30	Italian Lira
31	Japanese Yen
32	Korean Won
33	Malaysian Ringgit
34	Mexican Peso
35	New Zealand dollar

36   Norwegian Krone

37   Porteguese Escerdo

38   Russian ruble

39   Singaporean dollar

40   South African Rand

41   Spanish Peseta

42   Swedish Krona

43   Swiss Franc

44   Taiwan dollar

45   U.S. dollar and U.S. cert.

46   Venezuelan Bolivares

ELECTRONIC (electrnc.ppt)

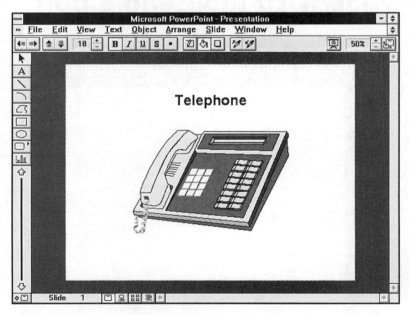

Telephone, slide 13 in the file.

1   Television monitor

2   Digital clock radio

3   Portable CD player

4   Portable cassette player

5   Radio

6   Television

7   Video camera

8   8MM camcorder

9   Audio cassette

10   8MM video cassette

11   Video cassette

12   Answering machine

13   Telephone

14   Pay phone

HOUSEHOLD (household.ppt)

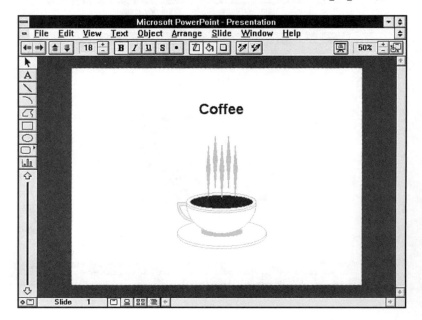

Fig. C.7

Cup of coffee,
slide 7 in the file.

1   Spray bottle

2   Squeeze bottle

3   Container

4   Paper carton

5   Sack

6   Mug

7   Coffee

8   Salt & pepper

9   Soda can

10   Six-pack of soda cans

11   Cheeses

12   Apple

13   Grapes

14   Plum

15   Ear of corn

16   Wheat

17   Grain

18   Cotton

19   Shopping cart

20   Umbrella

21   Key and door lock

22   Key

23   Light bulbs

24   Barrel

25   Balloon

26   Scissors

27   Scissors cutting paper

28   Paper and push pin

29   Bandage

30   Medicine

HUMOR (humor.ppt)

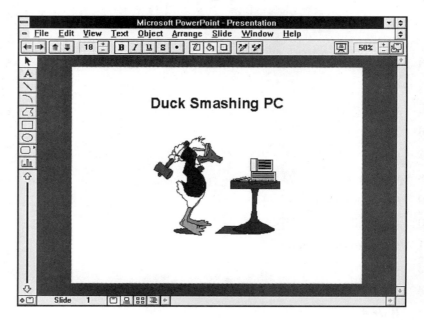

Fig. C.8

Duck smashing a PC, slide 22 in this file.

7   Man pointing

8   Man with too many hats

9   Man on phone

10   Ghost man one

11   Ghost man two

12   Ghost man three

13   Ghost man four

14   Tightrope walker

15   Dart thrower

16   Tug of war

17   Teamwork

18   Teamwork in a maze

19   Sherlock Holmes

20   Hooked

21   Swamped

22   Duck smashing PC

23   Men fighting

24   Computer choking operator

25   Fortune teller

26   Magician

27   Under the thumb

28   An idea

INTERNATIONAL MAPS (intlmaps.ppt)

1   Africa

2   North America

3   Central America

4   South America

5   Europe

6   Middle East

7   Southeast Asia

8   World map

9   United Nations flag

10   African continent

11   Australia and New Zealand

12   Eurasia

13   European continent

14   North American continent

15   South American continent

16   World Globe (Western hemisphere)

17   World Globe (Eastern hemisphere)

18   European community

19   Australian states

20   Provinces of Canada

INTERNATIONAL MAPS AND FLAGS (intlnatn.ppt)

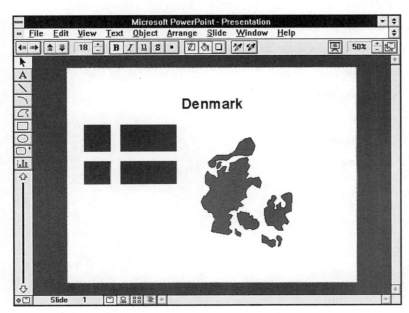

Fig. C.10

Denmark, slide 14 in this file.

9   Brunei

10   Canada

11   People's Republic of China

12   Cuba

13   Czechoslovakia

14   Denmark

15   Egypt

16   Estonia

17   Finland

18   France

19   Georgia

20   Republic of Germany

21   Greece

22   Hong Kong

23   Hungary

24   India

25   Ireland

26   Israel

27   Italy

28   Japan

29   Kazakhstan

30   Kyrgyzstan (Kirgizia)

31   Latvia

32   Lithuania

33   Luxembourg

34   Mexico

35   Moldova (Moldavia)

36   Netherlands

37   New Zealand

38   North Korea

39   Norway

40   Poland

41   Portugal

42   Puerto Rico

43   Russia

44   Singapore

45   South Korea

46   Spain

47   Sweden

48   Switzerland

49   Taiwan

50   Tajikistan (Tadzhikistan)

51   Thailand

52   Turkey

53   Turkmenistan (Turkmenia)

54   Ukraine

55   United Kingdom

56   United States

57   Uzbekistan

58   Venezuela

59   Yugoslavia

LANDMARKS (landmark.ppt)

1   Statue of Liberty - United States

2   Mount Rushmore - United States

3   Lincoln Memorial - United States

4   United States Capitol

5   U.S. flag

6   Empire State Building - United States

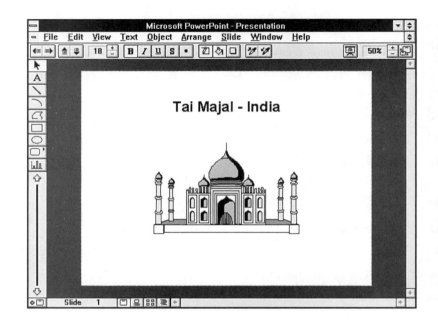

7   Liberty Bell - United States

8   Houses of Parliament - England

9   Eiffel Tower - France

10   Windmills - Holland

11   Taj Mahal - India

12   Leaning Tower of Pisa - Italy

13   Mt. Fuji - Japan

14   St. Basil's Cathedral - Russia

PEOPLE (people1.ppt)

1   Woman with briefcase

2   Women in busines suit with briefcase

3   Woman with portfolio

4   Woman in tailored suit

5   Woman sitting

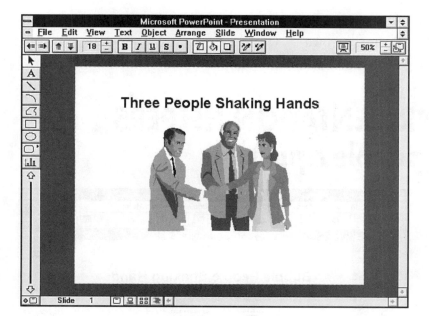

Fig. C.12
Three people shaking hands, slide 17 in this file.

6   Woman with binder

7   Woman with binder - close up view

8   Woman holding paper

9   Woman looking at watch

10   Two women sitting

11   Man with tan blazer

12   Man with briefcase

13   Man sitting at desk

14   Man leaning on box

15   Man at automated tellers

16   Two men meeting at desk

17   Three people shaking hands

18   Two men in discussion

19   Man and woman in discussion

20   Panel discussion

21   Business meeting

22   Group meeting

23   Business crowd

24   Business woman

PRESENTATION HELPERS (people2.ppt)

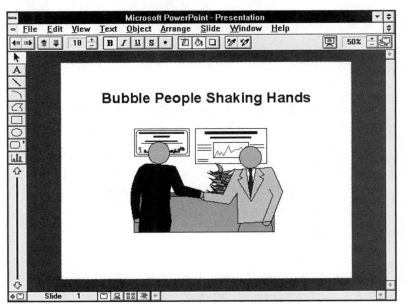

Fig. C.13

Bubble people shaking hands, slide 6 in this file.

1   Crowd

2   Meeting

3   World map and men

4   Bubble people

5   Business men at desk

6   Bubble people shaking hands

7   Bubble person in computer room

8   Bubble person at computer

SCENIC BACKGROUNDS (scenic.ppt)

Fig. C.14

Desert, slide 1 in this file.

8   City skyline at night

9   Sailing in the tropics

10   At the beach

11   Telephone poles

12   Spring

13   Summer

14   Fall

15   Winter

16   Perspective Grid #1

17   Perspective Grid #2

18   3-D perspective background

SHAPES (shapes.ppt)

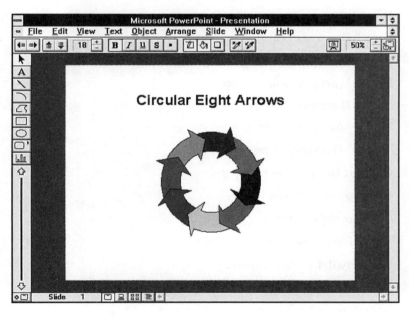

Fig. C.15

Circular arrows, slide 26 in this file.

1   Vertical circular arrows

2   Vertical curved arrows

SIGNS (signs.ppt)

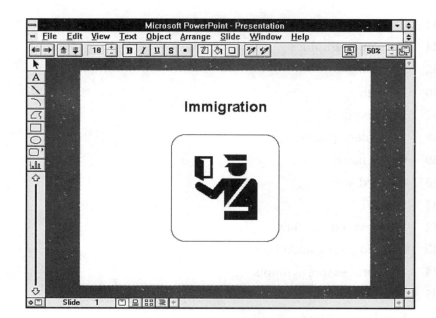

Fig. C.16

Immigration,
slide 9 in this file.

9   Immigration

10   Ticket purchase

11   Currency exchange

12   Hotel accommodations

13   Elevator

14   Restrooms

15   Men's room

16   Women's room

17   Handicapped

18   No smoking

19   Lost and found

20   First aid

21   Taxi

22   Ground transportation

23   Air transportation

24   Bus

25   Rail transit

26   Water transportation

27   Helicopter transportation

28   Swimming

29   Picnic

30   Play area

31   Pedestrian crossing

32   Bike path

33   Do not enter

34   Yield

35   Parking

36   No parking

37   Stop

38   One way

39   Flipping the switch

40   Plug

41   Radioactive

42   Woman

43   Man

44   Telephone icon

45   Electrical icon

46   Gas icon

SPORTS (sports.ppt)

1   Football & goal post

2   Basketball & hoop

3   Baseball & bat

4   Hockey stick & puck

5   Darts

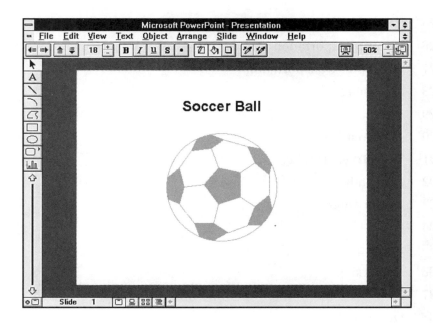

6   Soccer ball

7   Volleyball

8   Golfer

9   Skiing

TRANSPORTATION (transprt.ppt)

1   Red sports car

2   Blue sedan

3   2-door van

4   Ambulance

5   Police car

6   Fire engine

7   Truck

8   Tanker truck

9   Airplane

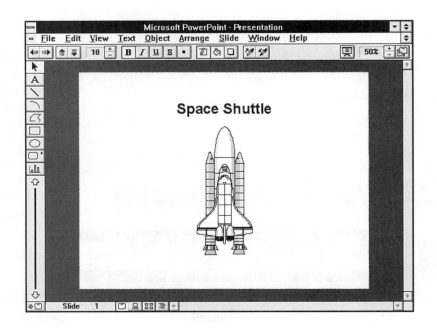

Fig. C.18

Space shuttle,
slide 25 in this
file.

10	Helicopter
11	Blimp
12	Hot air balloon
13	Train
14	Locomotive
15	Bulldozer
16	Hydraulic shovel
17	Forklift
18	Hand pallet
19	Yacht
20	Steamboat
21	Cargo ship
22	Jet fighter
23	Fighter plane
24	Combat aircraft
25	Space shuttle

26   Tank

27   Battleship

28   Bicycle

29   Gas station

30   Gas pump

31   Gears

U.S. MAPS (usmaps.ppt)

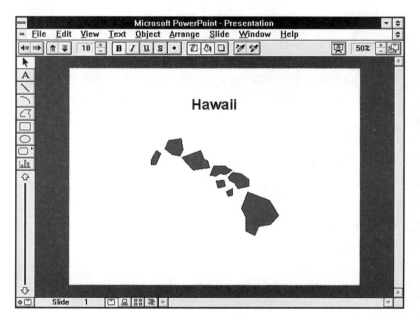

Fig. C.19

Hawaii, slide 14
in this file.

1   United States

2   3-D U.S. map with state boundaries

3   3-D U.S. map

4   Alabama

5   Alaska

6   Arizona

7   Arkansas

8	California
9	Colorado
10	Connecticut
11	Delaware
12	Florida
13	Georgia
14	Hawaii
15	Idaho
16	Illinois
17	Indiana
18	Iowa
19	Kansas
20	Kentucky
21	Louisiana
22	Maine
23	Maryland
24	Massachusetts
25	Michigan
26	Minnesota
27	Mississippi
28	Missouri
29	Montana
30	Nebraska
31	Nevada
32	New Hampshire
33	New Jersey
34	New Mexico
35	New York
36	North Carolina
37	North Dakota

38   Ohio

39   Oklahoma

40   Oregon

41   Pennsylvania

42   Rhode Island

43   South Carolina

44   South Dakota

45   Tennessee

46   Texas

47   Utah

48   Vermont

49   Virginia

50   Washington

51   Wisconsin

52   West Virginia

53   Wyoming